A Woman 🖋
Wanders through
Life and Science

SUNY Series in the Voices of Immigrant Women

Maxine S. Seller and Rudolph J. Vecoli, Editors

A Woman 〜
Wanders through
Life and Science

IRENA KOPROWSKA

State University of New York Press

Cover portrait of Dr. Koprowska was painted in 1970 by Alice Neel.
Photograph courtesy of Karen Mauch.

Published by
State University of New York Press, Albany

Printed in the United States of America

For information, address the State University of New York Press,
State University Plaza, Albany NY 12246

Production by Bernadine Dawes • Marketing by Nancy Farrell
Library of Congress Cataloging-in-Publication Data
Koprowska, Irena, 1917–
        A woman wanders through life and science / Irena Koprowska
            p.   cm. — (SUNY series in the voices of immigrant women)
        ISBN 0-7914-3177-0 (hc : alk. paper). —
        ISBN 0-7914-3178-9 (pb : alk. paper)
        1. Koprowska, Irena, 1917–   . 2. Women pathologists—
United States—Biography. 3. Women pathologists—
Poland—Biography.
        I. Title. II. Series.
        RB17.K67A3   1997
        610'.92—dc20
        [B]   96-18625
                                                    CIP

1 2 3 4 5 6 7 8 9 10

Contents

Preface

As a wartime refugee from Poland, and as a woman immigrant, I had to struggle for many years before adjusting to life in the United States and becoming a successful physician, scientist, and family woman. Now many young women continue to ask me, "How did you do it?"

Reading my story will not provide anybody with a recipe for success. But, hopefully, it may stimulate the ingenuity of the readers as to how to deal with their own problems.

I couldn't wait until retirement to begin writing my autobiography. This has not been easy because English is not my native tongue and because, being used to the rigors of scientific discipline, I didn't realize how to go about creative writing. I had to accept the fact that my recollection of past events is not exact and at times varies very much from the remembrance of members of my family, friends, and other witnesses.

Seeking to reveal the truth about myself and those I love, I became concerned that some of it may be painful to important people in my life. I had to decide what to conceal and what to reveal. In sacrificing the completeness of my story, I tried to minimize the disagreement of the members of my family, friends, and acquaintances with their image created in this book. I apologize for hurting anybody's feelings, though this may be unavoidable when I describe my own emotions in our relationship. Despite many ups and downs my marriage has become good and strong and a basis for the happiness in my life. Also, I am grateful to my husband for his patience and understanding in agreeing not to read my manuscript until its publication.

I am much indebted to Joan Mellen, professor at Temple University, for accepting me to her tutorial in creative writing in 1988. I also wish to thank Judith Wisdom, the professional editor who revised my book, for helping me to better understand the development of my own personality.

I recognize my debt to my secretaries, Eileen Dorsey and Julie Zahn-Schrader, whose skills allowed me to continue using old-fashioned handwriting for these memoirs, knowing that they would be printed in a presentable form. In addition, Julie has been invaluable in helping me with final editing of the book.

I am grateful to Maxine S. Seller, professor at the State University of New York at Buffalo, and Professor Rudolph J. Vecoli, Director of the Immigration History Research Center at the University of Minnesota, for their enthusiasm in submitting my autobiography to the State University of New York Press for inclusion in the series of books on women immigrants, of which they are editors.

Irena Koprowska, M.D.

Introduction

Irena Koprowska's autobiography spans her life from earliest childhood in Poland to her recent retirement from professional life in the United States. It opens with memories about her family, whose economic and social position within the bourgeoisie in pre-war Warsaw defined much of Irena's future outlooks and attitudes. Koprowska's father, Henryk Grasberg, was a successful entrepreneur, owner of flour mills and bakeries, and a member of the influential Warsaw House of Commerce. His wealth, as well as his caring protectiveness toward his only daughter, let Irena lead a comfortable and sheltered life. From the outset, nannies, governesses, servants, and private teachers filled her childhood. Education in an exclusive prep school for girls, and then at the medical school of Warsaw University, gradually expanded her social circles—although she never really crossed certain boundaries beyond the social class of her family. Economic security and the indulgence with which Irena's family surrounded her made her ill-prepared for the future struggles and deprivations of a refugee and immigrant life.

On the other hand, the same things that spoiled and disadvantaged Irena in some aspects of her everyday existence gave her a strong cultural and intellectual basis that contributed to her professional success and eased her transition to life in a foreign country. As a child, Irena used to spend vacations abroad, traveling with her family to fashionable European resorts. She continued to travel also as a college student. Her family's international social and business connections, relatives and friends living outside of Poland, and knowledge of foreign languages and cultures decisively contributed to Koprowska's

self-confidence and resourcefulness during the turbulent years of war
and displacement. A good education and the work ethic learned from
her father gave her an advantage that many of her contemporary
women refugees did not have.

Irena's childhood and young adulthood involved more than cultural and intellectual development. Relationships she established in
those formative years became an influence on the rest of her life.
Koprowska approaches these issues with openness and honesty. Her
family relations remain central to her psychological makeup.
Koprowska's mother, Eugenia, died during Irena's infancy, and her
father married his deceased wife's sister, Bronislawa. For a few years
Irena did not even realize that Bronislawa was not her birth mother.
With that realization came resentment of Bronislawa and competition for her father's attention. Despite the fact that the relationship
with Bronislawa remained a troubled one, Koprowska displayed a
great deal of loyalty towards her stepmother and half brothers,
whom she later sponsored to come to America and supported in
many ways.

There is no doubt, however, that her father became a major
influence in Irena's life. He was closest to her, and Irena considered
him a living connection to her dead mother whose absence from her
life she felt so deeply. It was he who encouraged and supported her
medical studies. As Koprowska reveals, her father "was fascinated by
medicine," and early on expressed his hopes that she go to medical
school. Responding to Irena's plans to become a lawyer instead,
Grasberg displayed a premonition as to his daughter's future. "Who
knows what wars are still ahead of us," she remembers him saying.
"You may need to leave Poland and emigrate to another country. You
won't be able to practice law because it's different in every country.
But diseases are the same everywhere." The father was also Irena's
confidante when she needed advice on her relationship with her future
husband and their marriage, and he was a source of wisdom about
men in general. Koprowska admits that her father was the person she
loved most and "felt loved by unconditionally."

Koprowska's autobiography includes more strong and complex
personalities, such as her mother-in-law, Sofia Semeonovna
Koprowska. Despite what was at times a difficult and stormy relationship between Irena and Sofia, the author repeatedly displays

respect toward her adversary as an educated and professional woman: "She looked like the married professional woman she was. Born and educated in Russia, Sofia Semeonovna had become one of the first women dentists in pre-revolutionary Russia. Later she had migrated to Poland where she continued practicing dentistry."

Irena competed with her mother-in-law for the love and attention of her husband, Sofia's only son Hilary. The power struggle between the two women for the position in the family became one of the main threads throughout Koprowska's story.

The question of the career and role of women in professions remains in the center of Koprowska's attention. Remembering her childhood in Poland, the author recalls her father's expectations for her "to get married and to have a profession also," as did many middle-class women in Poland at that time. Even though Irena did not have a role model in Bronislawa, whom she considered to be a traditional housewife, she decided to pursue her interest in biology and enroll in Warsaw University Medical School. The war disrupted her career, but she managed to find work related to her education, both during her stay in Paris and later during a sojourn in Brazil. After arriving in the United States, she immediately proceeded with advancing and developing her career. Koprowska worked in many prestigious medical institutions and research centers, conducting studies in pathology and early cancer detection. She published, presented papers, stayed active in the international arena, and taught medical college courses. Her work became recognized, and Koprowska achieved a great deal of success in the medical field. Her career remained a very important part of her life, defining many of her personal goals.

Her professional success did not come easy, and Koprowska had to cope with numerous obstacles. In France and Brazil she was young and inexperienced, and handicapped by language deficiencies. Once in the United States, she had to pass multiple certification exams and prove herself to her employers and colleagues. The intellectual challenge, however, was not the most difficult one. Koprowska admits that the hardest barriers were those connected to her gender. Having a career as well as family and children, she did not have many role models to follow. Nor was support for her efforts to combine work and family easy to find. Describing her experiences in work at the New York Infirmary for Women and Children, Koprowska concludes:

> Working at the infirmary was a mixed blessing. . . . The clinic employed women doctors only, and many of these women were what in those days were called "old maids." From my upbringing in Poland, I wasn't used to being confined to an exclusive female environment and, frankly, I felt ill-at-ease in this atmosphere. They, too, felt uncomfortable with me because I was different. Those who were married, like my boss Sophie Spitz, often refused to have children for fear it would interfere with their careers. (Ch. XVI, p. 145)

Koprowska felt very strongly about women's potential to successfully combine professional life and family, and she returned to this problem repeatedly. At one point, she had a chance to express her views publicly while interviewing women applicants to Cornell University Medical College.

> During my interviews, I questioned the women applicants about their plans and emphasized the desirability of their continuing to practice medicine after they married and had children. Although I understood it might be difficult, I tried to encourage these young women—future physicians—to find a solution to their problems by relying on their relatives, as many Polish women doctors did, or hiring help even at financial sacrifice.
>
> However, I went further. I let them know that if they couldn't work it out, and considered desisting from the practice of medicine, they would be wasting a training slot that someone else could use.
>
> "If you plan to quit after you find a husband, you shouldn't occupy a slot that might otherwise be given to a man; he won't give up his career because of marriage," I told the applicants firmly. They did not respond, but I suspect that they were shocked by what they heard from me. I don't know what they thought, but they may not have liked what I said and may have repeated it to the members of the admissions committee, because I was never again asked to interview the applicants. (Ch. XVII, p. 164)

As was the case with many contemporary women with both careers and families, Koprowska was not free from inner struggle and conflicting emotions about the amount of time spent with her children. The following story illustrates what kinds of pressures she had to face:

> One of Claude's (the author's son) friends, Walter Hammerle, a son of a baker, lived across the street from us. Claude loved to watch television at his house. Most American middle class women of my generation, the mothers of his classmates, stayed at home and didn't work. Claude was made uncomfortable by my having a career—it made him different from his friends.
>
> "Mummie, why do you have to work? Why don't you stay home and bake cakes like Mrs. Hammerle? Doesn't Daddy earn enough money to support us?" he asked me repeatedly.
>
> "Claude, I've spent years studying medicine and I want to practice my profession," I responded, although I realized that at his age he couldn't really be expected to understand how important my work was to my self-respect and my sense of myself as a person, how much pride I took in it, how I couldn't imagine giving it up. (Ch. XVII, p. 166)

The fact that Koprowska considered her professional career as a significant part of her life and displayed less esteem for the more traditional female roles resulted in her having few women friends in her adult life. Working in a profession dominated by men, however, was not always easy either. Throughout her life, Koprowska felt compelled to match the professional achievements of her husband, Hilary Koprowski, an internationally recognized scientist in the field of medical research. She also had a chance to be professionally associated with the famous scientist, Dr. George N. Papanicolaou ("Dr. Pap"), whose work on the so-called Pap smears revolutionized the area of early cancer detection in women. Koprowska reports her experiences of working with male doctors from the female point of view. Her story includes instances of lack of sensitivity and understanding, and even discrimination towards her as a woman scientist, but also examples of breaking through barriers and establishing successful work relationships in a field traditionally dominated by males.

Later in life, Koprowska joined the American Medical Women's Association and became active in that organization, as she focused her attention on work with female medical students. In the early

1980s, Koprowska felt that she could better communicate with them than with American women physicians of her own generation. "My reputation as 'role model' for the young women physicians and medical students became firmly established," she concluded.

Koprowska's personal story and her medical career constitute, no doubt, the backbone of her autobiography. Her life, however, is closely entwined with events of a broader scope: World War II and the post-war immigration wave reaching the shores of the United States in the late 1940s and early 1950s. Koprowska and her family exemplify the large refugee population from countries of central and eastern Europe, who refused to return to the communist-dominated states and chose life in exile. Displaced by the war, having lost homes and families, and burdened with traumatic war experiences, these refugees constituted a very specific immigrant population. The first refugee wave from Poland had already arrived in America in 1940. It included people who found themselves abroad at the outbreak of the war, or who managed to escape Poland during the early months of the Nazi occupation. Numerous politicians, artists, intellectuals, and representatives of the Polish social establishment who belonged to that group, entered the United States mainly through private channels.

A substantially larger group arrived under the 1948 Displaced Persons Act, amended in 1950, which enabled 400,000 European refugees to settle in America. The 1950 amendments to the Displaced Persons Act included an additional clause allowing 18,000 Polish ex-servicemen demobilized in Great Britain to immigrate to the U.S. The largest European group covered under the Act—about 140,000 Poles—found new homes in America. Other ethnic groups, such as Ukrainians, Jews, Russians, Czechs, Slovaks, Yugoslavs, Latvians, Lithuanians, Estonians, Greeks, and German *Volksdeutsche*, also arrived at that time, and joined existing immigrant communities in the United States.

For the Polish refugees, America was hardly their first country of immigration during their long and difficult years of war displacement. Many experienced deportation and slave-labor camps in Siberia, from whence they later journeyed through the southern Asiatic republics of the Soviet Union to the Middle East and North Africa. Others survived Nazi concentration camps, prisoner-of-war camps, prisons, and slave labor for the German war machine. Some were Polish soldiers who had fought in campaigns on many fronts of western Europe or members of the Polish underground army who had participated in the resistance movement and guerrilla warfare throughout the occupation years in Poland and during the Warsaw Uprising of 1944. Civilian refugees were sojourners to many European and other countries as they tried to keep ahead of the advancing German forces. There was also a growing number of people who escaped from oppression in Communist Poland. After the end of the war, the majority of refugees remained in the so-called "displaced persons" camps in Germany, Austria, Italy, as well as other locations on different continents. From there they emigrated gradually to countries that slowly and hesitantly opened their doors to the war refugees.

In the United States the refugees entered the Polish American community built and organized by the mostly economic immigrants of peasant background who arrived as a part of the great immigration wave at the turn of the century. Most of them remained in blue-collar occupations that were concentrated in the large urban centers of the East Coast and the Midwest. In the early–World War II years, the second generation was better educated and demonstrated stronger upward mobility. They assumed many leadership positions within Polonia, and worked on the maintenance and development of a network of Polish churches and parishes, numerous organizations, cultural clubs and fraternals, Polish schools, presses and publishing houses—all of which constituted a base for the Polish American community structure. By the time of World War II the "old Polonia" was considerably assimilated, and consciously accepted a "Polish American" rather than a "Polish" identity. The war mobilized Polonia's resources, rallied Polish Americans around the causes of independent Poland and humanitarian help for Poles within and outside of Poland, and at the same time facilitated the assimilation process.

The new wave of Polish refugees made it their goal to intensify the Polish American community's politicization in order to influence American foreign policy on behalf of Poland. In 1944 the Polish American Congress was established (the largest Polonia umbrella organization which claimed support of six million followers) and quickly became an active and successful Polish lobby. Cultural and scholarly organizations, such as the Polish Institute of Arts and Sciences in America and the Jòzef Pilsudski Institute for Research in the Modern History of Poland, were also formed as a result of the newcomers' initiatives.

From a social point of view, the diversified Polish population included a high percentage of *intelligentsia,* the Polish professional middle class. Their initial encounter with the old Polonia in the environment of the resettlement process and increasing Cold War atmosphere resulted in social conflict stressing differences in social class, background, education, the degree of assimilation, and political involvement. As a consequence, some of the displaced persons with middle-class backgrounds initiated separate organizations and attempted to isolate themselves from the "peasant" and "Americanized" part of Polonia. After the initial hardships related to the period of adjustment and assimilation in the United States, many members of that class, relying on their education and knowledge of English, achieved notable social mobility and joined the American middle class. The process of social negotiations that took place on all levels of the community's internal structure transformed the Polish American identity in a considerable way. Polish Americans responded in mass to the political challenges of the Cold War and later supported the anti-communist movement in Poland. The process of assimilation as well as the need to redefine their identity in front of the incoming new immigrants contributed to the formation of a social consensus within the Polish community. The contribution of the post-war *intelligentsia* newcomers to those changes within Polonia cannot be overestimated.

As a whole, the post-war immigrant wave distinguished itself by its activism within the Polish American community and by its avid interest in international politics related to the situation in Poland. We know little about the particular experiences of Polish middle class women who belonged to that immigrant population. The handful of literary accounts by Danuta Mostwin, scarce biographies of some artists, as well as ethnic press and archival sources do not provide much insight into Polish women's lives in America. Many women, burdened with the dreadful war past and post-war displacement, faced long periods of economic insecurity and social degradation as they struggled to provide for their families and put together disrupted lives. Some of them did manage to establish themselves successfully in professions, while others succumbed to the changed and unfavorable conditions of the immigrant life and never re-entered the ranks of the middle class.

The Koprowski family's war experiences reflect those of the first wave of civilian refugees. Koprowska, her husband, and mother-in-law escaped Poland and traveled first to Italy, then France, where her son was born, and through Spain and Portugal to Brazil, where they spent most of the war years. During each stage of their journey they were a part of spontaneously formed Polish expatriate communities whose members, like the Koprowski's, mostly middle class, shared the hardships and uncertainties of refugee life and supported each other in difficult circumstances. Koprowska's descriptions of her war years vividly portray various aspects of the refugee existence.

In 1944 the Rockefeller Foundation in New York sponsored Hilary Koprowski and his family to immigrate to the United States in order for Koprowski to continue his scientific work for the Foundation in America. The Koprowski family, who found themselves in New York almost four years before the major influx of Polish displaced persons, had a head start due to Hilary's secure job situation and his professional connections.

Since the very beginning, both Hilary and Irena concentrated on their professional careers and organized their social lives to include American friends and associates. Koprowska's story does not include much reference to participating in Polonia's life; be it established old Polonia communities or the new refugee circles. In fact, Paul Koprowski, Irena's father-in-law, several years after their arrival in the U.S., was the first to connect them with the Poles he knew in New York. Koprowska does mention some Polish friends, but it seems obvious that the family remained isolated from the mainstream of Polonia's life in the United States. Their lack of interest in politics, as well as their lack of religious affiliation, further separated the Koprowski's from activities of the Polish American community at the time, which were highly political and mostly Roman Catholic. Only in 1977, when Irena Koprowska was named Woman Physician of the Year by the Polish American Medical Association in New York, did she come into contact with the Polish Institute of Arts and Sciences in America. In some respects, Koprowska's isolation from the active Polonia life, although uncharacteristic for the major part of the displaced persons wave, constitutes an excellent example of the rift between the Polish American reality and the goals and aspirations of the upwardly mobile professional middle class.

While analyzing her experiences in the workplace, Koprowska sees greater hindrance for her career because of her gender rather than because she was an immigrant. However, she does allude to some instances when her or her husband's origins played a role in establishing work relations and receiving recognition for their achievements. In 1946 Koprowska lost her fellowship at Cornell University because preferences for research positions were then given to returning veterans. The author noted frustration of some American women who were forced to give up their jobs to the men. She, however, did not feel hurt:

"Perhaps it was easier for me to feel this way because, as an immigrant, I considered myself less entitled to such privileged opportunities than they were. After all, I was still an outsider, new to this country, and not yet a citizen."

Koprowska also felt a special rapport with her mentor, Dr. Pap, and emphasized the fact that he was a Greek immigrant.

The author's connections to her home country are mostly expressed through her support for her family and friends whose daughters she employed as domestic help, giving them an opportunity to come to the United States. Hilary Koprowski's generous contribution to the polio vaccination program in Poland enabled the entire family to visit Poland in 1958. The trip became an occasion to revisit some old places and renew old friendships. Later on, Hilary Koprowski maintained contact with scientists and researchers from Poland coming to the United States on exchange programs.

Koprowska's autobiography is, from the historical point of view, an interesting contribution to our knowledge about American society. The author was both a witness to and a participant in significant historical events and processes, which she describes through the eyes of a woman, a professional, and an immigrant. Even though Koprowska's book is a private autobiography and does not attempt to present and analyze broader social issues, it does reflect an important aspect of American social history in the post-war years. It carries special significance for Polish American history, since most of the existing scholarship about Polish Americans focuses on the largely working-class mass immigration of the late-nineteenth and the early-twentieth centuries. Much less attention has been paid to the more highly educated middle-class immigrants of the post–World War II years, and especially to the experiences of professional women like Koprowska within that group. As a precursor to the young women who entered the professions in the United States as a result of "second wave" feminism of the 1960s and subsequent decades, Koprowska is of interest to scholars in women's history as well as immigration history. Koprowska's is a positive and successful experience presented to the reader in an open, honest, and highly readable form.

Anna D. Jaroszynska-Kirchmann, Ph.D.

A Woman Wanders through Life and Science

Thou shalt prove how salty tastes another's
bread, and how hard a path it is to go up and
down another's stairs.

—Dante Alighieri, *Paradise Lost*

First
Discovery

I was born on May 12, 1917 in Warsaw, Poland, which was then occupied by Russia. My childhood was contemporary with the beginning of the European and Polish post-war order and the transition from the Victorian order to Modernity. My paternal grandparents lived and died in Warsaw before I was born. My father, Henryk Grasberg, in an apparent act of rebellion against his parents' attempts at his strict upbringing, left home at sixteen and got a job. He put himself through business school and continued to support himself.

During the Russian occupation, the government declared the Russian language obligatory in its schools. The socialists fought against this rule, and my father, who was active in this movement, was imprisoned for taking part in a strike over the use of Russian in school. After his release from prison he went to Germany, where he worked for several years in a grain importing business. After his return to Warsaw he purchased a flour mill and a bakery. Then he acquired a large, stone-fenced waterfront property on the Vistula River where, in addition to the steam-powered mill and bakery, there was a small, one-story office building, stables, a hayloft, a carriage house, and a two-story building where he lived in an apartment on the second floor.

The mill was equipped with modern, efficient machinery. Only a part of the flour that it produced was used by the bakery; the rest was sold outside. His business became very successful. In time he bought an additional mill, several more bakeries, and two large apartment houses. Henryk Grasberg became a rich man. He was invited to become a member of the Warsaw House of Commerce.

This allowed him to participate in making decisions about the rules by which business was conducted in the city.

Living in such close proximity to a mill, my father became allergic to the flour dust and began suffering from bronchial asthma. He developed a barrel chest, which is typical of the emphysema that often accompanies asthma. Except for this slight deformity, he was a good-looking man of medium height and weight, with a round face, dark eyes, dark hair and bushy eyebrows. He was manly and strong looking, yet had a gentleness to his demeanor.

My father employed his sister Zosia and their nephew in his office. After a while, when he needed more help, he hired Eugenia, an attractive young woman, to become his secretary.

Eugenia had been born in Warsaw in 1888, but several years after the birth of her younger sister Bronislawa, the family moved to Scotland where both girls went to school. Their mother, Anna, came from Zamosc—a town 143 miles southeast of Warsaw known for its renaissance architecture modeled on Padua. Both Eugenia and her younger sister were good students, but Eugenia was the brighter of the two. At graduation she received a gold medal, the highest academic honor, and Bronislawa a silver one. Several years later their father, Herman Cui, a watchmaker who failed to establish a good business in Edinburgh, returned to Warsaw with his family.

Eugenia was not only attractive and smart, she was a good secretary. She was well liked by all the office and mill workers, in whose welfare she always took a great interest, and she became good friends with Henryk's sister Zosia.

Eugenia and Henryk fell in love and became engaged. Henryk had already become a rich man by then, and he bought Eugenia a beautiful engagement ring with a large diamond mounted in platinum and gold. After they were married, they lived in Henryk's apartment, which they remodeled, for a year or two before I was born there on May 12, 1917.

They named me Irena after my deceased paternal grandmother. But the family's happiness was very short-lived. Eugenia died of a pulmonary embolism within three weeks of my birth. My father's grief was intense. He turned his affection to me, for he saw me as all he had left of Eugenia. One of my earliest childhood memories is of waking up at night on the floor of my nursery and being picked up and put back to bed by my father in his loose white-linen sleep shirt. Our wet nurse, my mother's parents (Grandpa Herman and Grandma Anna), and my mother's younger sister Bronislawa helped him take care of me. They all showered me with attention.

My unmarried aunt, Bronislawa, whom I thought was my mother, had a bird-like face, narrow brown eyes, dark hair, and very smooth, doll-like pale, pink skin. She was neither as attractive nor as intelligent as her deceased sister, according to what my father told me in my teens. At one time there had been a man in her life whom she had hoped to marry. I never learned what happened to that romance. But when my mother died, Bronislawa spent most of her time watching over me and supervising my care.

Then, when I was almost three years old, my father married Bronislawa. Their quiet private wedding took place in the center city apartment of my maternal grandparents on Marszalkowska Street. My memory is of a small group of people standing around my father and Bronislawa while a man pronounced some words over them. Then everybody was congratulating and kissing them. In retrospect I think that both of them had been lonely people and when they began to spend much time together taking care of me they probably developed a physical attraction to each other.

In 1920, when I was three and a half years old, Bronislawa gave birth to my half-brother, Eugeniusz (Gene), named for my mother. A few days later, Grandpa Herman died suddenly of a heart attack. This was the second time that death followed birth in my family. Bronislawa was lying in bed with an infant in her arms crying bitterly over her loss. I felt a sense of curiosity and gloom, not really understanding the meaning of death. I remember Grandpa Herman as a stocky man who used to bring me spice cookies, the taste of which still makes me think of him.

After Gene's birth, Wikcia, a peasant woman with dark blond hair, gray eyes, a prominent jaw with big teeth, and a cheerful disposition, was hired to be our nanny and to help Bronislawa. Wikcia was a sensual, vivacious and very warm person; Gene and I loved her. While she bathed us, she told us scary stories about Gypsies stealing children from people. We never tired of listening to Wikcia's stories. She was quite different from Bronislawa, who cared about our health, cleanliness, and food, but was very calm and reserved.

When I was four years old, I was taken to the funeral of Gabriel Narutowicz, the president of Poland and a great liberal. I sat high up on the shoulders of my father, overwhelmed by the sight of burning torches and the sounds of drums accompanying the funeral procession. I realized that I was witnessing an important and solemn event. But I did not know that he had been killed by a mentally deranged political opponent.

Grandma Anna, my maternal grandmother, was a short, slim, sweet-tempered lady with white hair and blue eyes, but whose head shook involuntarily. Grandma Anna used to come to visit us often at our Solec Street apartment. During the day, when father was downstairs in the office, she sat and chatted with Bronislawa, the two of them sitting on the beige sofa in the master bedroom. This bedroom had connecting doors to the nursery, the dining room, and a spare room with green wallpaper that was always called the "green room." I could see into the green room from the doorway of my nursery, and they also could see into that room through the doors that connected it to the bedroom, where they sat.

In the green room, over the piano, hung an oval portrait in a heavy gold frame. It was a large black-and-white photograph of a young woman with regular features. Her long hair was parted on the right side, pulled to the back of her head, gathered together there, then pulled up to the top of her head, and piled above her high forehead. Her face was very serene and had a slight smile. Grandma often looked in the direction of this portrait during her conversations with Bronislawa and then would turn her gaze toward me.

The conversations between Grandma and Bronislawa were usually fragmented and interrupted by long silences, sighs, and English words I didn't understand. I played with my toys, not paying much attention to what they said. However, the words "she has Genia's eyes" caught my attention one day. I looked at myself in the mirror and saw a round-faced girl with short dark brown hair and green eyes. I was plump and had thick legs. I struggled to understand what they were talking about. Slowly I realized that the portrait of the unknown but beautiful young woman hanging in the green room was a photograph of Genia and that Grandma thought that I looked like her.

I was five years old when suddenly I understood that Genia was my mother who had died. I don't know how I acquired this understanding, and I can only speculate that it was more like an intuitive perception of my physical similarity to the woman in the big photograph and the sadness with which my grandmother looked at her must have meant that that woman was dead and that I was her child. My real mother was dead! She must have been buried under the earth just like President Narutowicz, and I would never see her again. I was shaken by the horror of my loss. Now I understood that Bronislawa wasn't my mother. The discovery that I had no mother filled me with emptiness. I burst into tears and ran to Grandma Anna.

"Why did my mammie die?" I shrieked, crying. "Why don't I have a mammie?" I thrust my small body tight against her chest, wrapping my little arms around her neck. I wouldn't let go of her for a long while, as I cried uncontrollably. But neither she nor Bronislawa succeeded in providing the consolation I needed. They didn't really respond to my despair. They were restrained by their fear of my father's anger, for it was their careless words that had led to my painful discovery. I never doubted the truth and, feeling resentful that my father had kept it secret from me, I wouldn't seek any consolation from him. I thus had no one to turn to, and I had to keep my grief to myself.

At once my attitude toward Bronislawa began to deteriorate. With her cold personality, Bronislawa never succeeded in evoking my unreserved love for her. I was probably always jealous of the attention my father had given to her, knowing how much I meant to him. I considered her an impostor. I continued calling her *mamusia* (mama), but my feelings towards her now oscillated between love and hatred. I knew that I had my mother's beautiful eyes, and I began to identify with her, feeling superior to Bronislawa. That's when I started to become competitive with her for my father's affection. I resented any attention he would give Bronislawa, and I enjoyed listening to every demeaning remark he directed to her in my presence.

When I was six-and-a-half years old, my second half-brother Gabriel was born. I was moved to the "green room" from the nursery, which my brothers shared from then on. I knew that Gene and Gabriel, being her own sons, were very special to Bronislawa. I resented no longer being the exclusive center of my father's and Bronislawa's attention. However, I felt confident that I was still the most important member of the family to my father.

After moving to the green room, I had my mother's portrait constantly before my eyes. I looked at her each night as I was falling asleep and would see her as soon as I woke up in the morning. Around this same period, I started to have bad dreams and feared ghosts. These ghosts were white, extremely tall objects resembling angular obelisks. As a child I saw no connection between my mother and the ghosts in my dream. In retrospect I am inclined to speculate that their appearance in my dreams was related to my moving to the green room. It may have represented an unconscious attempt on my part to establish connection with my dead mother.

A small room at the end of the apartment adjoined the green room. Stray cats from the courtyard would climb the stairs that led to the doorway of this room. I liked cats, and whenever I heard them me-owing at the door I would let them in and give them milk. Bronislawa was none too happy about my turning our apartment into an animal shelter. That did not displease me, as I felt a malicious pleasure in exasperating her in this manner.

During my preschool days, Bronislawa took me to Grandma Anna's large apartment in the center of Warsaw where a regular nursery school had been organized primarily for my benefit. There I met children from good neighborhoods, and we played games, danced, and sang. Except for going to this nursery, I lived in relative isolation from other children. Solec Street, which was located at the periphery of the city, was not considered a good neighborhood. My parents felt that they couldn't find suitable local playmates for me. Only Irka T., a neighborhood girl of my age, the daughter of one of my father's employees, was invited occasionally to play with me. She and I liked to cut out paper dolls. Once, our maid inadvertently threw these dolls out with the trash. I cried bitterly and complained to Bronislawa about the maid. Bronislawa scolded her, but I didn't forget my loss for a long time.

It was customary among bourgeois families in Poland to have a governess take care of the children. Even after I went to school, I had governesses and tutors. But our nanny, Wikcia, remained the only one I loved.

On Sunday mornings, workhorses, which were used to pull the wagons distributing the flour from my father's mill to other bakeries, were scrubbed clean and brushed in our courtyard. Sometimes I was given a ride on these horses alongside the courtyard, and I would imagine that I was an adept horseback rider.

Sunday afternoons my father and Bronislawa took a nap on a couch in their bedroom. During this time I would retreat to a small room at the end of the apartment, hoping to hear the meowing of cats at the back staircase. I also liked to sit at the window watching colorful processions of saints carried out of the church across the street from our property. I was fascinated by this spectacle, which was particularly elaborate on big holidays. When my father, who was an agnostic, became aware of my fascination with these rituals, he ridiculed religious beliefs. I don't think he understood or cared that religious rituals and pageantry could easily fascinate a little girl, even one who, like me, was raised in a nonreligious home. I felt uncomfortable listening to his comments and had a sense that they were wrong. I didn't then know what blasphemous meant, but that is what best describes what I felt about his remarks. In spite of the total absence of religious practice in my family, as a child I had been clearly responsive to symbolism and the passion of ritual. Therefore, I was sensitive to my father's violation of something considered and felt to be sacred by many.

There was a tradition of throwing garlands of flowers into the Vistula River on June 23 (called St. John's night, the longest night of the year). Many such garlands were tossed from the top of our mill, and our house was a wonderful place to watch this spectacle.

With the Sunday make-believe horseback riding, a choice view of the processions, and St. John's night, our property offered many attractions to a growing child. Living there, I felt more important than other people. I didn't know anybody else who lived in such a grand place. Just the entrance itself was spectacular. The horse-drawn carriage in which we rode out and then back to the house would stop in front of the entrance, and its driver, in his blue uniform with a long coat, gold buttons and a blue hat, would loudly shout, *Brama!* (gate). The gate would open to let the carriage into the cobblestone front yard. Immediately afterwards, the gate would close and the carriage would proceed to the front of our residence, where it would again stop to let us out. We would walk up the stairs to our apartment, entering it through a long corridor. The carriage would then leave, passing under an arch to the backyard, and the horse would be set free and put in a stable.

In Poland, people were in the habit of going away on long summer vacations. The first one I remember was when I was six years old. I went with my father and Bronislawa for several weeks to Zoppot, a Baltic Sea resort near Gdansk. The Baltic Sea is cold. So although I played a lot in the sand, I wasn't allowed to go into the water. In the morning for breakfast I ate tasty rolls; in the afternoon I sampled cakes with whipped cream. I remember the smell of cigars and coffee in outdoor cafés. One day after eating eel, which was considered a great delicacy in Poland but which I had just sampled for the first time, we went for a boat ride and I became seasick. From that day on I wouldn't eat eel, but I continued getting seasick on boats.

Sometimes I played with a boy whose mother knew my father and Bronislawa. "Why do women's swimsuits cover more of the body than men's suits?" I asked his mother one day. "Because women must hide such ugly parts of their body as their breasts, which men don't have," she said. Her answer left me puzzled.

In those days young girls were raised in complete ignorance of sex. In my sheltered life I was told nothing about sex. Having two brothers, I was aware that boys have different genitals than girls, but I didn't know that these anatomical differences were related to their respective sexual functions. The lack of openness of adults to children about sexuality didn't help me gain the necessary understanding. Early in my life I recall experiencing feelings of sexual arousal, the nature of which I didn't understand because I didn't know about the existence of sexual life. But I don't recall any preoccupation with women's breasts; I was surprised by their description as ugly. This made me feel shy about my little girl's body, even though I didn't yet have breasts. But I had to wait for another three years before I learned something about the facts of life.

When I was seven, we vacationed in San Remo, Italy. Gabriel, who was only six months old, was left in Poland under the care of a nanny and the supervision of Grandma Anna. I was glad that we didn't have him with us. I would have liked it even better if Gene had also been left home. But he came with my father, Bronislawa, a governess, and me by train to Paris. We then traveled south in a rented car with a driver.

In Nice we saw a magnificent carnival parade of flowered carriages and people in fancy clothes dancing in the streets. My father and Bronislawa bought new clothes for all of us. I wore three coats, one on top of the other, to make them less apparent to the Italian customs officials; in this way my parents tried to avoid payment of import duties, which made me feel ashamed of their cheating. I also got a beautiful doll. I called her Lena because I had always liked that name, and she slept in her own box next to my bed at the Grand Hotel in San Remo. Every night after dinner a waiter peeled an orange for me; then he made a basket from the orange peel and filled it with candies. I liked the taste of Italian ice cream, which was served in silver goblets at the hotel's restaurant. After a few days in San Remo, my father and Bronislawa left me and Gene with the governess, and they went off by themselves to Egypt and Jerusalem. I didn't like being left with the governess. I kept running away from her to look for lizards and to play in the hotel gardens with a boy I met there and befriended.

One day after our return to Poland, a little Tatar[1] girl named Zaira, with slightly slanted black eyes, approached me in Warsaw's Ujazdowski Park.

"Little girl, would you like to play ball with me?" she asked, and we started playing together.

Zaira came to the park every day with her grandmother, a tall, black-haired Tatar woman who always held herself erect. Zaira's mother was Polish; she was a physician, an assistant professor of pathology at the Warsaw University Medical School. Zaira and I became play companions, and so began our lifelong friendship.

At eight I was tall for my age and had big, dreamy green eyes. My dark hair was short and parted on the side. I wore simple but pretty dresses, even for play. Unlike today's American girls, I did not own any play clothes.

My father had a large family with numerous siblings, but he maintained contact with only two sisters—Aunt Zosia and Aunt Nathalie. Aunt Nathalie was his youngest sister. I liked her very much. She was always smiling, cheerful, and ready to do things for other people. Her husband supported his family by making hand-painted

---

1. The Tatar are members of one of the numerous chiefly Turkish peoples probably originating in Manchuria and Mongolia and now found mainly in the Tatar republic of the U.S.S.R., the north Caucasus, Crimea, and sections of Siberia.

decorative trays. He considered himself an artist and dreamed of living in Paris. Their only daughter, Irene, was one year younger than I.

One afternoon, when I was eight years old, they all came to take leave of us before going to France. Although I liked Aunt Nathalie, I saw her and her family so rarely that I didn't feel any pangs about their leaving. But I did notice that the departure of my aunt Nathalie was painful for my father.

Whenever I made a remark that my father and Bronislawa considered clever, they looked at each other and nodded. "Grandma Irena," I heard them say, implying that I had inherited my paternal grandmother's brains. This made me feel proud and increased my feelings of superiority, which often bordered on arrogance. Although I can't be sure, I think my feelings of superiority were related to the special place I had in my father's heart because of the death of my mother. These feelings might also have been my attempt to identify with her. Besides that, I think they were part of a hard shell I had built up around me to hide the unhappiness that stemmed from the fact that I had no biological mother.

I inherited my father's fierce temper and stubbornness. This made me sympathetic to his occasional outbursts of anger. I loved and respected him. But one day when I was nine years old, in spite of my admiration for him, I approached him as he sat at the dining room table, said some curse words, and spat at him! I have no idea why I did it, unless I resented his Sunday naps on the couch with Bronislawa or was still angry that he didn't tell me about my mother and I had to learn it from Grandma Anna and Bronislawa quite accidentally. When I did this awful thing, I was wearing a pretty, new, sheer wool red dress with long sleeves and a white satin collar and cuffs. Very slowly my father pulled the hem of my dress to his face and wiped my saliva from his face onto the dress. He said nothing. That was his punishment. My new dress was now soiled. I was shocked and angry. However, only a few days later, when he heard me using curse words not addressed to him, but just said in the thin air, he didn't punish me.

The mill and bakery workers constantly walked through the large plaza surrounded by the house where we lived, the mill, the bakery, and the wall with the gate to the street. The horse wagons carried flour from the mill through the gate to the city. They returned empty to the backyard behind the house. The workers and the drivers were in the habit of cursing and my father tried to prevent my hearing them by keeping the windows closed. In spite of his efforts, I managed to pick up some curse words.

Now he was ashamed that those people would hear his own daughter swearing. "In the past, I kept the door to the balcony closed so that you wouldn't learn cursing from the mill workers. Now I have to keep this door closed so the workers won't hear you swearing!" my father said. At once I felt the full force of his despair. And on top of the remaining shock and anger, I now felt ashamed.

Jealous of the attention they were getting, sometimes I tortured my younger brothers when there were no adults around. Gene, the oldest, with his round face, dark hair, and dark brown eyes, looked much like our father. Once, when he was five years old, I took advantage of the momentary absence of the governess from the room to convince him to lie down on the floor. I proceeded to cut his eyebrows with a pair of scissors. I know I resented how Bronislawa favored Gene. In retrospect, I also wonder if this torture was an attempt to get revenge for my father's recent punishment of me.

"What are you doing, naughty girl!" I heard the voice of the governess, who had just entered the room. With her entrance onto the scene, I was given no chance to cut the eyebrows of Gabriel, my wiggly two-year-old brother.

School Starts

By the time I was nine I had become a heavy-hipped, thick-boned, plump girl. My eyes were still my best feature. They were of an unusual yellowish-green-gray mixture of colors, framed by long black lashes and my father's thick black eyebrows. Nobody ever referred to me as a pretty girl, but I was often spoken of as "the one with beautiful eyes." Bronislawa liked to buy me expensive dresses. I was aware that I attracted attention. My eyes, the especially lovely dresses I wore, living on a large property with horses, having a rich father and no mother, all made me different both in the view of others and in my own feelings about myself.

Most children in Poland started school at the age of seven. But I still had private tutors at home. This may have had to do with difficulties in arranging convenient transportation for me from the outskirts of Warsaw where we lived to the center-city location of the private school my parents selected for me. I was nine years old when I was finally sent to the first class of the Popielewska Roszkowska Gymnasium,[2] a private school, in 1926. The school year had already started, and I was placed in a class of older girls, although I never knew why.

"What's your religion? What's your father's occupation?" These bigger girls bombarded me with questions.

---

2. The Polish and most other European educational systems differ from the American system. Americans who graduate from high school may go to a junior college (2 years) or fully pledged four-year college before they go to a professional school such as medical school, which is also a four-year educational facility. In Poland, graduates of Gymnasium which is either a 6 or 8-year institution may go directly to a professional school only from an 8-year Gymnasium. In Poland, medical schools are 6-year institutions, with the first two years corresponding to American pre-med.

"I have no religion. My father's an atheist, and he's a mill owner," I replied.

"But you must have a religion. Everybody does. Are you a Catholic, Russian Orthodox, Protestant, or Jew? You must be one! What do you mean that your father's a mill owner? He must be a rich man. Is he?"

"Miss Grasberg has arrived in her carriage!" I overheard one of my classmates say. I was painfully aware that this was hardly a casual observation, but a remark of derision and ridicule. These girls might have been jealous. Children often, when jealous of someone they perceive to have it better than they do, will ridicule them to cover their envy and as a way of showing their resentment.

They surrounded me and made me feel uncomfortable. Until then, being different had been a source of pride, but now it became a handicap.

From that day on, as soon as the carriage stopped in front of the school, I got out as fast as I could and ran indoors quickly, hoping that no one saw the carriage. Whenever I was teased, my feelings of superiority and being special gave way to feelings of inadequacy. I wasn't prepared for their intolerance, for in the past I either played with children in a closely supervised environment (in the nursery school at Grandma Anna's) or with just one other child like Zaira, my Tatar friend.

To escape from my uneasiness in this new situation, I developed a habit of daydreaming. I would stare into space without listening to what the teacher was saying. When I was suddenly brought back to reality by the teacher asking me "Do you know the answer?", I would realize that I didn't even know the question. But when I wasn't daydreaming, I often knew the answer and was praised.

After school I had French and German lessons at home. Zaira and I attended classes in rhythmic dancing at the famous Mieczynska Dance School. In addition, I had private art and piano lessons. I was neither a gifted artist nor a talented musician. I didn't enjoy going to concerts, and none of my teachers succeeded in arousing my interest in music. My musical education did not progress much beyond the "Solvegi's Song" by Grieg, which I would hammer out for hours. Like most children who are neither particularly gifted in the arts nor interested in learning a foreign language, I didn't appreciate my expensive private instruction, which I now realize most of my classmates couldn't afford but maybe would have loved.

The school we attended was very strict. We all had to wear navy blue uniforms. The hygienist was instructed to measure the length of our skirts and inspect our underclothes. She scolded me for wearing silk panties and suggested that Bronislawa ought to buy me cotton underwear. She was expected to report on any signs that our brassiere straps had been chewed on, although I never knew why anybody would want to chew on brassiere straps.

Gradually I became used to school and my classmates, and began establishing friendships. Halinka H. became one of my friends. We used to call her Heksa, which means "witch." She was a shapely, medium-sized girl with reddish-brown curly hair. Her parents were divorced. She was the first person to acquaint me with the facts of life. For some reason, despite their reticence about talking of sex to me, as soon as I got home from Heksa's "lessons" I went to Grandma Anna and Bronislawa with questions about all the new and exciting information I had received. I'm not sure why I did that, but I suppose I wanted some confirmation from the female adults in my life. Maybe I also wanted to let them know I was growing into a woman and, on my own, was learning some of the secrets they were determined to keep from me.

"This isn't what little girls should be thinking about. When you grow up, you'll find out," Grandma Anna said.

Bronislawa became red-faced. "Isn't it horrible what kind of conversations these girls have at school?" she said to Grandma Anna. Bronislawa didn't like to talk. I never heard her tell a story, although she was in the habit of interrupting other people's conversation by her remarks.

Besides my grandparents, I had never met anybody from her family except her cousin, who was a dentist and treated my teeth. Then, when I was ten, I found out that she had another cousin. One day Bronislawa and Grandma Anna took me to Milanowek, a small industrial town known for producing artificial silk. It was located a few miles away from Warsaw. That cousin, a pleasant dark-haired, middle-aged woman, was engaged in conversation with other women when we arrived at her villa. "This is how you look at life when you are fifty," she said as I entered her living room.

Looking at my new summer shoes, I tried to imagine what could be meant by *looking* at life, and why you would look at it any special way when you are fifty years old. Until then, I had lived a fairly insular life, and this visit to Milanowek was a strange experience for me. I didn't know how to behave. I wasn't used to listening to the conversation of adults other than in my immediate family and, listening to the unfamiliar topics discussed by these strangers, I couldn't understand what they were talking about.

They never spoke about my mother in my presence. If they had mentioned her name, I know I would have become interested in what they were saying, and I thus might have become more interested in my mother's relative. But this didn't happen. Their conversation seemed boring. Just as I did at school, I started to daydream, my habitual escape from what I didn't understand, or didn't interest me, or was difficult to deal with. I never did find out why Bronislawa and Grandma Anna had taken me to Milanowek on that particular occasion or never brought me there again.

In contrast to the prudish attitudes towards sex of Grandma Anna and Bronislawa, our nanny Wikcia spoke to me freely about the body and its desires. When I was ten, she called attention to my developing bosom and praised its beauty. On several occasions she embarrassed me with the question, "Wouldn't you like someone to put a good length into your body?" I hadn't experienced such desires. I liked Wikcia, but I considered her question vulgar. Wikcia's healthy openness about sex was just one example of her ability to enjoy life and all its pleasures. In spring, she returned from her Sunday outings bearing heavy branches of white and purple lilacs. She would distribute them throughout the house in vases, filling the apartment with their fragrance. Whenever I smelled these flowers, I associated their scent with a then popular song about lilacs blooming in Pennsylvania. At the time I had no idea that Pennsylvania is in the United States. I just loved this song, which I heard sung at one of Warsaw's cabarets called *Morskie Oko* (Eye of the Sea). My parents took me to this cabaret because of the many lovely songs they sang there and the witty political jokes.

Except for political jokes, which my father enjoyed, I never saw him laughing at any forms of entertainment, certainly not at the slapstick comedies. He didn't have a good sense of humor, and considered stupid many jokes that made other people laugh.

"Everybody laughs except for us," he said with pride on such occasions. Because of his example, I too didn't laugh easily.

Our family went on a long summer vacation in France when I was ten years old. On the way to Biarritz we stopped in Paris to visit Aunt Nathalie and to see the International Colonial Exhibition. It was a craft exhibition of people living in what were then French colonies. It was the first of its kind that I had seen, and I must have been impressed by its novelty because I still remember the silver bracelets I saw there.

We took my cousin Irene with us to Biarritz. She and I had very different personalities. I was outspoken; she didn't talk much, but I thought that she was manipulative. I was raised in wealth, and she in modest circumstances. However, she had a mother she loved without any reservations, and I had lost mine and had mixed feelings about Bronislawa. At the age of nine, she competed with me successfully for the attention of boys. This aroused my jealousy and resentment. As a result of all this, we didn't become close that summer.

The weather in Biarritz was much warmer than in Zoppot, and I was allowed to bathe in the sea at noon. One day, a good-looking, muscular man stood in the water at some distance from the shore. He seemed to be teaching children to swim, and he offered to teach me how to float in the sea. He took me into deeper water and supported my back with his hand, while I stretched out on the surface. I became aware that the outline of my budding bosom showed through my swimming suit and, surprisingly, that pleased me. The water was warm, and having discovered that I could float on my own, I had a feeling of complete happiness. Still, every now and then, I had moments of fear, during which my instructor's hand would provide a welcome support.

Soon I had a sense of something touching me between my legs. Could it be his hand? I rejected that notion at first and thought I must be imagining things. But one thing I was sure of: I liked this new and pleasant sensation. As it continued, I felt ashamed of myself because I wanted it to continue. I enjoyed it. Then, suddenly, I became frightened. I stood up in the water and started walking towards the shore. I kept my eyes straight ahead, not wanting to look at my swimming instructor. My unsuspecting family was waiting for me with the lunch brought by our governess, Miss Waclawa. I remember well this welcome repast—a Swiss candy bar inside a crisp French roll and a peach for dessert. The memory of this first sexual experience continued to return during my daydreaming long after my return to Warsaw.

During our vacation in Biarritz, there was some labor agitation among the French hotel servants which didn't mean anything to me at the time. But years later, when I sought accommodation in a luxurious hotel in Biarritz, not as a paying guest but as a poor refugee, I realized the importance of money.

My French had improved from this stay in Biarritz. Then in the fall I continued private lessons at home with a tutor, Madame Marguerite de Revillon-Rogóyska, who became a friend of the family. In winter I went with her for a vacation to Krynica, a resort where I had skiing lessons. Madame Rogóyska taught me how to knit, which I liked and kept up for many years. Whatever we did together, she spoke only French with me, and soon I became fluent in this language.

In contrast to the pleasant Madame Rogóyska, my private German teacher was an obese man who had a tendency to spit while he talked. This made his lessons very annoying. I studied German for two years, but I never learned to speak, read, or write German properly.

At school, aside from Heksa, who had aroused my curiosity about the facts of life, I had three other friends. Halina S. was by far the most intelligent and cultured. She was also a good sportswoman. We called her "Szpilka" which in Polish means "a pin." She earned that name because of the sharp, cutting remarks she was in the habit of making.

Vera L. was very different from Szpilka. Vera was always very well groomed, and she was interested in social life and feminine domestic activities. When Vera visited me on Sundays, we often went to the movies. At other times, we would climb a ladder leading to the hayloft in our backyard and sit on the hay, gossiping about the girls and boys we knew.

Krysia O. was another friend and a classmate of mine. She was a short, blond girl with black eyes whose parents were divorced. She matured earlier than the rest of us, and she understood people's emotions and motives better than we did.

These three girls—Szpilka, Vera, and Krysia—satisfied different needs in me. With Szpilka I was an intellectual and a sportswoman; with Vera I was a silly gossip; with Krysia I became a more compassionate person with insight into the loneliness of children from broken homes.

One of our classmates, Zolka Dowbor-Musnicka, was a girl from an aristocratic family. At sixteen, Zolka had a much more active social life than the rest of us. On one summer evening, I sat on the balcony of Krysia O.'s apartment and watched Zolka in her evening gown waltzing with a handsome young man at a party across the street. Krysia and I felt excluded from the grown-up world that she had entered.

A sense of not belonging, of being an outsider, had been familiar to me ever since I entered school. But out of shyness, I never discussed my sense of isolation with any of my friends. Instead, I continued to escape by daydreaming.

My family practically never had guests or accepted invitations to other people's homes. Although my parents sometimes took me to the circus, a ballet, an opera, or even to a cabaret, most of the time we spent our evenings at home. Cigarette or cigar smoking, alcohol, and the mere excitement of social gatherings easily provoked my father's asthmatic attacks.

Although I was making some progress in forming friends, my feelings of inadequacy persisted and were exacerbated by my family's lack of social life. But aside from the limited exposure to the opportunity of learning and stimulation that contact with others provides, other factors also contributed to my social uneasiness and lack of self-esteem. I never had to prepare food, clean dishes, or wash my own stockings. My friends from less affluent homes had to help at home; they had an opportunity, which I didn't, to learn how to cook, serve dinner, clean house, and launder. Although they might have envied my relative leisure, by not knowing how to do these things I was deprived of a sense of independence and competence, and when I compared myself to my friends, in this respect, I came up short.

Once, when Miss Popielewska, the director of our school, invited our class to have tea at her apartment, the girls divided the chores among themselves. Some poured, others passed the cups, sugar, lemon, and cookies. Someone gave me a tray with a cup of tea to take to Miss Popielewska. Without removing the cup from the tray, I put the entire tray on her lap when I should have simply handed her the cup and saucer. I saw the raised eyebrows of my classmates, and I knew immediately that I'd done something wrong, but I didn't know what.

When I was twelve I contracted a middle ear infection, which was a complication of an undiagnosed case of scarlet fever. I got sick with it first, then passed it on to Gene, Gabriel, and Bronislawa. Bronislawa, with the aid of a nurse, took care of all of us in her usual self-sacrificing manner, although she was very sick herself. At the time I thought that my father had married her primarily for my sake. But later there was no limit to the efforts she would make for him, Gene, and Gabriel, as well as myself.

Infatuation

After the family recovered from scarlet fever, we spent the summer in Srodborow, a popular vacation resort surrounded by pine woods not far from Warsaw. I was twelve, and I fell in love for the first time. Janek G. was a tall, lanky young man with dark hair, gray eyes, a slightly curved mouth, and a pleasantly smiling face. The uncoordinated motions of his long arms made him look awkward and not particularly attractive. However, that didn't bother me because his intelligence, which seemed extraordinary to me, and his wonderful sense of humor were more important to me than his appearance. He was sixteen years old and wanted to become a physician, like his father.

During that summer, Janek and I stole apples from a private property adjoining the boarding house where we stayed. Although still plump and wide-hipped, I had become a more attractive girl, with big gray-green eyes and short dark hair. I wore a satin, pink-striped peasant dress with big sleeves that were held tight to my arms by elastic bands—an ideal hiding place for our stolen fruit. At the slightest noise in the orchard we would lie down on the ground and keep very quiet. In spite of these precautions, we were discovered. Fortunately, the owner of the orchard knew our families and seemed to be more amused than angry at our appetite for his apples.

I never spoke to Janek about my feelings or made any gestures that would betray them. I was quite sure my affections were not returned and that I held no special place in his heart. In fact, I really think that he spent time with me simply because there were no other young people his age around, and I was his only available company. I looked up to him and made no demands. He was a loner and seemed to be more interested in books than in girls anyway.

When I was thirteen I sometimes would wake up in the middle of the night in the green room, hop out of bed, turn the light on, and out of some inner need compose poetry. After I wrote down my poem, I would go back to sleep. Most of the time I didn't remember what I wrote about. But I was always thinking of Janek.

The summer I was thirteen, I went with my family to Spain. In Barcelona we saw a bullfight, which I found repulsive and extremely cruel. The sight of blood made me nauseated. "I feel faint," I complained to my father and Bronislawa, holding their hands, as we left the arena. But my parents were very intent on exposing me to the traditional spectacle of Spaniards.

I was bored visiting art museums, perhaps because neither my father nor Bronislawa spoke to me enough about art to arouse my enthusiasm. My father usually rushed through museums. Bronislawa was more interested in art than he was, but had no inclination to articulate her views. In spite of this, our sightseeing in Spain was not entirely wasted on me since I retained a vivid memory of the country, especially the streets in Barcelona and the appearance of the Spanish people and their clothes. Visiting St. Ignatius Loyola Convent, I was most impressed by a room with walls made of silver panels.

My parents enjoyed the opera and, in Warsaw, took me to see Moniuszko's *Halka,* Smetana's *Bartered Bride,* and such popular operas as *La Bohème, Madame Butterfly,* and *The Barber of Seville.* My father delighted in singing the well-known aria from *Il Pagliaci*—"Ridi Pagliaco." My half-brothers loved music and, at a very young age, became familiar with classical composers and famous operas. But music did not become an important part of my life until my later years, when I did come to enjoy going to concerts and listening to classical music in my home.

At our school each class had an annual dance. Since the girls in the lower grades were only allowed to dance with each other, my classmates and I used to watch the older girls dancing with boys. Standing in the hall and looking through the open door at the swirling couples, I admired an attractive girl from a higher grade, Janeczka Polakowna, waltzing with her partner. I thought that her long, pearl-gray sheer skirt, a burgundy velour top, and an elegant matching bag swinging from her shoulder were the most beautiful clothes I had ever seen. I sighed with envy, hating my navy wool school uniform. I wished I could look as pretty as she did and that I too could dance with boys.

At fourteen I was still shy. I never volunteered to speak when a teacher asked the class a question. "Irena, do you know the answer?" our history teacher asked one day. This time I had a chance to exhibit my knowledge. I spoke about the emergence of the Renaissance after centuries of medieval obscurantism.

"Just listen to her! She sits quietly, as if she couldn't count to three; but once she starts talking, listen to the words of wisdom coming from her mouth!" Mrs. Ada B. said.

Her praise reminded me of the reaction of my parents to those remarks of mine that they considered clever. It was on those occasions that they would inevitably compare me to my long-deceased paternal grandmother, who was known for her intelligence and wisdom. My teacher's remarks strengthened my growing reputation as a good student.

When I was fourteen, I developed a low-grade fever. I tired easily and perspired. A chest X-ray revealed a small tuberculosis lesion at the top of my left lung. Dr. Maliniak, our family physician, advised my parents to take me to the mountains for summer vacation and make sure that I had plenty of rest, fresh air, and good food. We spent that summer at a well-known Polish resort called Ciechocinek. I was an avid reader of poetry, so I became very excited when I discovered that a poet I admired, Julian Tuwim, was staying at our pension. Seeing him sitting alone at a table on the porch, I forgot my usual shyness and approached him. He looked at me with a smile when I told him how much I enjoyed his poetry. Then we discussed religion, and I told him that I was an agnostic. Later I heard Tuwim say I was a very intelligent girl. His praise made me proud and happy. The impression I made on Julian Tuwim added to my growing realization that I had a good mind.

At the end of the summer I had another chest X-ray, and it showed that my lung lesion had healed.

My half-brothers, Gene and Gabriel, were now attending the Gymnasium named after Mikolaj Rej (a famous Polish writer), which is the same school my first love, Janek G., had graduated from. Gene and Gabriel now differed dramatically in appearance and behavior. Gene was always immaculately dressed, gentle, and sociable. He also had a well-developed appreciation of gourmet meals. At home he cut his food into small pieces and ate each bite slowly. By the time we all finished eating, he still had some choice morsels left on his plate. Sometimes it made Gabriel and me envious. Gene was also a bit of a *bon vivant.* At the age of eleven he told Bronislawa that he had joined a society of boys devoted to looking at pictures of naked women; she made him resign immediately.

Gabriel was interested in books and in the violin, but he couldn't care less about what he ate or how he looked. Although both boys got new clothes at the same time, Gene's suit still looked new after a year of constant wear, whereas within a few days Gabriel's tailor-made new suit looked as if he had slept in a gutter.

I differed from both of them in appearance and behavior. I lacked Gene's elegance, social grace, and gourmet tastes, but I was not so sloppy and absent-minded as Gabriel.

We were all avid readers, but both of my half-brothers knew literature better than I ever did, and I wasn't as knowledgeable about music as either one of them. They were good to me, gladly complying with my requests for errands and sometimes doing chores for me. But they were so much younger that I didn't have much in common with them. I regretted that I had no older brother, whose classmates or friends could provide a source of boyfriends.

When I was fourteen a classmate, Anka Przysiecka—a big girl with black hair and dimples in her cheeks—recited her poetry for us, which she often did. One of her poems started with the words: *Jam jest powietrze czyste, przejrzyste* (I'm pure transparent air). For some reason these words have remained forever imprinted on my memory. When I returned home from school after hearing them, I dug out the poems I'd written the night before and, remembering the beauty of Anka's verses, I tore mine to pieces. A few days later I tore up and discarded all my previously written poems. But I didn't live by writing poetry alone. Reading it still meant a great deal to me, and I also got a lot of pleasure from mysteries and adventures.

Wikcia, our beloved former nanny and housekeeper who had left us to marry a much older widowed iron monger, maintained contact with us. She, her husband, and her younger sister, who was married to Wikcia's husband's son, lived in a small but very tidy apartment in the Praga section of Warsaw on the left bank of the Vistula River. One day, when I was fifteen, I skipped school with Szpilka, and we went to visit Wikcia in her Praga Street apartment. In spite of her concern that Bronislawa would be angry if she knew that I had played hooky, Wikcia made us feel very welcome. Then Szpilka and I went to visit a gypsy who told our future with cards.

At school we had heard the older girls talking about what they planned to do after graduation. Most of these girls were daughters of educated professional families who varied in their economic resources. Other girls had fathers who were businessmen. Some wanted to have a profession, as many women at that time had in Poland. Not surprisingly, I had begun to wonder what future occupation I should choose for myself. My father expected me to get married and to have a profession also. It hadn't occurred to me to consult any of my teachers on the choice of my further studies. Having made no choice as yet, I naively expected help from the gypsy, who would predict my future. But when this gypsy said that we would have a long life, be rich, and happily married, both Szpilka and I were disappointed. Her prediction threw no light on our future careers.

Neither of us had a role model at home. Szpilka's mother and Bronislawa were housewives; her father was a businessman and my father was an industrialist. Ala, Szpilka's friend whose father was a lawyer, wanted to follow in his footsteps and also become one. In fact, she already knew that she wanted to defend juvenile delinquents. Looking at Ala, a smiling girl with beautiful black eyes, I became so impressed by her determination that I was inspired to follow her example. "I would like to be a lawyer defending juvenile delinquents," I too would reply during the next several months whenever anyone asked what I wanted to do in the future.

Although many girls from well-to-do Polish families wanted to acquire university educations, have professions, marry yet remain economically independent, this wasn't a universal rule. Almost as many girls from comparable families didn't seek an education beyond the Gymnasium and didn't plan careers. They wanted only to marry well and be supported by their husbands. Women from poor, mainly peasant families, which formed the bulk of the population in Poland, had to work for a living. They dreamt of a day when

Irena at fifteen with a classmate on a school excursion to
Wigry Lakes

they would marry, stop working for money, and only keep house
for their husbands.

After Wikcia married and left our household, we had an illiterate
live-in cook who worked for us for a long time. In anticipation of
getting married, every evening she sat at our kitchen table and practiced signing her name so that she would be in a position to write on
the wedding certificate. So, a huge pile of pages with an endless
succession of "Julia Abramowicz" written on them covered our
kitchen table.

Some of the girls in our school were already much more sexually
precocious than Szpilka and I. One was a girl in a class just above
us, Irka K. Her parents owned a large, well-known chocolate factory
in Warsaw. Irka, their only daughter, was very spoiled. She dressed
in expensive, sophisticated clothes and wore perfume and makeup
whenever I saw her outside of school. Once I noticed her at a public
swimming pool in Warsaw being literally carried to a chaise lounge

in the arms of the popular movie actor Witold Conti, the Cary Grant of Poland. This sight made me feel as if I were still a child, and I fervently wished I were more grown up. Irka K. wasn't troubled about what profession she would enter. Her future was clear—she would get married and run a household.

One day, when I was fifteen years old and in a hurry to go out, I noticed that a dress I wanted to wear on that occasion needed to have a button sewn on. But when I asked Zosia, our maid, to do this for me, she didn't want to interrupt her work. I was determined to have my way, showed her my gold watch, and offered to give it to her as a reward. Zosia obliged, and I gave her my watch. But she felt uncomfortable about this deal and told Bronislawa about it. Bronislawa immediately demanded that she return the watch to me. I became very angry that Bronislawa challenged my right to dispose of my own property, and I made Zosia keep the watch. I won a silly battle with Bronislawa in an attempt to assert my independence from her. Although such behavior is typical of many teenage girls, in my case I think it was also evidence of my continued ambivalence toward her; after all, this woman was not my mother, she had participated in keeping my mother's true identity from me, and she stood between me and my father in the special way that only a stepmother can.

I remained indifferent to Bronislawa's thoughtfulness, even when she tried to please me and suggested that we go to buy new clothes. When we went shopping, she liked to buy me expensive dresses, for which I never showed any gratitude even though I was glad to have them. During our visits to fine stores, I looked critically at the dresses until finally one of them appealed to me.

"I want that one!" I would say in a demanding tone of voice. I never asked Bronislawa's advice. If she suggested that some dress other than the one I wanted would be more practical, I ignored her. She wasn't trying to force her choice upon me and, usually, I got what I wanted.

Bronislawa liked good clothes and always dressed well. She was proud that she was the wife of a rich man, and it showed, especially when she would be driven out in our carriage wearing her finery. She was aware that being Mrs. Grasberg made her thought of by others as being someone above ordinary people.

I had never considered her an intelligent woman, and I thought that her pride in her social status was silly. What made me feel superior to her now was that I already had an ambition to be somebody in my own right rather than merely someone's wife. I looked down on Bronislawa because she was only a housewife, taking for granted everything she did for me, as if it were her duty. At every opportunity, I undermined her identity, as I competed with her for my father's affection. I sometimes attempted to play the two of them off against each other.

As I look back on all this I am not proud of my behavior, for Bronislawa was a good mother to me. I realize that I was behaving like a rebellious teenager, and that, unknowingly, I was also taking out on her my hurt over the loss of my biological mother, for which she was hardly responsible. That pain didn't stop with my adolescence, but the early loss of a mother rarely does.

My father was fascinated by medicine. I think he was really a frustrated physician. He used to treat us with sodium bicarbonate for virtually every symptom we had. Each Sunday, like clockwork, he painted our gums with iodine so that we wouldn't develop the gum infection from which he suffered. He sought out the care of a physician's assistant named Pan Jan (Mr. John), who applied hot suction cups to my father's back to deal with his frequent pulmonary problems. Such applications created a vacuum that caused blood to be drawn from his congested lungs to the skin. This by now long-abandoned procedure was very popular at the time, and usually was administered by paramedical personnel rather than a physician. Pan Jan had a wide range of skills, and he also gave us pedicures.

In contrast to my father's love of playing doctor and joy of being a patient, I hadn't the slightest interest in caring for my own or other people's afflictions. My father attempted to stimulate such an interest in me and, by the time I was fifteen, he had already expressed his hope that I go to medical school: "Medicine is as noble a profession as there is. Wouldn't you like to become a physician?"

"Daddy, I'm not interested in diseases," I replied each time.

But he persisted telling me what a gratifying future I would have being a physician and treating sick people. "I would establish free clinics for poor patients if you would become a physician," he offered. My father was a wealthy man capable of securing my future, but well aware that great fortunes are more easily lost than acquired. He knew that if medicine were my profession, my financial independence would be more certain. I suspected that there was also another reason why he wanted me to become a physician. He was still mourning my mother, and may have wished that I could prevent unnecessary deaths of other young women.

"But Daddy," I repeated, "medicine doesn't appeal to me. I would rather study law."

"Who knows what wars are still ahead of us," he persisted. "You may need to leave Poland and emigrate to another country. You won't be able to practice law because it's different in every country. But diseases are the same everywhere," my father continued. I could detect in his voice more emotional involvement than usual.

My father had a realistic view of the history of Poland. It was then 1932, and he felt that Poland hadn't seen the last of hostilities — that another war was not only possible, but likely.

"Daddy, I may not study law. But I'm still not interested in diseases. I abhor the sight of blood and the smell of urine. Please let me find out what I really want to do," I insisted with the usual stubbornness of a teenager.

On Sunday mornings, after our gums were attended to and, weather permitting, we would often travel in our horse-driven carriage outside Warsaw to Wilanow, a seventeenth-century royal residence which King Jan Sobieski had built for his beloved wife Marysienka. On such occasions we would all be together as a family.

Mickey, our black miniature pinscher, accompanied us on those outings. He was our only pet and an important member of the household. Father used to take him out for walks. Mickey wiggled a lot during my father's attempts to put on his collar and leash. "Mickey, please stay still! Be a man!" Father would tell him. Having no responsibility for any domestic chores, I never volunteered to take the dog out for a walk.

While my father was trying to stimulate my interest in medicine, my attention was directed elsewhere. I wrote an essay entitled "A Child with Black Eyes Writes Balladyna"[3] about the great nineteenth-century Polish poet, Julius Slowacki. A new teacher at our school read it and praised my talent for literary criticism. This made me euphoric. I loved writing. But I never knew what I was going to write until I

---

3. Balladyna was a character from a poem by Julius Slowacki.

actually started. Then I thought that I could write faster than I could think. Whenever we were assigned essays at school and my classmates asked me what I was going to write about, I had no plan and my honest answer would be, "I don't know." Then I wrote under a sudden impulse, and my ideas would often come out of the daydreams.

I was then fourteen, read avidly, and wrote more essays, neglecting all my science homework until I flunked the first test in physics. This was a serious blow to my pride, since I was a good student and had never failed a test. My reaction was to put aside my literary ambitions for the time being and direct my attention to physics until I felt at ease with this subject. This effort was well rewarded. Soon I was at the top of my class in physics, and with that began my interest in the sciences.

Eagerly, I read popular books by Infeld and other physicists and started attending lectures of the visiting professors at the University of Warsaw, whose rector Professor Pienkowski was a physicist. I became interested in the contrasting structures of atoms and the universe. My new fascination with basic science changed my attitude toward religion. Although raised as an agnostic, I had been so impressed by church rituals in my childhood that I had considered myself a silent believer. I now experienced that same awe over the mysteries of existence that until then I had associated with religion, which now began to lose its meaning for me.

I was fifteen when my father and Bronislawa told me about their plans to move from Solec Street to another, more centrally located, apartment. My father owned two big apartment houses on Hoza Street. In one of these, a second-floor apartment and first-floor office space had become available. Although the decision to move was a natural outcome of my father's growing prosperity and his important position with the Warsaw Chamber of Commerce, Father and Bronislawa felt that this new location would be better in two important respects: it would be easier for Gene, Gabriel, and me to get to school, and the neighborhood was more convenient and more congenial for our friends to visit us.

During the selection of the furnishings for our new apartment, I was amazed at the extent to which my preferences for the style of our furniture influenced my parents' final purchases. This reinforced my realization of how much the move had been made for the sake of my future. My father and Bronislawa wanted me to participate in furnishing the new place so that I would feel comfortable with the way it looked when my friends would come to visit.

When we discussed outfitting the living room, the more practical-minded Bronislawa favored comfortable modern chairs and sofas, whereas I preferred furnishings that I considered more elegant. The type I liked was traditional, gilded, Louis XVI-style furniture that I had seen in palatial residences, including Wilanow. I didn't care if the pieces were reproductions, as long as they resembled what impressed me in visiting castles. This more luxurious furniture contrasted sharply with the simple oak tables, chairs and beds, which we had on Solec Street, and was far more uncomfortable. But comfort—so important for adults—would not be of equal concern to a girl my age. So, being as obstinate as teenagers tend to be, I would be unlikely to change my mind about my preference.

My own room was custom-designed by a decorator and furnished with beautiful *czeczot* furniture, which looked like spotted amber. There was a small safe built into the wall of a closet, and in it I kept souvenirs from my mother: a golden locket pendant, and a silver pendant in the shape of a fish with ruby eyes.

Whenever I had the need to talk about my classmates or school events, I spoke to Bronislawa freely. She listened eagerly, although rarely offered any comments. But I continued to keep my inner life secret from her. I never showed her my poems, nor confided in her my amorous feelings for Janek.

After we settled in to the Hoza Street apartment, Father moved his office to the floor beneath our new living quarters. There was no elevator in the building, so he had to walk up a flight of stairs when he came home for lunch and dinner. This was a big effort for him. Although he was only forty-seven and wasn't a smoker, his asthma bothered him increasingly. As soon as he entered our apartment, he walked straight to his oxygen tank, which was located in the bathroom. After breathing through the mask for a while, he would cough and expectorate, then inhale an Abyssinian powder that he had to ignite and then burn on a metal ashtray, before he regained the ability to breath normally and talk.

The summer after moving to Hoza Street we went to Vulpera Tarasp in the Swiss Alps and stayed there for several weeks because the clear mountain air was good for my father's asthma. It was also beneficial to me after the previous year's mild case of tuberculosis. When a spa physician, who was a woman, examined me and drew a drop of blood from my finger, I fainted. After I recovered consciousness, she asked me what I was planning to study after graduation from the Gymnasium. I told her that my father wanted me to study medicine, but I hadn't made up my mind as yet.

"You will never make a physician—you faint at the sight of blood," she stated emphatically. Even though I did not want to study medicine at that time, her remark upset me. I feared that her statement was intended to limit my future choices.

On my sixteenth birthday, my father took me to the cemetery and pointed to my mother's black tombstone, which had a weeping willow engraved on it. "Now this tomb belongs to you to cherish your mother's memory," he said, wiping tears from his eyes with a white linen handkerchief. I felt deeply moved by this scene and accepted my mother's tomb as my father's recognition of my maturity and, in a way, his birthday gift to me. I understood then that he had never ceased to love and mourn my mother and did not want to hide it anymore from me.

My other birthday gift was more materialistic. It was a dark oak chest with sterling silver cutlery for twenty-four, which I accepted as my dowry. For I had no doubt that I would someday marry. Only very ugly and poor girls had trouble finding husbands.

Although I used to see Janek G. only once or twice a year, I was still infatuated with him during my last year at the Gymnasium of Popielewska-Roszkowska. Then I met Witold K., who was known as Witek among his friends; he was a younger student at Janek's school, and they knew each other. But I met Witek through Szpilka, my classmate.

Szpilka, Witek, Kazik—another boy she knew—and I would spend the evening together discussing current events, literature, or politics. At other times, we would go in a group to a theater. There were usually many interesting plays to choose from. Polish actors like Junosza-Stepowski and Osterva were wonderful. Watching them perform, whether it was Shakespeare or a modern play, was always a memorable experience. Polish playwrights such as Stanislaw Wyspianski or Alexander Fredro wrote patriotic plays as well as satires on the nobility. *Wesele* (The Wedding) and *Zemsta* (Revenge) are two plays I remember.

Other times we would go to the movies. There were few, if any, good Polish movies at the time, but we did have French, German, British, and American films, as well as some from other countries. We became admirers of Maurice Chevalier, Greta Garbo, Marlene Dietrich, and Charlie Chaplin. I was enchanted with Maurice Chevalier, and fascinated by Marlene Dietrich's vampish performances. Charlie Chaplin was my favorite comedian. In Warsaw, at the time, there was no dearth of all sorts of cultural entertainment, but I liked going to the theater and movies more than I liked concerts and operas.

After a while, Witek and I started going out alone. By then, I had given up any hope that Janek G. would ever return my affection for him, and I wanted to have a boyfriend because it wasn't easy for a girl of my age to have any kind of a social life without a liaison with a young man. Soon, Witek and I began to embrace and kiss each other in a funny and childish manner. Neither of us — I at sixteen and Witek at seventeen — really knew how to kiss. I remember that Witek used to kiss my teeth and not my lips, and that I felt something missing in his kisses that prevented me from enjoying them.

On the way back from the theater or movies, we walked and chatted for hours. We wandered back and forth on Hoza Street just to prolong being together. We discussed the books we read, or the plays we saw, and exchanged our thoughts. I liked spending time with Witek, but I never felt he was a man with whom I could be in love in the same way I was with Janek.

It was a clear night and the moon was shining on one of our late night walks. We noticed a small wooden bench in front of a house near where I lived. We cuddled together and felt very strongly that the bench was meant just for us. I wanted desperately to feel in love with Witek, and I almost succeeded then.

"We are in love with each other. Don't you see it, Irena?" he said. "I really love you, Irena, as you are, with your big fat legs," he added, completely destroying my romantic mood. My fat legs were my Achilles' heel. In spite of wanting to be, I wasn't in love with Witek. But I didn't want to say so and hurt his feelings. He had a good reason to believe that I shared his feelings ever since I had allowed him to kiss me.

We ended our evening soon after his awkward declaration of love. The next morning, to my surprise, the small bench was gone. Its disappearance was so mysterious that both of us wanted to believe that it had been put there just for the two of us, and I forgot then my resentment of his reference to my fat legs.

Bronislawa, who was aware of my late returns home, was none too happy about my frequent dates with Witek. "Witek is nice, but you shouldn't limit yourself to seeing only one man," she said, entering my room the morning after my late night walk with Witek. "You're only sixteen, too young for a serious commitment. Anyway, Witek wouldn't be the right choice for you. His mother is a widow with a modest income, and he doesn't impress me as the kind of man who could provide you with the style of life you're accustomed to. Furthermore, he doesn't look manly enough to me. You would always have to nudge him to arouse him."

"I don't like your remarks, mother. Please keep your criticism to yourself," I replied. "I see whom I want to see."

Bronislawa left my room without another word while I pondered how little she knew and understood me. I thought that only men wanted to have intercourse and that women derived no pleasure from this. Therefore, I wouldn't care to "arouse" Witek. I was way too inexperienced and shy to initiate any sexual play. I was still interested in Witek only as a social companion and as someone to talk to and to whom I was special. For I didn't feel interested in any sexual activities with him except for some kissing, in which I was disappointed anyway.

Fearing she might be jealous of my relationship with Witek, I asked Szpilka how she felt about my growing involvement with him.

"It doesn't bother me because he isn't enough of a man for me," Szpilka replied. "But I wouldn't forgive you if you tried to steal Kazik from me."

Although I continued to see Witek, Szpilka's derogatory assessment of his weak masculinity—similar to Bronislawa's criticism—was not entirely wasted on me. The seeds of doubt about my relationship with him were already planted in my mind. I didn't cherish the thought of his sexual inadequacy in the event that I would ever want to marry him. I couldn't see myself trying to arouse him. So nothing was happening for a while.

Like many other teenagers, I was writing a diary where I described my impressions of the girls with whom I was friendly and of the boys I met at the school dances. I also wrote about my sporadic feelings of inadequacy and loneliness, about which I never spoke to anyone. But sometimes I felt depressed and unhappy for no particular reason. On one of these occasions I looked so miserable that Bronislawa summoned Dr. Maliniak, our family physician. After he gave me a physical examination, he asked me to sit down on a chair next to him.

"I can't find anything wrong with you, my dear child. Please tell me what is bothering you," he asked.

I liked him; he inspired my confidence. "I don't know myself, Dr. Maliniak, but I feel lonely and unhappy for no particular reason. I don't know what I want and it bothers me." I had told him a truth I had never confided to anyone.

Dr. Maliniak got up, picked up my chin with his right hand, and kissed me on both cheeks. "Don't worry, my child, everything will be all right and you'll get used to being an adult person, which you are now becoming," he told me. "Most adolescents go through a 'weltschmerz' period. It passes."

Janek G., who was now twenty years old, visited our family occasionally, and sometimes he and I would go out for one of our sporadic visits to Lazienki—the most beautiful park in Warsaw. We never kissed, and only rarely would he put his arm around my shoulders, which I enjoyed tremendously.

Once he gave me a biology book about the life of amoeba, a single cell protozoan organism, wonderfully written by a Polish professor of biology named Dr. Dembowski. I became fascinated by amoeba and wanted to know more about its life. The sudden urge to learn about this organism was the first manifestation of my interest in biology. It took place two years after the awakening of my fascination for physics. With this, my inclination toward the sciences became firmly established.

I asked Janek whether biology was taught at the medical school, because I wanted to learn more about protozoa.

"Yes, of course. It's a first-year course."

As soon as he answered, I became silent and thoughtful. My new interest in biology was genuine. But should I pursue it at a medical school? I knew I didn't want to be a doctor but didn't realize that I could study biology independently of medicine, getting a Ph.D. instead of an M.D.

Janek, a medical student, was my role model, and he guided my reading and intellectual pursuits. Partly as a result of his influence and partly to please my father, I reconsidered my objections to medicine. I still had no interest in the study of diseases or the treatment of sick people. But after this conversation with Janek, the idea of going to medical school became appealing. I also felt, although I wouldn't admit this, that my following Janek to medical school might bring us closer together.

When I woke up the next morning, I had made up my mind that I would study medicine. I immediately went to tell my father.

"That's a wise decision," he said in his usual undemonstrative manner. "Now you should submit your application to the school of medicine as soon as possible."

Once I knew what I wanted to do, I ceased feeling inadequate. I now had a goal. I felt that I was outgrowing my adolescent "weltschmerz."

I continued seeing Witek, but I ceased to cut myself off from seeing other young men, who now sought me out frequently. Soon, however, I became preoccupied with doubts about whether my growing popularity with men was due to my beautiful eyes or to my father's fortune. I had no idea whether I was more popular with men than other girls were and, if so, why. These doubts made me distrustful of the men who pursued me.

I was certainly suspicious of Mr. Z., a thirty-year-old assistant professor of law, who began to visit me. Even though I wondered about his motives, I knew I wasn't at all interested in him as a suitor. He was too old for me and not good-looking enough. Although I felt that my true feelings about him showed, he didn't give up easily. On one of his visits, when he discovered that I was planning to go that summer to Jastrzebia Góra for a vacation, he said, "Maybe we'll meet there."

Our graduation was approaching, and my classmate Hanka F. and I were told by our parents of their gift to us—several days vacation on our own at a Jastrzebia Góra resort hotel. We were among the few girls fortunate enough to be treated so generously and given so much independence.

Hanka had an aunt in Stockholm and planned to go by boat to Sweden after our Jastrzebia Góra vacation. I wanted also to go there with her, but fearing that my parents wouldn't let me go, I didn't tell them that I borrowed money from our cook, got a passport, and bought a boat ticket to Stockholm.

Our vacation in Jastrzebia Góra on the Polish seashore was memorable because of an incident with Mr. Z., who stayed at the same resort hotel where Hanka and I shared a room. One evening, he and I went for a walk together. While we were resting on a bench, he put his arm around me. I suspected that something more was about to happen.

"You're such a quiet girl, Irena. You're still asleep. But one day you'll wake up and reveal your passionate nature. I'll wait. I love you," he blurted out. Then out of the blue he said, "Will you marry me?" He tried to kiss me, but I wouldn't let him.

"No, I won't marry you. First of all, I'm too young for marriage. Furthermore, I don't love you." With these words, I ran to the hotel. Fortunately, Mr. Z. didn't pursue me.

Once in our room, I told Hanka what happened. We were chatting late into the night when I suddenly became concerned that my rejected suitor might attempt suicide. Fearing responsibility for his death, I told Hanka that I would go to his room to see if he needed to be rescued. But I was also worried that my unexpected appearance in Mr. Z.'s room at night would put me in danger of being seduced. Sensing the risk I took in going to his room, Hanka simply prevented me. Without a word, she walked to the door, locked it, and hid the key. And that was that.

The next day, I left some money with a newspaper boy to mail pre-addressed, stamped postcards to my father and Bronislawa every day. I wanted them to believe I was still in Jastrzebia Góra. Then Hanka and I boarded a boat for Sweden. When we arrived in Stockholm, Hanka visited her aunt, while I stayed on at the boat. That evening I walked along the pier in search of adventure, moving my hips in what I believed was an effective way to attract attention. I must have looked more ridiculous than alluring because not a single sailor gave me a second look. Disappointed, I retreated to my cabin where I promptly fell asleep.

The next day Hanka came to take me with her to her aunt, who offered us a sightseeing trip. Hanka was to stay with her aunt part of that summer. But I had to go back home. So, two days later I returned alone by boat to Gdynia, where I took a train to Warsaw. As I entered a second-class train compartment, I immediately recognized its single occupant, Irka K., that sophisticated girl from our Gymnasium. Her face was beautifully made up, her hair attractively arranged. She wore an elegant, blue silk printed dress, smelled of exquisite perfume, and was smoking a cigarette. She nodded to me without smiling, making it clear that she didn't want me to join her. In fact, we hardly spoke during our long journey of several hours. This really made me aware that I still looked very much like a schoolgirl, in contrast to this grown-up young lady only a year older than myself. I was jealous and wondered if I would ever look as attractive as she did.

Upon my return to Warsaw, I was pleasantly surprised that my father and Bronislawa, who had discovered my plot, were happy to welcome me back and forgave me for my subterfuge.

Later that summer, Bronislawa, with whom by then I had established a more peaceful coexistence, took me to Francesbad, a spa in Czechoslovakia, where she took mud bath cures to relieve her from menopausal symptoms. I took natural mineral baths. Both of us drank spring water, which was said to have therapeutic value. However, despite the increased ease between us, our conversations there, as at home, were usually monologues with me talking and Bronislawa eagerly listening.

After our return to Warsaw, I spent the rest of my vacation learning how to make marzipan candies and fruit compotes, both of which I liked and, having much time, wanted to learn how to make. I developed this fancy taste even though I didn't know anything about basic cooking.

The year was 1934. Shortly before I was to take the fall entrance examination to the medical school of Warsaw University, Janek G. told me about a boy from his school who was also taking this exam. His name was Hilary Koprowski.

Janek seemed excited about the prospect of his two younger friends following in his footsteps to medical school and was eager that we should meet each other. Janek said that Hilary was very capable and intelligent, and that I would enjoy meeting him. What he told Hilary about me, I don't know. I was still infatuated with Janek,

Irena at eighteen enters medical school.

Hilary meets Irena at the entrance
examination to medical school.

although I continued to believe that he wasn't aware of it. It never occurred to me that he might have known about my feelings all along and that by trying to get me interested in Hilary, he possibly was making an effort to get rid of me.

Janek sought us out at the entrance to the examination hall and introduced us. Hilary was blond and had steel blue eyes, but my initial reaction was that he was too plump to be physically attractive. Nevertheless, the very fact that he was Janek's friend aroused my curiosity about him. In the examination hall, Hilary sat in the first row; I sat in the back in the top row. When the list of our names was read before the examination, and my name was called, Hilary looked up and his eyes met mine.

I wondered what he thought of my appearance. I had a suntan from my summer vacation, which contrasted with my big, green-gray eyes and pearly white teeth. My smooth and shiny dark brown hair was parted on the left side, and the right side of my forehead was partially covered by a single wide wave. I wore a lightweight, soft, blue woolen suit and a white and blue collarless blouse. I looked radiant and the picture of health at eighteen.

V

Secret Romance

Stanislaw Kryszek, a tall, dark-haired, slim young man with eyeglasses, stood ahead of me in line at the dean's office. Both of us had been accepted by Warsaw University Medical School and had come to register. We would be classmates, but at the time we had no idea that fate would bring us together repeatedly in the future.

A guard standing at the entrance to the office approached us. "You're lucky to be entering medical school. Physicians have a good life. In all the years I've been here, I never saw one who starved."

Although his words were reminiscent of those of my father, that was not what was on my mind at the time. It was September 1935, and with classes about to begin I knew that a new life was opening up for me. Listening in the big university halls to lectures given by a very colorful faculty, having male classmates for the first time in my school career, and spending hours dissecting cadavers in the Anatomicum would be exciting and stimulating experiences, unlike anything I had ever known before.

When I was at medical school, anatomy was the backbone of our first two years of study. Currently its importance is somewhat overshadowed by a more recent emphasis on other areas of basic sciences, such as molecular biology and genetics. But we had classroom lectures on this subject every morning, five days a week, and on three afternoons for three hours at a time we worked in the lab dissecting corpses. The anatomy of bones was taught at the beginning of the first year. Our instructors were very exacting and required us to know every bone in the body. To drive this point home with us, they would throw the bones of the wrist up in the air one at a time and make us identify each one of them. And their expectations were just as high for the rest of the body.

The nauseating smell of the formalin-fixed cadavers permeated our hair and clothes. Bronislawa had bought me some nice new clothes, and I hated that they absorbed the odor of the decaying corpses. My skin and hair would also pick up that smell, so as soon as I got home I would shower and change.

Our anatomy teacher, Professor Loth, was extremely popular, mostly because of his last lecture of the year, when he would invite nude male and female art school models for a live demonstration of human anatomy. Not surprisingly, at this lecture his audience was huge. Loth would enter the large auditorium with a big smile on his face and say, "I welcome today the entire student body of Warsaw University."

Biology was taught by Professor Kopec. He was obsessed with his experiments and could be found in his research laboratory examining mice as early as seven o'clock in the morning. He would explain to us the purpose of his research, but in doing this he was very modest and never bragged about his scientific accomplishments. Although we had to pass oral examinations in every subject, most were formal and impersonal. But Professor Kopec's examinations took place in his laboratory and seemed more like friendly conversations than tests. They were opportunities to talk about what we had learned. I liked him best of all our faculty.

Our class was made up of 150 students. Fifty were from the Army Medical Corps (Sanitarka), and they would come to school dressed in military uniform. Of the remaining one hundred students, forty-five were females. Our male classmates treated us as their equals in the classroom, but outside the university they behaved in the same courteous manner young men did at that time in Poland. They gave us their seats on streetcars, opened doors for us, and helped us into our coats and on with our boots in winter.

My best friend in the class was Zaira P., the Tatar girl I had met when I was seven, playing in Ujazdowski Park. She and I had remained close, and we now often studied together for our examinations in medical school. But gradually my circle grew larger and included male as well as female students.

Shortly after the beginning of the school year, Hilary Koprowski, the young man Janek had introduced me to, began to telephone me every day to check on our assignments. He knew what our assignments were, so these were simply excuses to make contact with me. We usually chatted about the lectures we attended and the professors who delivered them. I was amused and pleased by his calls. One day I took a better look at Hilary. He now seemed more attractive to me than he had when Janek first introduced us. I no longer minded that he was plump. What I saw was a pleasant, boyish-looking young man with blond hair, blue-gray eyes, a prominent nose and rosy skin. Quite frankly, I found the overall effect appealing. I liked his attention, became accustomed to it, and found myself beginning to expect it. Despite this budding attraction, and deaf to Bronislawa's warnings, I continued to see Witek, with whom I had started going steady while still in the Gymnasium. I found myself still dreaming of the elusive Janek. Discounting the Jastrzebia Góra summer episode with the thirty-year-old lawyer, thus far Witek was the only man who had ever said he loved me. Although I wasn't in love with him, he was with me. That was flattering and not something I was willing to relinquish all that easily. Yet, no matter how much that meant to me, because I didn't love him, I had decidedly mixed feelings about our entanglement. In retrospect I think that this growing ambivalence of my feelings may have been aggravated by the pleasure I began to derive from the steadily increasing attention given me by Hilary.

I soon became annoyed by Witek's unscheduled appearances at the Anatomicum, where I spent long afternoon hours dissecting cadavers. During a lab break one day, Witek met me, and we stood in the lobby talking. I was hoping he would leave and, nervously, I fingered the sapphire ring that was a birthday present from my father and Bronislawa. It became loose, slipped from my finger, and fell into the cracks between the wooden planks of the floor.

I sensed that Witek was about to leave. I knew he would offer to help me look for the ring, and I didn't want to give him any excuse to remain. So I postponed looking for it till he was gone. But he didn't leave and instead stayed until the bell rang, when I had to return to class. I was annoyed, feeling he had remained out of stubbornness, since I am sure he sensed my growing impatience with him. But probably he was trying in the only way he knew to hold on to me. My need to rush back to class and my annoyance with Witek made me forget about the ring. Later, when I remembered and returned to search for it, my ring was gone.

"Where's your ring?" Bronislawa asked that evening.

"It slipped off my finger and disappeared through a crack in the floor in the Anatomicum when I was playing with it," I answered, ashamed of my carelessness and annoyed that Bronislawa had discovered my loss. She didn't say anything then, but a few days later she resumed her inquiry.

"You're together with Witek all the time," she complained. "You haven't enough time to study. Did you give him your ring instead of losing it, as you said?"

"You know that I don't lie," I answered, annoyed by Bronislawa's interrogation and her suspicion that I lied. She said no more, and I continued to see Witek.

"You have no idea how difficult it is for me to control my desire for you," he said one night after kissing me. It now was at least clear that Witek had no problems being sexually aroused!

I didn't want to tell him that I didn't love him enough to marry him, so instead I said, "I'm sorry, Witek, but I could allow you more liberties only if we were married."

"So let's get married," he replied quickly.

"My father and Bronislawa wouldn't approve of our marriage," I told him evasively.

It was early spring 1936. I was eighteen and Witek was nineteen. Aside from the fact that I didn't love him — which he didn't know — the idea of our marrying was quite unrealistic. We didn't know or discuss how we would support ourselves, what would happen to my medical studies, or where we would live. Witek was a second-year history student at the University of Warsaw. It was unlikely that he would be earning money for at least two more years, and then his expected income would be very modest. My parents wouldn't approve of our marriage, as I told Witek, and I didn't love him enough to go against their will.

"Let's elope," Witek suggested. "But remember to take your pillows with you because pillows are expensive and we wouldn't be able to afford new ones."

When I heard this, I felt as if someone had poured a bucket of cold water over my head. Whatever little romance there was in our talk of marriage was squelched completely. It reminded me of his comment about my fat legs! This brought me to my senses and also reminded me of Bronislawa's warning that poverty awaited me with Witek. I simply didn't love him enough to face that prospect. Without saying anything to him, I made up my mind what I would do.

The next day I wrote Witek a letter, telling him that I had decided to end our relationship and that my decision was irrevocable. Breaking up with Witek marked the end of my adolescent feelings of inadequacy and insecurity. My decision to study medicine had already brought with it a new capacity for knowing my own mind and making independent decisions.

I sent Witek back all the letters he had written me during his courtship and requested that he return mine. In reply he wrote that he was heartbroken, but he refused to return my letters, insisting that they were his property and he intended to keep them. He did not return my diary, which I gave him to read at one time.

When I revealed to Bronislawa that I had broken up with Witek, she hugged me and cried with relief and joy. Yet, although I hadn't loved him, he had been an important part of my life, and our abrupt breakup was a stressful experience.

I was further disturbed at this time by the death of Marshal Josef Pilsudski, a very powerful military hero for Polish independence who practically had ruled Poland since 1926. I was raised in admiration of this man and felt his death to be a personal loss. Pilsudski's funeral took place on my birthday, May 12. The military parade honoring him, the beating of drums, and the burning torches reminded me of the funeral of President Narutowicz, which I had watched from my father's shoulders when I was four years old. When I returned from the funeral, Bronislawa put a lovely clock on my desk—a birthday gift from her and my father.

The following day we had beautiful spring weather. I wore a new, navy blue, collarless, wool spring coat with a silk print scarf. I felt happy and attractive. Suddenly, Witek caught up with me in the street calling out "Iru," his favorite term of endearment for me. His voice was full of emotion. When I reminded him of my request that he not try to see me again, he replied, "You have a stone in place of a heart," and walked away. I was crushed by his words, but with approaching tests and examinations my mind became absorbed with school, which helped dispel my lingering sadness.

Shortly after that, Hilary told me that he feared we wouldn't remember the first year's chemistry laboratory experiments well enough to pass the combined chemistry-biochemistry examination at the end of the second year. He insisted that we repeat these experiments. There was ample storage space in the basement of the building where I lived with my parents, and Hilary suggested that I ask my father's permission to use it as a laboratory. He was determined, and when he set his mind to something he was very persuasive.

My father and Bronislawa were glad to see me recuperating from the sadness caused by the breakup with Witek, and they encouraged my involvement in this project. Soon a complete laboratory was installed in our basement. Since this laboratory was considered to be my parents' birthday gift to me, my father paid for it all and I made all the purchases in consultation with Hilary and Heniek U., our classmate and Hilary's partner in dissecting corpses whom Hilary wanted to work with us.

By fall, we had a fully equipped laboratory in good operating condition, but we had to delay beginning our experiments because, quite unexpectedly, Hilary announced that he had to accompany his ailing mother on a trip to Vienna. She had breast cancer and was being operated on by a famous Viennese surgeon. Hilary remained with her for several weeks, not only during the surgery but also through her convalescence. I was impressed by his filial devotion but somewhat surprised that he, rather than his father, was the one to be with her all this time.

Immediately upon Hilary's return from Vienna, we began working in our newly furbished basement laboratory, repeating the chemistry experiments and completing them just in time for Christmas recess. One evening Hilary and our classmate Heniek, who was Hilary's best friend, came over with a record player, records, snacks, and wine, for an impromptu dancing party. I enjoyed dancing with Heniek as much as with Hilary, and when they offered me cigarettes, I felt very grown-up, accepted one, and began smoking until I started to choke.

"This happens to those who have their first cigarette and don't know how to smoke," Hilary said, teasing me. After our Christmas party, I was determined to become proficient at smoking. I succeeded so well that I soon became addicted.

Once the holidays were over, Hilary and I started studying histology together at my house. Then one day he asked me to study in his parents' apartment. I wondered why and I hoped that he wanted to introduce me to his parents, but when I arrived nobody was home except for Hilary. Besides feeling that his apartment wasn't warm and bright like ours was, I was also disappointed that his parents were not there. My feelings became very mixed. I wanted to be introduced to his parents as a sign of his growing affection and seriousness about me as his romantic partner, but he did not seem inclined to do so. But he revealed what probably was his reason for inviting me home. He had to practice the piano for his examination at the Warsaw Conservatory of Music, and the time he had to spend at the piano would have to be taken from our study time for the histology test at medical school. So he brought me over to sit next to him and read aloud our textbook while he played the piano. When I finished reading the assigned histology chapter, Hilary stopped playing. He mentioned that he could speak English—which was just beginning to become quite fashionable in Warsaw—and that he had traveled with his father to London. "You should learn to speak English, Irena. Our chemistry teacher's brother, Mr. Truszkowski, teaches it. I know him and will ask him to accept you as a student."

While I was still thinking about what to say, he abruptly changed the subject. "By the way, do you have any vacation plans?" he asked. "I'm taking a Baltic Sea cruise to England; you might enjoy going."

I was stunned by his suggestion that we take a long trip together. I hardly expected this after his reticence of the afternoon, although the prospect excited and pleased me. I also wondered how my parents would react to such an idea.

"I wouldn't mind taking English lessons," I said, avoiding any commitment to the cruise, still thinking and wondering why he hadn't made any romantic gesture toward me.

He did ask Mr. Truszkowski to teach me English, and I went for my first lesson. But it turned out to be a perplexing experience, perhaps somewhat typical when dealing with the authoritarian and controlling attitudes some teachers had towards their students. I started, worked earnestly and made impressive progress in my first three lessons, but then medical studies began to interfere with my English teacher's assignments, and I couldn't give it the constant attention it needed. Mr. Truszkowski refused to continue teaching me.

Hilary did not seem to mind that I had to discontinue my English lessons, and our relationship continued pretty much as it had been, with contact focused mainly on our studies. However, once, during a break, he put down his textbook, took my wrist in his hand and began playing with my gold chain bracelet, a birthday gift from Bronislawa and my father. Hilary wouldn't let go of it, as he persevered in pressing me to make arrangements for our summer cruise to England. I felt an unfamiliar spasm in my lower abdomen in response to his touch, a sensation I had never experienced before. I realized that this feeling was sexual. I had become very attracted to Hilary and was excited by his touching me and wanting me to spend the summer with him. It was a powerful moment. No further words were spoken.

Eventually I told my father and Bronislawa that I would like to spend part of my summer vacation on the sea. I was nineteen, a grown-up medical student, and they gave me the money and permission to take this expensive cruise. But I didn't tell them that Hilary also was going.

We boarded the same train to Gdynia as strangers board a train, and we remained apart so that my parents, who were there to see me off, would not know that both of us were going on this trip. Hilary had been seen off by his cousin who did not know me, but when Hilary was saying good-bye to him, he was recognized by my parents, and I saw through the window of the train a surprised look on their faces. But they were used to my independent ways and did not seem to be shocked.

It was evening when the train left Warsaw. I had my supper before leaving home, but it was too early to go to sleep and I was hoping that Hilary would knock at the door of my compartment and drop in for a chat. I was disappointed because he never did. I remembered the visit to his apartment when he also didn't use the opportunity of being alone with me to kiss me, which I had expected him to do. After waiting for him so long that I began to feel sleepy, I undressed, went to bed and turned off the light. But after expecting to fall asleep immediately, I tossed in my bed, wondering why Hilary would shy away from showing me any signs of physical affection and why I had to spend this evening all by myself. I didn't see him until the next morning in Gdynia when we greeted each other and went together for breakfast to a waterfront restaurant. Hilary made a big fuss when his boiled egg proved to be too soft. I remember very distinctly thinking that I wouldn't want to be in the shoes of his future wife.

I recalled that when his mother became ill, he took time off from medical school to accompany her for her surgery abroad and that he remained there through her post-operative convalescence. I was wondering why his father allowed him to take his place on this occasion. I also was thinking of my disappointment that Hilary had not introduced me to his parents. Was he afraid of his mother's reaction to me as his girlfriend? Was he overly dependent on his mother? I suspected and feared that this would explain his strange behavior.

The first evening on the boat, Hilary knocked at my cabin door. For a while he tried to get me involved in a conversation, but then we stopped talking. I saw his face approaching and wondered whether he was about to kiss me. I wasn't sure, because he took his time, and I wasn't feeling very confident about predicting Hilary's behavior. Then, ever so gently, he kissed me on the mouth. For a while we remained very still, both obviously quite happy. I was so pleased that this long-awaited moment had arrived at last.

The next day I became seasick on deck. Hilary, who was an excellent sailor, took care of me and then took me down to my cabin and told me to get into bed.

In London Hilary had a cousin, Simon, who was a practicing gynecologist, and we went to his house for dinner. Simon was the first and only member of Hilary's family I had met thus far. Later, when Hilary and I went shopping together, he presented me with a bottle of French perfume as a souvenir of our trip.

Our vacation had me quite exhilarated, almost as if it were a dream. However, parts of it clearly puzzled me. But I felt I had to wait to unravel some of its mysteries. Hilary acted quite proud when he pointed out that he was returning me to Warsaw a virgin.

vi
Abandoned Bride

In the fall we were back at medical school. I also attempted to become better versed in modern literature to discuss books with Hilary, and I began lessons with a private instructor, Mrs. Barbara Rafalowska. I remember reading Silone's *Bread and Wine* and Dos Passos's *Manhattan Transfer.* One day I noticed that Barbara's sister was lying on a narrow couch with her fiancé. Suddenly I remembered how angry I had been when my father and Bronislawa took their afternoon naps. It was then that I realized that some of my resentment of her was sexual jealousy. This had nothing to do with how she treated me or that she had taken my mother's place, although I wouldn't doubt that the latter was part of my resentment towards her also.

When Aunt Zosia's only son, my cousin Janek S.—who was three years older than I— became engaged to his future wife, Aunt Zosia gave his fiancee a lovely enamel compact. But the girl said that it was too small and refused to accept it. I was thrilled when Aunt Zosia decided to give this compact to me. "It wasn't meant initially as a gift for you, Irka," Bronislawa said, destroying my pleasure. "You received it only because somebody else didn't like it."

This kind of vindictiveness was not typical of Bronislawa, and it surprised me. It made me realize that there wasn't much love lost between Bronislawa and Aunt Zosia. It also became clear that Bronislawa resented the affection I had for my aunt. Beyond making me feel bad about the gift, Bronislawa went on to malign Aunt Zosia's character, adding that Zosia was a very envious person. I disagreed with Bronislawa's assessment. I had very tender feelings for my aunt, and great compassion, for I knew that she was an unhappy woman who didn't love her husband. Fortunately, though, she adored her only son, Janek.

When I was a second-year medical student, Aunt Zosia committed suicide. After her death, I sought out my grandmother. The sadness I felt made me realize how much Grandma Anna must have suffered when she lost her daughter Eugenia. Could her suffering be great enough to cause the shaking of her head which had never ceased? I finally asked her if the tremor of her head started after my mother's loss, and she confirmed my suspicions.

During my third year of medical school, Warsaw University students had an opportunity to work as voluntary assistants in the department of their choice. Zaira's mother had been an assistant professor in the department of pathological anatomy of Warsaw University School of Medicine before she died — ten years previously — of tuberculosis contracted during the performance of an autopsy. Zaira knew the chairman and other members of that department and decided to become a voluntary assistant there. Not yet committed to a specific area of medicine, I thought that a good background in anatomical pathology would prepare me for any medical specialty I would eventually practice. Hence, I chose the same department Zaira did. Hilary selected the department of experimental pathology, where from the beginning he became very involved in medical research. He even published a paper on blood ammonia in dogs.

Several months after our cruise Hilary and I began planning another secret vacation together. Shortly before we completed the necessary arrangements, my friend Krysia Orlanska became very ill and died of pneumonia in those pre-antibiotic days. Thus one of my school friendships came to a very sad end. The same feeling of emptiness that I experienced after Aunt Zosia died reappeared after Krysia O.'s death. It might very well have lingered longer if I hadn't been planning to go to Bukowina with Hilary just a week later.

Hilary met me in Zakopane, which is about 200 miles south of Warsaw. He arrived a few hours earlier so as not to be seen on the same train with me. As soon as I saw him, I threw myself in his arms. For a while we hugged and kissed passionately at the train station.

"I hired a sleigh to take us to Bukowina," Hilary said. A few minutes later we were installed in a comfortable horse-drawn sleigh, our legs touching beneath the furry blankets. Hilary called our driver "Gazda," which is how Polish mountaineers call themselves.

"Take us to Veronika Sliwowa," Hilary told him.

The sleigh began its smooth glide through the snow, its bells ringing. It took us forty-five minutes to get to Bukowina. By the time we reached our log cabin on the slope of a snow-covered mountain, it was already dark and the moon and the stars were shining brightly. Veronika Sliwowa, the owner of the cabin, emerged to greet us. It was a fairy tale environment. A supper of hot soup, bread, and *bryndza* (sheep cheese) awaited us on the table. A fire blazed.

After our hostess cleared the dishes and left for the night, we had a look at our surroundings. Through the windows we could see the distant lights of other cabins. We were now completely alone, with the entire weekend all to ourselves.

After our return from Bukowina, Hilary continued coming to see me at home everyday. But he continued to avoid any social demonstration of affection, any sign that we were a couple in front of other people. Even now, after our long weekend in Bukowina together, he would avoid me in school and at lectures. He still hadn't introduced me to his parents. All this bothered me enormously. But I was afraid that the spell between us would break if I asked questions or made any demands on him.

The summer when I was twenty, I planned to visit Aunt Nathalie in Paris for a few days and then to go with my cousin Irene for a vacation at Juan les Pins. My parents enjoyed providing me with such luxurious travels. Hilary had arranged a summer research fellowship at the University of Manchester in England, so we decided to meet and spend a few days together in Paris since he could easily stop there on his way to England.

Hilary took a hotel not far from where Aunt Nathalie lived. As soon as he called, I left her apartment to spend most of the day with him, until finally my cousin Irene came to fetch me for dinner. She realized what was going on and became the only person to whom I actually admitted that Hilary and I were lovers. She told my Aunt Nathalie. To my delight, rather than being upset or angry, her response was to invite Hilary to have dinners with us. But after his departure for England I cried at the airport, sensing the loneliness ahead of me. I realized that I had become dependent on him for my emotional well-being.

The day after Hilary left, Irene and I set out for the French Riviera. When we arrived at Juan les Pins we checked our luggage at the train station and began searching for accommodations. All the hotels were full. Finally, we spotted a small house on the beach with a red light on and a sign "Rooms for Rent." The landlady took us to a small, modestly furnished room for which she asked what seemed to us to be a ridiculously low price. When Irene and I looked at each other in surprise, the landlady mistook our reaction and thought that we felt it was too expensive. She then told us she could lower the price or even let us have the room free if we would take good care of her customers and see to their entertainment and consumption of alcohol. We realized then that it was a house of prostitution and we fled into the night to resume our search.

When my cousin and I returned to Paris from Juan les Pins, I spent several more days with Aunt Nathalie. Her warmth made me feel good, and to my added delight she began talking to me about my mother.

"I loved her. She was a wonderful person," Aunt Nathalie said. "If she were alive, you would be able to talk to her about Hilary," she added, knowing that I didn't confide in Bronislawa. Talking to Aunt Nathalie about Hilary consoled me. But I still couldn't bring myself to talk about the extent to which his hiding our relationship bothered me.

I returned to Warsaw from my summer vacation before Hilary came back from his research fellowship. On his way back from England, he stopped again in Paris, this time to visit his cousin, Leon Gerber, who was a physician and practiced medicine in France. Leon took Hilary to a *Bal des Internes*, an annual event at which young French physicians—women and men—undress and then dance on the tables. This upset me but after mentioning it Hilary showed no interest in discussing it with me.

One day, unexpectedly, Heniek U., who had worked on our experiments with us in our basement, dropped by to see me. We were sitting on the couch in my room when he suddenly took me into his arms and began to kiss me passionately. I had never experienced so great a passion as I felt at that moment. For the briefest possible moment I enjoyed total abandonment in his strong masculine arms. But I didn't dare prolong it. I belonged to Hilary. Heniek was his best friend. We couldn't possibly betray Hilary. I pushed Heniek away from me gently.

"Stop it, please, Heniek. We can't do it. I'm Hilary's girlfriend," I told him.

Heniek was stunned. He had no idea of what was going on between me and Hilary. Hilary hadn't revealed our involvement even to his best friend! Heniek left promptly and never again approached me in an amorous way. I blamed Hilary for this enjoyable but upsetting romantic incident with Heniek. Not only did I feel frustrated and rejected, I now felt more strongly than before an emotion that vacillated between annoyance, anger, and sometimes even rage.

Other young men who had girlfriends were proud of that fact and happy to be known as part of a romantic pair. Why was this not the case with Hilary? Why did he want to retain the image of being an unattached young man in the eyes of our friends and his family? This behavior made me feel very insecure about his feelings for me, despite so much other evidence of his affection and desire. Those feelings were not the ones I doubted — I felt them to be authentic — but I wondered if there was something about me that dissatisfied him and made him wish to be free to attract someone else. Sometimes I thought he felt me too much beneath him intellectually. But I was grasping at straws. I simply did not know or understand — I had no real answers to this puzzle.

Upset and uncertain about what to do, I quite naturally did a lot of thinking. I recalled Hilary going to Vienna with his mother for her cancer surgery and wondered if she might be unduly dependent on him. I also recalled that on our cruise he told me that she always shampooed his hair, which had seemed odd to me then and still did. I became afraid that maybe he was so dominated by his mother that he had to conceal his love for me from her, and thus from others. Or, equally as bad, he was fearful that his love for me might threaten his tight bonds with his mother. Whatever the truth was, the more I thought about their relationship, the more it seemed strange and abnormal.

One day, when I was feeling very unhappy about all this, Bronislawa entered my room. Seeing my tears, she pressed me for an explanation. I had never talked to her about my relationship with Hilary, but in this moment of weakness I admitted to her that I was Hilary's lover and that I was disturbed by his carefree attitude to our relationship. She didn't say much, but I could see how distressed she became by my revelation. Later that evening, she repeated what I had told her to my father. I felt it to be disloyal of her to tell him, but I wasn't surprised that she had done so.

The next morning she told me what my father had said: "I can't stand Irka's acting like an easy woman." I knew immediately that I had caused him pain by my behavior, and I was sorry. At the same time, I felt relief. Since my father knew the truth, now I could talk to him about my problems and he would be able to help me, although I didn't go to him right away.

One day when I was going with Bronislawa to buy a hat, Hilary joined us, pressing Bronislawa to buy me the one he liked best. He seemed to care a lot about my appearance and would act very possessively. This hardly seemed like the behavior of a man who was casual about a woman. Like a chameleon, he was forever changing his skin. But in a sense he was consistent, and this particular incident was a sign of his caring and involvement.

When "Kuznia Mlodych," a young people's literary club, had their annual dance, I asked Hilary to take me. He refused, and I was enormously disappointed. A few days later Szpilka, who attended this dance, casually remarked that she saw Hilary there dancing with a girl in a red dress. I suspected that Szpilka, who had been very critical of the way I had broken up with Witek, derived malicious pleasure from telling me about Hilary being out with another girl. I was very angry at him, and when we were together next I reproached him for having refused to take me to this dance, then going there himself. I asked him who the girl in the red dress was.

"My cousin was visiting us, and my mother forced me to take her. I was so angry that, out of spite, I let her sit by herself while I danced with another girl whom I didn't even know," Hilary said calmly. He acted as if I would believe this story—true or not—and that I would accept it with no pain or concern, as if his unwillingness to take me—his girlfriend and lover—to the dance would have no effect on my feelings. He tried to sound as if I should accept his behavior as being entirely appropriate and natural.

Listening to his words, and realizing that he had no understanding of my feelings, made me even more annoyed. He seemed to have no sense of the importance of this event to me, and of my desire to meet the young writers and other intellectuals at the club. That should have pleased him. He should have wanted to participate with me in that. But he did not. What could this mean about him or about his feelings for me? Again, I felt suspicious that Hilary didn't want to be seen in my company. Besides that, I was extremely unhappy that he lied to me about going to the dance in the first place. But short of breaking up with him, there didn't seem to be anything I could do.

Fortunately, now that my father knew that Hilary and I were lovers, I felt free to seek his advice about how to evaluate and react to Hilary's behavior. One afternoon I found my father sitting at a small round table in the master bedroom. He was taking a teaspoonful of baking soda for his heartburn and washing it down with tea. I noticed that he was going bald and felt sad to see this sign that he was growing older. Noting that he didn't feel well, I approached him with some reluctance, not wanting to be a nuisance. He offered me some baking soda, which I refused.

When I confided to my father that I was so unhappy with Hilary's behavior, I was shocked by his response. He said to me that most men are polygamous. Although I didn't expect or like what he said, since it came from my father I didn't reject it out of hand. In fact, after I did some reflecting, I reluctantly decided that if this was the way things were, accepting it would be the only realistic and sensible thing to do.

Hilary's unpredictable behavior continued. Close and warm to me in private, he was cold and distant socially. So it was very unexpected when he suggested to Bronislawa that I should have a big party for my twenty-first birthday. He even took the initiative, compiling a list of the friends and classmates who ought to be invited. This oscillation between intimacy and distance had me utterly perplexed. I even wondered if, despite his role in making this party, he would allow himself to appear to be my boyfriend when the party took place.

During this party we played a modified hide and seek game. Instead of individuals, couples were supposed to hide together. Hilary and I hid together under the dining-room table. One of the guests, who knew how shy and inhibited I was, discovered us. He smiled and looked at me knowingly. He now knew our secret, which is just what I had so longed for. Now maybe others would learn about my relationship with Hilary.

My feelings towards Hilary, however, remained mixed. I felt a strong physical attraction to him. I became excited at the sound of the telephone or doorbell whenever I expected it was he. I was certain I was in love with him. But because his efforts to distance himself from me socially often made me hurt and angry, it complicated our relationship in ways I didn't like.

In June of 1938 our intimacy reached the stage that when I missed my period we decided to get married without any pregnancy test. Hilary insisted on a secret wedding. When I told my father and Bronislawa about our plans to get married, they encouraged the marriage and agreed to pretend no knowledge of this. I was very unhappy that it never occurred to Hilary to buy us wedding bands, and so I asked my father for the money and bought them myself. To me this was still more evidence of Hilary's failure to accept our relationship fully.

We had our blood tests and made arrangements for a civil wedding ceremony, with strangers as witnesses. Then, only a few hours before the wedding, I started menstruating. I ran to my father and asked him whether I should cancel the ceremony. His advice was to ignore the bleeding and proceed with my wedding plans, as if nothing had happened. And that is what I did. I was also relieved to know that legalizing my relationship with Hilary would eliminate my father's concern about my being an easy woman. Somewhere inside of me I knew what I was doing was not right, but with the intensity of my desire to be Hilary's wife, my father's recommendation, and Hilary's unpredictability, I paid no attention to those doubts.

It was an awful way to be married. His parents were not told, and although mine knew, Hilary assumed that they didn't. Hence, neither were present. We were declared man and wife by a judge at the city hall.

That night I approached Hilary and gently took his arm.

"A miracle happened. I'm not pregnant," I said. Hilary didn't ask me when I had discovered that I wasn't pregnant, but must have become suspicious that our wedding was not unavoidable—that I knew in advance.

In the morning, to my dismay, Hilary went back "home" to his parents and didn't take me with him. I wondered how long he expected to hide from them that he had a wife. But I felt so guilty at having lied to him that I didn't dare ask.

A few days after our secret wedding, my former boyfriend Witek telephoned to tell me that he had married a medical student named Nina J. My heart stopped when I heard this news. Maybe I cared for him more than I ever admitted to myself. With great satisfaction, I told him that I too already was married. It was Witek's turn now to become silent. Then we exchanged wishes of happiness.

When an acquaintance of Hilary's father read a municipal publication of newly registered weddings, he called to congratulate him that his son had married the daughter of so rich and prominent a man. I assumed that was how they found out, although Hilary never told me, nor did he say what happened at his home when our marriage was discovered. And, of course, I didn't dare ask. But a few days later, Hilary announced to me that his mother invited me to tea.

When I arrived, my new mother-in-law received me at the door. Sofia Semeonovna, whose maiden name was Berland, was a short, stocky woman with smooth blond hair, steel-gray eyes, and a flat nose with a rounded tip that curved slightly to the left and widely spread nostrils. She had on a simple, navy blue dress with short sleeves and a belt. I noticed that she was wearing a diamond bar pin and an emerald ring. She looked like the married professional woman she was. Born and educated in Russia, Sofia Semeonovna had become one of the first women dentists in pre-revolutionary Russia. Later she had migrated to Poland, where she continued practicing dentistry. My mother-in-law had her dental office at home, as many Warsaw dentists did. At the time Hilary and I married, she was in her late fifties but was still seeing patients.

Hilary's mother came from an educated family with many physicians, lawyers, and musicians. But none were as successful financially as her husband, Paul Koprowski, a rich businessman. However, Sofia Semeonovna didn't respect him because of his lack of a university education. She married only because of her sister's insistence that she not remain an old maid. Despite all this, she expected her husband to help her family, and she tried to dominate him in every way. By the time I married Hilary, his father's affection for his wife had long since diminished, and he resented and resisted her constant demands.

When I arrived for tea at mid-afternoon, Sonia—as her family called her—first took me to her bedroom. "I'm sorry that I have only a few insignificant souvenirs from abroad I can offer you," she said, giving me hand-embroidered silk purse accessories she had acquired in France.

Her gift surprised me because I didn't expect to receive anything from her, given how little time she had known of our marriage. But it also annoyed me. For these were not the sort of gifts a mother-in-law in her circumstances gives to the bride, and she made no mention that these were just token welcomes until she had the time to shop for something more appropriate for me, her son's new wife. I wasn't mercenary, but I felt shortchanged emotionally.

"Thank you for these lovely things," I said, glad that she couldn't read my thoughts. And I put the comb and compact into my pocketbook.

"Let me introduce you to my family," Sofia Semeonovna then said, as she led the way to the dining room, where several of her relatives were sitting at the table having tea and pastries. They all looked at me with curiosity as I entered the room. Only one of these people, Aunt Hova, had a pleasant smile on her face.

After tea, when my mother-in-law and I were left alone, she asked me why I got married in such a hurry.

"You could have lived with Hilary as long as you wanted to without marrying him," she told me.

"Not at my parents' house," I said.

"Hm," was her only response.

I was offended by her suggestion, because in those days respectable women didn't live with men unless they were married. It was then quite clear to me that she was not at all happy with the marriage.

Hilary's father came home soon after my mother-in-law's relatives left. He was a short, gray-haired, balding man with protruding eyes, a big abdomen, and an irritating, loud laugh. Paul Koprowski shook my hand and handed me a beautiful cameo brooch. I thanked him and put it on. His gift consoled me for the disappointment caused by my mother-in-law.

Suddenly Hilary, who had been nowhere to be seen, appeared. "Hilary, remember to come back home early," I heard his mother call after him, as we departed.

I was shocked. Hadn't she expected her son to spend the night with his wife? Why did she ask him to come back early? To me this was further evidence that Hilary's mother didn't accept our marriage and was going to continue her domination over Hilary. I felt angry and began to wonder what I was going to do and whether I could change things. But I had no idea. I still lived with my parents and Hilary with his.

A few days later, Hilary's father came to meet my father and Bronislawa in our apartment, and he brought me six pairs of beautiful silk stockings. Stockings were considered an elegant gift, and the ones he gave me were nicer than any I had. "I would like my daughter-in-law to wear nice hosiery," he said simply.

Hilary never discussed his parents' reaction to our marriage with me, even after my visit to his home. Then a week or two after I met them, Hilary came to see me with a gift—a lovely cocker spaniel. But shortly after giving it to me he left. "I'll call you tomorrow and we'll arrange to get together," he said, kissing me and rushing off as he usually did at night, except for our wedding night.

Quite naturally, I became alarmed when Hilary didn't call me the next day. As the night approached, I telephoned his parents' home. The maid answered and said that Hilary wasn't home.

Seeing no other way of learning Hilary's whereabouts and ashamed of finding myself in this position, I went to see Hilary's parents the next morning. They were both home and asked me to join them in their dark drawing room. My father-in-law sat in a tall, comfortable armchair upholstered in brown leather. Hilary's mother sat in a straight chair behind a table, and pointed to another chair for me. I apologized for my intrusion. At once I came to the point.

"Can you please tell me if you know where Hilary is?" I demanded.

"He's in England. He flew to Manchester yesterday," Hilary's father told me.

"That's strange," I answered. "I don't understand why he didn't tell me anything about his plans; he even misled me, asking me to await his call. We're married and should be together."

Inside I was trembling. I was shocked by the devious way that Hilary had kept me in the dark about his plans—that he had left the country without telling me or taking me.

"You can fly to Manchester and be with him there. That may be the best solution," Hilary's father said at last.

"No, thank you. I'm too proud to impose my unwanted presence on him," I said.

My in-laws remained silent after that.

"When he saw me last, he gave me a dog," I added. "I didn't realize that this animal was meant to be his substitute. Now that I have no husband, I don't need or want a substitute. I'll just find another home for the dog. Please forgive me for bothering you with my problems."

My mother-in-law didn't say a word. When I got up to leave, it was Hilary's father who saw me out. I thought that their behavior was very strange—that they knew a lot more than they were saying.

I became so furious with Hilary that I didn't even miss him. Perhaps I was just numb. I felt I didn't care how long he would remain in England, although I was humiliated by our classmates' questions about where Hilary was and how much longer would I remain alone since our marriage was no longer a secret.

"Oh, I don't know, but I hope that it won't be very long," I answered, trying to smile and hide my embarrassment.

Although I now found it difficult to concentrate in class, I continued to attend lectures and pass examinations. My schoolmates' questions continued to upset me. But more significantly, I even began to consider divorce.

Honeymoon

Several weeks after Hilary's disappearance, I received a large bouquet of red carnations. A few hours later, the doorbell rang and there stood Hilary.

"I'm sorry I left you alone so long," he said, putting his arms around me. "I will never cease to love you." He tried to kiss me, but I pulled away. I was too angry and upset to kiss him. I had to let him know how I felt.

"Why did you go to Manchester without talking to me about your plans?"

"Because you changed your maiden name to your married name at school without letting me know about it. This made me so angry that I decided to go away. I went to visit my cousin in Manchester."

While he was saying this I noticed he wasn't wearing his wedding band, so instead of responding to his reason for leaving, I asked him why the ring wasn't on his finger.

Calmly, as if he expected me to easily accept this explanation, he said, "I lost it. It must have fallen out of my pocket."

I had a difficult time believing that he had lost the wedding band unless he had lost it as a result of having purposely taken it off when he fled. But lost or set aside, I considered his not having it on a very bad omen for our marriage. Nor was I persuaded that he was telling me the truth about the reason for his travel to England. Why would he mind my using my married name at school? To me, this was more evidence of his wish to hide our relationship. For if that was the reason—that he had minded my using his name—why hadn't he discussed it with me, even argued with me, rather than flying away with no explanation? All this had me feeling very uncomfortable about our marriage now. For as angry and hurt as I was, I still felt love for Hilary and, on seeing him, I saw signs in him of authentic affection for me. I also felt the power of his charm and attractiveness. I was relieved seeing him back. I hadn't expected his return, and although I had contemplated divorcing him, the prospect wasn't a pleasant one. Divorce is rarely easy emotionally and socially, and at that time it was far more difficult than it is now. Aware of all this, I decided to continue our status quo as it had been before, and for a few days after our wedding. It meant that we did not live together, but each with our parents, and that Hilary came every day to study and spend evenings with me in my room.

During the fourth year of medical school we were busy studying and attending clinics. Our schedule didn't leave me much time to brood about my disappointing marriage. I was hoping that, sooner or later, some arrangements would be made for us to begin living together as man and wife. But neither of us had money nor felt that, considering the way we got married, we could make demands on our parents for a separate apartment. Actually, I may have been the only one who felt the need to normalize our situation. But after all the humiliation and disappointments, I did not discuss it with Hilary.

I still didn't know many of Hilary's friends. Those I had met were gifted young writers or musicians, but Hilary usually preferred to meet with them alone. One of them, Lova Abeljowicz, was a musician of whom Hilary was very fond. Lova was a quiet, polite young man who always wore dark suits. Because he was poor, Hilary gave him money out of his allowance from time to time, and would then have to turn to his parents for more funds for himself. Although I realized that it was nice of Hilary to help a friend who had no money, I could not help wondering why he had not used his allowance to buy our wedding bands, instead just accepting the one I bought him and then making light of its loss.

I was impressed by Lova's knowledge of music and consulted him when I decided to buy Hilary records for his birthday gift. Following Lova's advice, I bought a recording of the Brandenburg Concertos. Hilary looked with obvious pleasure at the album I presented him, although he may have suspected or actually heard from Lova that this was his selection. Since music was the basis of their relationship, and I knew so little about it, Hilary and Lova continued to meet together without me. Observing their relationship gave me a chance to see a generous and caring aspect of Hilary's nature, which I liked.

Hilary took me to several concerts at the Warsaw Philharmonic at which such well-known pianists as Vladimir Horowitz, Robert Casadessus, and Miecio Horszowski played. Although I knew these were outstanding performances, my appreciation of them was still very limited. Nor did I feel particularly motivated to learn more about music.

In May of 1939 I missed a period and, this time, after getting a positive result of a pregnancy test, I knew that I was definitely pregnant. But now that I was a married woman, the prospect of having a baby didn't frighten me. I knew that I wouldn't have to worry about finding support for the child.

"Are you ready to be a mother?" Hilary's mother asked me when I told her that I was expecting a baby.

"Yes, of course I am," I retorted. Although I wouldn't admit it to her, inside I had my doubts.

I continued attending classes, even though the pregnancy caused me to feel nauseated at the sight of the vermin-covered corpses that were used in our medico-legal lectures. I was glad that at least I didn't have to perform autopsies on them.

The family physician who had diagnosed my pregnancy later discovered that I also had hepatitis. After I recovered from it, arrangements were finally made to have my father and Bronislawa meet Hilary's parents. When they did, one of the things they discussed was the subject thus far not addressed and now the most pressing issue of the moment — getting us an apartment, where we could live together with the baby.

Neither Hilary nor I were present at their discussion. But later my parents told me that Hilary's parents had very different ideas than they did about our needs. Hilary's parents spoke of a large, elegantly furnished apartment with two separate bedrooms. My father and Bronislawa were more concerned about my studies and thought that a smaller and simpler place would be easier for me to take care of. Nobody asked us what we wanted, and I am not sure that I knew what I wanted. But to the best of my recollection, Hilary and I did not discuss the matter and assumed a "wait and see" attitude. As it turned out there was nothing to see.

Both parents did agree that Hilary and I should go away on a honeymoon. August seemed to be the best time for us, and the Polish Tatra mountains a suitable place to go. But the idea of our honeymoon apparently wasn't easy for Hilary's mother to accept.

"Would you mind if I joined you and Hilary?" Sofia Semeonovna suddenly asked me shortly after our parents met. "I wouldn't disturb you at all," she added. To put it mildly, I was shocked.

"I always thought a honeymoon was intended for a husband and wife to be alone, and I've been looking forward to it for a very long while," I answered coolly. In her reply she showed absolutely no recognition of how inappropriate her request was. For she said, "I'm sorry that you feel that way," almost as if it were some quirk of mine or selfishness on my part to take this position in response to her outlandish request. And beyond her words, her behavior conveyed something even stronger—that she felt it was ruthless of me to expect and want to go on my honeymoon with her son, leaving her all alone. On top of her previous actions and attitude concerning our marriage, combined with the history of Hilary's reticence to acknowledge our relationship socially, this felt like the final straw and, at that moment, did considerable damage to my emerging, newly found happiness.

But before we went off on our August honeymoon, Hilary became very busy preparing for a piano recital prior to his graduation from the Warsaw Conservatory. I don't recall whether my parents were invited, but I don't think they would have come because of my father's asthma. I was asked to come to Hilary's parents' apartment from where I presumed I would go with them to this recital. On the day of the performance his father was not at home, and I went to the concert alone with his mother. I wondered why he wasn't coming with us. Later I noticed him entering the concert hall and taking a seat at a location quite distant from us. He made no attempt to join us. I had already suspected that Hilary's parents' marriage wasn't very happy. Now I was virtually certain. But what I had also suspected earlier was likewise becoming more apparent—that Hilary's mother leaned on her son for the companionship, affection, and moral support she no longer received or expected from her husband. And I had a premonition that this would interfere with the happiness of our marriage. I also felt that this explained a great deal of Hilary's ambivalence toward me and his unconventional efforts to distance himself from me socially.

The march of events in my personal life—our marriage, Hilary's disappearance, and our reunion, my worries about his ability to commit himself to our joint life, the pregnancy, plans for getting settled, and the demands of my studies—all quite naturally had me totally preoccupied so much so that I was hardly aware that the Nazi movement had reached full bloom in Germany.

One day, however, I heard Hitler's booming voice on the radio in the dining room of my parents' apartment. His voice was frightening and seemed almost unreal. *Ein Reich, ein Volk!* were the words I remember hearing. I felt he sounded like a fanatic and a demagogue, but many young Poles were attracted by his call for the restriction of civic rights of the Jews. In doing this they were completely ignoring the past occupations of Poland by Germany. They also did not realize the growing danger posed by having Hitler's dictatorship next door to our country. Some university students went so far as to stage anti-Semitic incidents, and they demanded separate benches for the Jews in lecture hall. These demands became so strong that part of the faculty and administration gave in and agreed to assign special seats to Jewish students, who then were required to sit on the left side of the lecture hall. The majority of students didn't support this decision but were afraid to oppose the Nazi sympathizers. Only a few of the liberal students were courageous enough to even just voice their indignation.

Although Hilary and I had never been involved in political activities, we were horrified by these events. We were concerned about the development of the Nazi movement in Germany and frightened to see it spread to Poland. When the movement reached our own university, we really became alarmed. It signaled to us that educated people, who should have learned the lessons of history and resisted such irrationality, had succumbed to Hitler's power, with its attendant prejudice and hatred. We felt helpless. To organize a counter-movement was dangerous and would have required a lot of time and effort, which we, as students constantly studying for examinations, couldn't afford. In retrospect I now feel that this was selfish and shortsighted but, at the time, we felt it was safer not to undertake such dangerous actions. I suppose, like many, despite our worry and opposition, we didn't realize the enormity of what was ahead. Even our bravest classmates—members of the Communist Party—who subsequently risked their lives hiding Jews during the war, weren't yet ready to fight against the demand for separate seats for them.

We still did not have an apartment of our own and had not had our honeymoon, but one spring weekend I went with Hilary and his parents to their country place in Celestynow. At the Warsaw train station, Hilary's mother, smelling of jasmine perfume, was in a very good mood. I remember her smiling at me. Although I didn't like her, I did respect her because she was Hilary's mother and, unlike Bronislawa, a professional woman.

When we arrived at Celestynow, which was only about ten miles north of Warsaw, a carriage awaited us at the station and took us to the house. The house was small, but old and beautiful, and it was surrounded by cherry and pear orchards. Hilary and I were given a bedroom on the second floor where he retreated after lunch for a long nap.

Not knowing what to do, I began wandering through the property until I came upon Hilary's father, who was tending roses in the front of the house. Feeling comfortable with him, I stopped and helped him with his gardening. After Hilary finished his nap, he chatted with his cousin Leon Gerber. Leon, who was three years older than Hilary, was already practicing medicine in France and was here on a visit. Leon's mother had died when he was young, and he had been raised by his aunt, Hilary's mother. So Hilary and he felt some of the closeness of brothers.

Sunday evening we returned to Warsaw, taking with us several crates of cherries for Rozalia, Hilary's parents' cook, to make compotes and preserves for the coming winter.

After this weekend in Celestynow, Hilary and I began to prepare for our long overdue honeymoon. During the last week of August 1939, when I was in the fourth month of my pregnancy, we arrived in Zakopane, a mountain resort in southern Poland. A famous piano teacher, Egon Petri, happened to be staying at the same hotel, so Hilary took several lessons with him and also began spending many hours playing the piano. One afternoon, as I saw him surrounded by a small but admiring audience, I realized that when Hilary played the piano, only music existed for him. I might as well not have been there.

I felt lonely and excluded. It was unfortunate that music still didn't interest me very much, for if it had I might have enjoyed listening to Hilary play and thus would have been a participant, albeit a passive one. I think that would have made me feel better, although I still retained my feeling of unimportance and neglect. This feeling was much diminished during our honeymoon because Hilary had paid more attention to me than at other times. But I found it difficult to share Hilary with his admirers, and I realized that a new feeling of possessiveness towards him began to grow in me. I wondered whether or not I was beginning to take on my mother-in-law's domineering attitude. Was it my subconscious effort to arm myself for future battles with her?

Unfortunately, circumstances beyond our control occurred that interfered with and ultimately interrupted our honeymoon; it turned out very differently from the relaxed and lovely weekend in Bukowina of two years before. Just two days after our arrival we received a very disturbing letter from my father. He was urging us to return to Warsaw because of the imminent threat of war. I sent a reply, protesting. Notwithstanding the history of Poland, I refused to believe that a real war could occur in our country in modern times, although I knew that Hitler had already annexed Austria. And so we remained.

Except for Hilary's piano playing, we kept to ourselves, avoiding the company of other people. We didn't even listen to the radio. Like an ostrich, I put my head in the sand and focused only on our personal life.

It didn't matter. Our honeymoon was ill-fated. Even though we decided to stay in spite of my father's entreaty to return, the very next day we received a telephone call that Hilary's mother had had a stroke. It occurred during her visit to her nephew's house. Her face and her arm were partially paralyzed. We then had little choice but to end our honeymoon and return. Hilary, quite understandably, wanted to return to her bedside immediately. But instead of taking the very short time it would have taken to pack up all our things so that we could return together, he hired a car and went off by himself, asking me to pack and return alone by the first available train. I did not see the need for such an arrangement, even given the emergency, since we could have gotten to Warsaw almost as quickly together. Thus, our honeymoon was not only cut short by several days, but I was also left, unnecessarily, separated from my husband and had to return home alone. Our honeymoon lasted only a week. By August 31, both of us were back in Warsaw, where arrangements had already been made for transporting Hilary's mother the next morning by car to their country home—the one we had visited in Celestynow—and he would accompany her there.

I announced that I was going with him. At this critical moment I was able to overcome my shyness and intimidation and express my will. When I did—although I don't know what they felt—nobody raised a voice in objection.

The next day, September 1, 1939, at eight
o'clock in the morning, I left my parents'
house to meet Hilary at the apartment of his
mother's nephew. On my way I heard an air
alarm. But knowing that for some days there
was an anti-air attack defense program in
Warsaw, I didn't think it was real. I wasn't
frightened as I followed the people going to the
street shelter, which was located in the basement of a nearby building. I learned there that
Poland had been attacked by the Germans, and
that this wasn't a drill but a real air attack. I
began to feel fear. Half an hour later, the alarm
stopped and I left the shelter with great relief
and went on my way.

Hilary's father was standing in front of the
nephew's apartment house. He had come to see
us off. I asked him why he wanted to remain in
Warsaw all by himself. "There isn't enough
room for everybody," replied my mother-in-law
who, just coming out of the house, had heard
my question.

She was accompanied to Celestynow by
her two nieces, two children, and her nephew.
Somehow her answer made me feel that my
coming along was the reason for her husband's
exclusion. However, it was perplexing to me
and disconcerting that nieces, their offspring,
and a nephew were more important than her
husband and the new and pregnant wife of
her only son.

Annoyed by the implication, I spoke up:
"I'm sorry if my presence is causing a problem,
but my place is with my husband." I probably
felt insecure and I was trying to cover my feeling of insecurity by this harsh statement. To
my relief, Hilary didn't seem either shocked or
annoyed at my response, nor was he surprised

that his father was not coming with us. Half an hour later, my mother-in-law, her entourage, Hilary, and I were assembled and ready to go.

By the time we left the city, life in Warsaw had been totally disrupted and the university closed. Outside the city on both sides of the road, houses were burning and the charred bodies of dead horses in grotesque positions were scattered everywhere. It was several hours before we reached Celestynow, where for the next few days our ears were practically glued to the radio as we listened to the news. In contrast to what we had heard and already sampled of the horrors of the war, the house in Celestynow was peaceful and lovely, surrounded by the beautiful pear and cherry orchards. The pears were almost ripe. I had never seen any quite so big.

On September 4 a general mobilization was announced on the Warsaw radio. All healthy young men were ordered to join the Polish military forces, which were concentrated near the Soviet border. A nonaggression pact between Molotov and von Ribbentrop, made on August 23, 1939, involved secret protocols according to which parts of Poland, as well as the three independent Baltic nations—Lithuania, Latvia, and Estonia—were to become part of the Soviet Union. Because at that time our government didn't expect the Soviet army to invade Poland, it selected a location near the eastern border of Poland furthest away from our Western invaders for the mobilization of Polish troops. Hilary and his cousin Julian decided to follow the orders and join the Polish army. Foolishly, Hilary's mother and her nieces declared that we (along with the two children ages three and five) should accompany them rather than remain alone in Celestynow. So, like figures out of Brecht we started on this strange journey, with no idea what would happen to us when we reached our destination.

Our transportation was primitive and inadequate. We rode in a horse-driven farmer's wagon. Its sides were made of long wooden ladders, and its bottom was lined with hay. We put the children to sleep on the hay, and we walked behind. There was room in the wagon for one adult, and we alternated so each of us could get a little rest in the carriage. Hilary's mother had recovered well from her stroke and insisted on walking most of the time. I was usually offered more rest than the other women because I was pregnant.

During the day the Germans bombed the roads, and their low-flying planes shot at the peasants working in the fields. Mostly we moved at night, resting and hiding in peasants' huts in the daylight. We would try to get some food in a village store before retreating to our primitive accommodations. Sometimes we could get eggs or potatoes, and we felt lucky if we got fresh hot bread just out of the oven. Being very hungry, we ate it immediately; and afterwards, our bellies became painfully swollen with gas. Sometimes we were still on the road when the German planes approached, and we had to hide in ditches by the side of the road. I was horrified by the way we had to live, scared of the bombs, and all the time physically uncomfortable. Eventually I became apathetic, realizing that there wasn't much we could do to change our situation. One night I tried to sleep on the floor of a peasant's hut between my husband and his mother, who kept chasing rats from my abdomen. As my pregnancy progressed, Hilary's mother became more solicitous of my well-being than she had ever been before. I was glad and appreciative, especially given the harsh circumstances. But in truth I must admit, after all that had transpired before, a part of me remained suspicious and wondered if her kindness was not so much toward me but evidence only of her concern for her son's child. Only the future would tell.

We traveled in this way for several nights. Although our purpose was to join the Polish military forces, unbeknownst to us, they had moved away from the frontier with Soviet Russia, having dispersed when the Russians invaded Poland.

Seeing returning troops, we never reached our destination. There wasn't much choice for us but to return to Celestynow. On the night of September 25, 1939, on the return trip, we could see the sky over distant Warsaw glowing red from the fires, and we heard the distant thunder of bombs falling on our city. Horrified by these sights and sounds, we stopped to watch what had been going on, thinking of those who remained in Warsaw, exasperated by fear of what may have happened to my family, Hilary's father, and other relatives. Feeling helpless, we had little choice but to continue our journey, hoping to find in Celestynow a place where we could get a night's rest. But upon reaching our destination, we were shocked by the extent of the vandalism that had occurred during our absence. At first we just noticed that all the fruit had been picked and removed from the orchard, but then we realized that the house was wrecked. The silver and linen were missing, the furniture smashed, and piles of excrement had been left on the floor. It must have been done by local hoodlums, encouraged by the chaos of the war, since the Germans had not yet arrived in that area. It took us hours to clean up the mess and to improvise primitive overnight accommodations. Although back in familiar quarters, there was no peace. All the time we heard the echo of German bombs falling upon Warsaw.

That night Warsaw fell into the enemy's hands. And so began the German occupation of Poland. The Gestapo arrived a few days later. Train transportation back to Warsaw had been disrupted. We had no car, and the wagon we traveled in to the frontier was in disrepair. Also, the telephones didn't function. Our clothes were filthy. I tried to wash Hilary's shirts in a basin. It was the first time in my life I had ever attempted to wash a shirt, and I had no idea how to do it. I rubbed my knuckles until they bled and became sore.

As soon as the temporarily disrupted train service between Celestynow and Warsaw resumed, we decided to return home, find our families, and assess the safety and conditions of staying in the city.

When we reached Warsaw there was a lot to learn and deal with. In our absence, my father-in-law had gone to visit my father and Bronislawa. Shortly after he reached them, there was an air raid and they all went to the basement shelter. The house was hit by a bomb, which exploded in our kitchen. In the shelter, my father-in-law was hit by falling plaster, causing pain, bruises, and bleeding. When I saw him with all those bruises, guilt that I hadn't protested when he had been left alone in Warsaw came bubbling to the surface. I felt great compassion for him and found it touching that he had sought the company of my family, and that they had welcomed him.

But along with my concern about Hilary's father, I had something more tragic to confront. My parents' cook, Zosia, had refused to hide in the shelter, insisting on getting dinner ready. The remnants of her body had been found scattered all over.

As I surveyed my parents' apartment and the building it was in, I first noticed that the kitchen, as well as the kitchens on the floors above it, had disappeared. Amazingly, the china in the dining room buffet was undamaged. Then when I felt the need to use the bathroom, I discovered that it too had disappeared. There were no longer any toilet facilities in the apartment. Bronislawa produced a chamber pot and when I was finished with it, very kindly covered it and carried it away to dispose of the contents. As in the countryside, the war had made life very primitive and frightening in Warsaw.

Looking at my large abdomen, Bronislawa was anxious to take care of me, just as she had been doing since I was a small child. During the next two months, she anticipated all my needs. By then, I was more appreciative than I had been in the past of the efforts she made on my behalf, and now accepted them with gratitude. How ironic it was that, just when I needed and appreciated her help so much, it was to come to an end. For after twenty-two years of being mothered by her, I now had to leave and go off to live with my husband at his parents' apartment.

While living with Hilary's parents, I became frightened of my mother-in-law and her temper. Once I witnessed an ugly and painful scene between her and her niece, Niuta, who had been with us in Celestynow. Niuta was a frail woman in her early sixties, who came to visit my mother-in-law lugging a bag full of ripe, red tomatoes. She had to carry it to the fourth floor because the elevator was out of order, and some of the tomatoes were squashed as she walked up the stairs. Instead of thanking her for her thoughtfulness in bringing fresh vegetables or apologizing for her having to make the difficult trek up the stairs, Sofia Semeonovna shouted words of abuse, accusing poor Niuta of saving the nicest tomatoes for herself and bringing her, Sofia, the damaged ones. It was behavior like this that created fear in me and made me hate the general atmosphere she created. I so wished to be living elsewhere, but there was no way Hilary and I could now get an apartment of our own during the German occupation.

During this period I became very aware of the extent to which Hilary did everything his mother asked him to do, without ever objecting to any of her demands. This worried me and was a source of my continued concern and unhappiness.

My feelings about my father-in-law were different. He had been kind to me from the time I met him, although I was somewhat annoyed by his unattractive appearance, his frequent criticism of other people, and irritating laugh. But I felt empathy for him to have to endure Sofia.

My father-in-law had been a representative of the British textile industry for the past twenty years and had spent considerable time every year in England. He was a staunch Anglophile and always maintained a valid English visa. He had a large number of business associates and friends in England, and he had some capital located in English banks. He had an apartment in London, and another in Manchester.

He wanted to leave Poland—by now totally occupied by the Germans—and go to England as soon as possible. Because England was now at war with Germany, however, he couldn't travel there directly. But since he was a wounded man, he could get the Gestapo's permission to convalesce in Italy. With that in his favor, his enterprising niece Lotta managed to obtain an Italian visa for him. To aid in the project, a woman physician who lived in my parents' apartment house helped me cover my father-in-law's wounds with bandages in a manner that would exaggerate their severity, hiding his face and much of his torso beneath the dressings. I then accompanied him to Gestapo headquarters where he asked permission to travel to Italy.

The building was full of Germans in uniform, moving in all directions as they went about their business. We had done such a good job that Hilary's father really looked frightening. In fact it was fairly clear that the Germans feared he might be a source of infection. The result, I'm quite sure, was that they were glad to be rid of him. Prodded by a ten dollar tip, which would be roughly the equivalent of one hundred dollars today, a Gestapo official readily authorized his departure. Two days later Hilary's father took a train to Rome, where he remained to await our arrival.

After his departure, Lotta opened my eyes to how, in desperate times like the ones we were in, one had to devise deceptive schemes to survive, and how pregnancy could be used as a way to gain sympathy. Lotta became acquainted with a Miss Trevisani, the employee at the Italian Consulate who had provided the visa for my father-in-law. Miss Trevisani, a native of Trieste, Italy, had an Italian father and a Polish mother. She had told Lotta the name of a girls' school in Warsaw from which she had graduated. Lotta then devised an ingenious scheme. She suggested that I should give Miss Trevisani best regards from Bronislawa, pretending that Bronislawa went to the same school and remembered her well. Anticipating that Miss Trevisani would be embarrassed to reveal that she didn't remember Bronislawa, she would pretend that she did. And out of her guilt at having forgotten, combined with her concern over my very obvious pregnant state, she wouldn't refuse an Italian visa for me, Hilary, and his mother.

I was amazed by this scheme. But having nothing to lose, I went to see Miss Trevisani to give her those bogus greetings from Bronislawa, making sure to mention the name of the school. Miss Trevisani was indeed embarrassed that she didn't remember Bronislawa. Just as we hoped, she became interested in me and my very pregnant state. Noting that reaction, I followed up on it. "Please help me so that my child can be born on Italian soil, outside the horrors of German-occupied Poland," I pleaded.

Although Italy and Germany were political allies at this time, the Italian people disliked and feared the Germans and were helpful to Poles whenever the opportunity presented itself. When I saw evidence of Miss Trevisani's interest in helping me, I was quick to hand her Hilary's passport as well, hoping she would understand that in my state I wouldn't want to travel alone and would very much want to be accompanied by my husband. But when I also handed her my mother-in-law's passport, she raised her eyebrows.

"Once the baby is born, I'll need her help," I said. But I wondered what would have happened had she refused the visa to Hilary's mother, and why I made the effort to keep us together. I must have feared her and Lotta's criticism for not having tried hard enough to get her a visa. I also was convinced that Hilary would never agree to go away with me and to leave his mother alone in Poland.

Miss Trevisani acceded, but she wanted to know how many more passports I had in my pocketbook! My heart was beating very fast, and I assured her that I had no more. I walked out of the Italian consulate with three visas, hardly able to believe what I had accomplished. All that we needed now was the Gestapo's permission to leave Poland.

In the meantime, we began our preparations for travel. As soon as the dean's office at the medical school reopened, Hilary and I went in search of our professors to get their signatures, attesting that we had passed our final examinations. We were in the last class to finish medical school in Poland before the Second World War for which we were honored at the Polish Royal Castle fifty years later and awarded anniversary medals.

Besides readying ourselves to leave Poland and resettle in Italy, I had something else to concern myself with—the birth of the baby. I had to learn how to care for a newborn, and even about the birth process itself. At medical school we were taught only about childhood diseases. So before we left, every morning at dawn, I went to a foundling home to learn how to handle infants. Since nobody was allowed out of the house between seven o'clock in the evening and seven o'clock in the morning on account of a curfew, I obtained special permission to be in the street before seven. Bronislawa ordered a maternity dress and girdle custom made for me, and she bought a complete layette, including several dozen linen diapers, for my baby. I felt awful about leaving her, my father, and brothers and having a baby away from them. But once I made this decision, I began to act like a machine programmed to carry out the mechanics of our departure.

We purchased train tickets and then went to Gestapo headquarters to seek permission to leave the country. Although by now we were used to seeing Gestapo men marching through the streets of Warsaw, it was always a frightening experience, and going to their headquarters was even worse. They were still accepting bribes, though this practice continued only during the first few months of the occupation and then was stopped. We did what we had to do, and we were granted permission to leave Poland under legal and even reasonably comfortable conditions.

My family had no plans to leave Poland. While my father, like my father-in-law, had no illusions about the oppressions to which the German occupational forces would subject Poles his situation was very different. In spite of his liberalism, politics had no influence on his decision to remain in Poland. It was because of his health and economics.

He had been a chronic invalid who suffered from frequent attacks of bronchial asthma most of his life and he feared the hardship of leaving his home for an uncertain fate abroad. He had neither capital nor business connections outside of Poland. Nor did he have the strength and stamina to hope for the beginning of a new life in a foreign country. We had never lived for a long time abroad, and his family, settled in France a long time ago, barely made a meek existence from their earnings. Bronislawa had no profession, and my two brothers were still of school age. In contrast to the decision made by my father-in-law, my father had made a difficult choice to remain in Poland, even though he realized that the Germans were planning to expropriate Polish businesses and properties.

However, my parents accepted my decision to go in order to be with my husband, and also because it was in the best interests of my soon-to-be-born baby. They looked towards my departure with resignation but at least on the outside maintained their calm. When my father and Bronislawa expressed their concern about my future, though, my brother Gene declared that my prospects looked brighter than theirs. To tell the truth, I was somewhat hesitant to place my fate in the hands of my newly acquired husband's family and to leave my father, whom I adored, to his uncertain future in Poland.

My father gave me my mother's diamond engagement ring. "This is all I can give you now," he said. I put the ring on my finger, but I left all my other momentos from my mother in the closet in my room, feeling it was safest there. I had little knowledge then of what the future would actually hold. Just prior to finding out about our plans to leave Poland, my father had complied with the Germans' order that private citizens not keep foreign currency, and he sold all his American dollars. As a result, he couldn't give me more than a one hundred dollar bill when I left. To give me so little was a source of considerable pain for him, but it moved me greatly. At that moment I felt his sorrow that he wasn't able to help me more, and I was overwhelmed by his warmth and love for me. But even had he been able to give me more money, it was a risk to take it out of the country. I hid the note he gave me in my maternity girdle in order to prevent it from being taken from me by the Germans.

I was horrified when my mother-in-law, on learning how little money my father had given me, said, "They let you go with a bare ass!" I don't think she took a lot of money out of Poland, either, and she hid an emerald pendant that Hilary's father had given her before their marriage went sour in a large ball of knitting wool.

I was crushed by Sofia's unfair criticism of the father I so adored, showing no respect for his love for me or mine for him, no compassion for the circumstances of his inability to provide more for me. She completely disregarded our mutual pain in separating, especially with my being pregnant with his first grandchild and the grandchild of my mother, whose memory was so dear to him.

When the day of our departure arrived, my family came to see us off at the train station. As I kissed them good-bye, we were all composed. Nobody cried, but my father's cheeks felt uncommonly cold to my lips. "I'm afraid that we'll never see one another again," he said.

I didn't answer, since I feared it, too. He was still the person I loved most, and I felt awful leaving him.

The train moved west to the border, across Germany and through the Italian frontier to Rome. My suitcases contained only a few changes of clothing, a baby layette, and diapers. I was then in the seventh month of pregnancy. We carried little money. The only jewelry I took was my mother's ring, my wedding band, which I wore, and the cameo brooch which Hilary's father had given me. Taking valuables out of Poland was tantamount to risking your life because of the regulation of the German occupational forces. Even taking the few bits of jewelry we had was quite chancy. But luckily, although our train tickets, passports, and visas were examined, nobody ever looked inside our suitcases. We breathed a deep sigh of relief once we were on Italian soil, despite Mussolini and his fascist government. Italy wasn't yet involved in the war.

My father-in-law awaited us at the Pensione Milton in Rome. The four of us stayed there for one month. It was a comfortable place. Hilary and I shared a room, but each of my parents-in-law occupied a separate one. I don't recall anymore if we all had private bathrooms, but we certainly had at least a sink with running water in every room. We had no cooking facilities and ate out. I was very little interested in food during my pregnancy, but knowing Hilary's parents' appreciation of good food, I am sure that we must have eaten well. Our daily walks on the nearby via da Porta Pinciana alternated with visits to museums. But going to outdoor cafés to meet other Polish war refugees and discussing with them the progress of the war were our most important activities, since nobody knew from day to day what the future would bring us. Our fate was closely linked to the political situation of the world. We all anticipated that Italy would soon enter the war on the side of Germany. We needed to decide what to do next in light of the approaching birth of our baby.

Besides these major changes in my life, the war also affected small but important everyday personal habits and practices. Since the war started, I hadn't gone to a hairdresser on a regular basis to have my hair cut and set. Now in Rome, having no funds, I wasn't able to resume this habit. My hair grew longer, and I had to pull it back — which gave me a less elegant and more serious appearance. But Hilary didn't seem to notice or care.

During our stay in Rome in January 1940, family tensions surfaced. My in-laws treated each other with extreme coolness. It was pretty clear that my presence was a nuisance as far as my mother-in-law was concerned. But I was carrying her son's child and it became apparent that she wanted nothing to happen to me that could have a bad effect on the baby. She even went so far as to object to my seeing the mummies in the Egyptian section of a museum: "Irena, don't go looking at those horrible things. Your child will look like one of them!"

I ignored her advice and looked at the mummies with interest, surprised that my mother-in-law had the kind of irrational superstitious beliefs that I wouldn't expect to find in an educated professional woman. Only after getting to really know her did I learn that she did indeed have a superstitious side.

But, quite aside from all this, our main preoccupation was getting out of Italy. Hilary's father was anxious to get to England, where he felt he could best earn money to support us. All of us were increasingly concerned about the anticipated entry of Italy into the war. When this happened, we would once again find ourselves on enemy territory. With the delivery of my child rapidly approaching, the prospect of escaping from Italy with a small baby under unpredictable circumstances was frightening.

Hilary and his parents agreed that I must leave Italy and give birth to my child on Allied soil. France was the logical choice because my father's sister Aunt Nathalie, her husband, and their daughter Irene still lived in Paris. In addition, Irene was now a medical student and would be able to arrange for my obstetrical care.

Although the Soviet Union's invasion of Poland had prevented Hilary from joining the Polish army during the general mobilization in Poland, his military status changed when he started working as a physician at the Polish Consulate in Rome. He became a medical officer, examining recruits for the Polish army who would then be shipped to Coetquidan in France. As long as I remained in Italy we could be together, but if he were to accompany me to France, he would be treated as all Poles of military age, including civilians, and would be sent by the French to Coetquidan. His medical officer's rank was valid only at the Polish Consulate in Rome. I understood this situation but naturally was unhappy that his father, and not Hilary, offered to accompany me on my pending and difficult journey. In the end, I had to face the reality that, once in France, Hilary would not have been able to remain with me; and I was deeply grateful to and touched by my father-in-law offering to see me through the trip and to safety.

I spent the days preceding my departure from Rome as if I were wrapped in a cocoon, without seeing the world around me. I had played no role in the choice of my destination and passively accepted the decisions that Hilary and his parents made about my life. I felt helpless without my father to advise and protect me, and I was emotionally anaesthetized by what had been happening to me. Most of my pregnancy had taken place under such dramatic circumstances and under so much emotional stress that hardly any of my thoughts were focused on the baby I was about to give birth to.

When the moment of our separation came, there was no dramatic or emotional scene between Hilary and me. We weren't in the habit of publicly expressing our emotions, and Hilary's mother's presence had a restraining effect on us both. We were stunned by all that was happening to us. We didn't know what was ahead of us, and there was still a good bit of ambivalence in our relationship. We just kissed and held each other tightly for a few moments, without saying much. "Take care of yourself, Irena. Hopefully we'll see each other soon," was all Hilary said to me.

"Who knows when we'll see each other again!" was all I managed to reply.

"Dad, take good care of Irena," Hilary said to his father, putting an arm around his shoulders.

"Don't worry, son, I will," his father reassured him.

"I hope that you'll have a safe delivery of a healthy baby," my mother-in-law wished me with tears in her eyes, placing loud kisses on my cheeks.

As the train pulled away from the station, our true emotions mostly remained sealed in our hearts.

Once the train crossed the French border, I was approached by the French Intelligence Service who, seeing my Polish passport, questioned me about the movements of German troops in Poland. I told them what I knew, which was very little. They listened with interest, however, and saluted.

When I arrived in Paris, my father-in-law brought me to my aunt and uncle's apartment, leaving me under their care until the baby was born and I was back on my feet. He stayed in Paris and took up residence in a small hotel at the foot of Sacré Coeur. He probably didn't mind remaining in France for a bit, since it brought him closer to his ultimate destination, England.

My separation from Hilary led to the creation of two odd couples—Hilary and his mother in Italy, and Hilary's father and me in France.

Aunt Nathalie was as warm towards me as ever and took loving care of me. She had tears in her eyes as she, my uncle, and cousin Irene listened to my description of our experiences in Poland. "Oh la la! Poland is an ill-fated country! None of this could ever happen in France," Aunt Nathalie said. Personally, I believed the Germans might well invade France just as they invaded Poland, but I didn't say so. It was February 1940, and the fate of France was still unknown.

Four days after my arrival in Paris, I began to feel labor pains. My cousin took me to the Clinique St. Pierre in Neuilly sur Seine, a suburb of Paris, where her professor of obstetrics and gynecology, Dr. LeLaurier, offered to deliver me.

I spent that night at the clinic. The next morning, my pains ceased, so I was sent back home. But the following evening my pains recurred, and the sac of amniotic fluid burst, releasing the liquid. But by the time I returned to the clinic, I was very cheerful because I felt no pain. They were about to refuse me admission, but I fortunately had the presence of mind to request firmly that I be examined by a physician.

Professor LeLaurier arrived just in time to recognize that my uterine contractions had stopped and that I couldn't deliver a baby spontaneously. He rushed me in for an immediate forceps delivery. The head was already down low and the baby had been about to suffocate because of compression of its umbilical cord. That was averted, and in a very short time, my obstetrician held the newborn up by the feet and announced the birth of a boy. Suddenly I felt

Irena with baby son Claude in Paris at the balcony
of a hotel in Montmartre (February, 1940)

extremely happy and pleased to have a son. There was a mole on the
sole of his foot, but on the opposite foot from that of his father. I was
overjoyed by this finding, which made me feel that I was holding in
my arms a true genetic descendant of his father.

In response to our telegram from Paris announcing the birth of
a baby boy came a telegram from Rome, signed by Hilary and his
mother, requesting that the baby's name should be Claude. Although
I had not taken the time to select the name for my child and to
announce my choice, it somehow struck me as very wrong that nobody asked me if there was a name I wanted. I resented it. However,
I managed to summon up enough courage to add a middle name for
Claude — Eugene — after my mother, Eugenia.

Despite the distractions of my difficult circumstances, when I held
my new baby in my arms, I felt that wonderful maternal joy that is
almost impossible to put into words. And as I looked down at Claude's
face while I was holding him, I could feel a soft, happy smile come
over mine.

As soon as we notified my family in Warsaw about the birth of
Claude, we received a congratulatory telegram. I so wished my father
could have seen my son.

In the meantime, Hilary continued his medical practice at the
Polish Consulate in Rome. Recruits who were found fit for the Polish
army were sent across the French border to Coetquidan for military
training. Once trained in Coetquidan, they were shipped to England

to join the British forces. It was a source of satisfaction for Hilary that, barely out of medical school, he could be a physician in a foreign country and that his efforts contributed to the enlargement of Polish army units in France. He also was thrilled by the opportunity to continue his piano studies at Santa Cecilia Conservatory in Rome. He was advancing his career in medicine and his education and skills as a pianist, which were of enormous importance to him, even in the midst of war.

After leaving the Clinique St. Pierre, I spent a week with Aunt Nathalie and then moved to a comfortable room in the hotel where my father-in-law lived. He and I established a routine for Claude's care. I took him out to the park for fresh air each morning in a baby carriage he had bought for Claude. At noon my father-in-law would join me and stay with Claude while I went to have lunch, as it was not possible to cook in our hotel. We took turns eating to avoid bringing the baby carriage with us to the crowded small places we were eating in. We alternated places, going to different neighborhood restaurants, where food was cheap but excellent. That Hilary's father was taking such good care of me was a great solace, and one for which I was quite grateful. Although I didn't especially like him when I met him initially, during this period I grew very fond of him.

I nursed Claude, but didn't have enough milk to satisfy his needs. So I had to supplement my breast feeding with formula. This complex feeding procedure was a slow process, but at least it gave me an opportunity to feel the precious intimacy of breast feeding. My cousin Irene arranged for me to attend a weekly baby clinic, which in France provided instruction in child care for the benefit of young mothers and included pediatric consultation.

Claude was growing into a good and lovely baby, with big blue-green eyes resembling my own. He slept well at night. Because of all the difficult experiences I had been through during my pregnancy, I had had fears of not being able to experience normal emotions about my baby. But I had developed strong maternal feelings now that Claude was born. It was a joy to wake up in the morning, listen to his cooing in the crib, and call him *Kloduleczek mala zabka* (Claude, little froggy) and other endearing Polish names. For the first several weeks of his life, nothing else mattered to me. To my delight, I was very much able to enjoy motherhood and to love my new baby boy.

My father-in-law did not hide in his quarters in Paris. He was a very open man and, although in a foreign country, he was quite sociable and alert to the people around him. One day, when he was taking a walk, he noticed a familiar face and realized it was Stanislaw Kryszek, a former medical school classmate of Hilary's and mine. Stanislaw was serving in the Polish army and had come to visit Paris from Coetquidan on his day off. Hilary's father wasted no time in bringing him back to our hotel to see me. I was nursing Claude as they walked in, which I found embarrassing. But as soon as I closed my blouse, I jumped with joy and hugged my welcome visitor. It felt so wonderful and was such a relief to see a familiar face from my former life in Poland.

Stanislaw was in the position that Hilary would have been had he not remained at the Polish Consulate in Rome where they needed his services as a physician to examine recruits for the Polish army. Hilary's military rank of officer was an incidental bonus. But once in France, he would have been trained as a soldier and shipped to England as Stanislaw was about to be.

Although the war prevented graduation ceremonies from taking place, all the members of our medical school class who passed their final examinations had the status of doctors with diplomas, even though many never received the piece of paper. Luckily, Professor Halecki, professor of history and rector of the Warsaw University, was now in Paris. When I went to visit him, I obtained handwritten diplomas for Hilary and for me.

Another faculty member from our medical school, Professor Electorowicz, was in Paris, and I visited him. During our chat together, he had strong words for me, putting me to shame for allowing myself to be supported by my father-in-law instead of practicing my recently acquired medical profession. He gave me a list of jobs available in Paris for young Polish physicians. Our faculty was used to Polish women physicians practicing medicine when they had small children, and he probably did not stop to think that in France I had no comparable facilities for child care that I would have had in Poland. He wasn't used to such considerations and stressed the need for us to help the French in fighting the Germans. It did not occur to me for a moment to seek excuses for my comfortable life of leisure. My ambition to assume an active role as a physician was stimulated by his attitude, which to me seemed perfectly rational.

Since I spoke French fluently, I was in an especially good position to get work, and I started immediately to look for employment. I visited two prospective employers—Dr. de Martel, a famous neurosurgeon, and Professor LeLaurier, who had delivered my baby. Because young French doctors were in the army and, thus, France needed physicians, both of these doctors were delighted at my availability to join their staffs. Each offered me an internship, which meant that I would have to live at the hospital where no accommodations would be available for my baby. So I went for an interview at the Villejuif Lunatic Asylum, where I was accepted as an intern and given permission to keep Claude in my room with me. At the time Hilary was unaware of the situation, but I doubted if he would object to my decision. With Claude locked in my room, I began my work.

Villejuif was a very large and old-fashioned asylum that accommodated about two thousand inmates, including criminals adjudged insane who were chained and kept in isolated cubicles. I was responsible for the medical problems of eight hundred noncriminal psychiatric patients who were housed in two wards. In the afternoons I examined new admissions. The ward patients I was responsible for were affected by a variety of diseases, many of which may have been related to malnutrition and erratic behavior. Some had little resistance to infections. Although I didn't have the required experience, I collected cerebrospinal fluids, washed osteomylitis wounds, and, through gastric tubes, fed patients who refused food because they thought they had no stomachs. I prescribed medication for pneumonia, which was not uncommon among long-bedridden patients whose lungs tended to become congested and who had little resistance to infections. So many doctors were away from their civilian jobs and at the front that those who were hired to replace them were given responsibilities for which they often hadn't been fully or properly trained. I had to go to the library to learn how to perform some of the procedures that were unfamiliar to me, procedures that are usually taught in clinical situations by trained and experienced doctors, who then supervise the trainees as they get their first experiences actually performing the procedures themselves. But I didn't have that luxury. After reading about a procedure carefully, I would carry it out to the best of my ability while strong male attendants held down the patients, who were often angry and agitated. A woman with osteomylitis, whose wounds I had to wash and dress, constantly ripped off the dressings, and I then had to put them back on again. As a solution to this repeated problem, the attendants decided to tie the sleeves of her straitjacket securely to the sides of the bed.

Having many patients to take care of and learning how to perform necessary procedures, I didn't have much time to react to all this human misery, which I had confronted for the first time in my life. Even seeing a woman in a straitjacket, as distressing as her sight was to me, I had to agree with the attendants that this was the only way we could have the dressings left on.

One of my afternoon responsibilities was to see new admissions and give a first tentative diagnosis. An elderly non-violent patient served as my orderly. He was a quiet, melancholic, well-mannered, seemingly educated and articulate man. His duty was to file reports, keep order in papers, etc.

Psychiatry is a highly specialized discipline, requiring a great deal of study and practical experience. Like many young physicians, just out of school, I barely knew the basic textbook concepts and lacked any practical experience whatsoever. I found most of the cases of new patients baffling and nearly impossible to classify, unless this was already done by the doctor who referred the patient for confinement. At the occasion of the first examination, having described the physical state of a new patient, I sat bent over the admission form, worrying how to fill the tentative-diagnosis slot. My orderly, who observed me from his corner of the office, moved next to me and quietly murmured;

"This looks like an acute case of paranoia." Immediately I recalled my textbook and was struck by how right the man was.

This situation occurred more than once in the following two or three days, and finally I ventured to ask my helper how he acquired his knowledge of the matter. "Oh," said he, "I am a psychiatrist myself. I am here because of the jealousy of my professional colleagues who were envious of the therapy of mental diseases which I invented."

When I asked my colleagues about the antecedents of my helper, they confirmed that indeed he used to be a practicing psychiatrist, even an outstanding one. However, he started to treat his patients with colored water, using different colors for different kinds of mental disorders. After he presented the results of his treatment at an annual meeting of the local psychiatric association, he was confined to the Villejuif asylum.

I had the shock of my life when I first saw the Salle de Guarde, which was the Villejuif staff dining room. The walls were covered with life-sized frescoes of different types of sexual acts between men and women, people and animals, and various other lewd combinations of species and sexes. There was no place on the wall free of these pictures, and I felt ill at ease eating and talking to people with these frescoes constantly before my eyes. I was curious about who executed these frescoes, but was too embarrassed to ask, and to this day I don't know. This *was* France, and perhaps, unlike Poland, its culture allowed a greater openess about sex. However, given my background, I found it distasteful, as I did the signs in the hall stating that intercourse was prohibited on the stairway. Although I already was a physician, my sheltered and apparently prudish upbringing in Poland had failed to prepare me to deal with such circumstances. Nevertheless, in spite of some of my feelings of discomfort, I was pleased to be working at Villejuif. After all, I was practicing clinical medicine, enjoying it, and earning money. I was proud of my situation.

While dividing my days between patients in the wards and new admissions, I managed to go back to my room every three hours to feed Claude. Fortunately, he wasn't left unattended all the time I was gone. The wife of the asylum truck driver lived on the premises and was employed as a laundress. She did her laundry in an outdoor stream, and I was able to leave Claude with her each day for a couple of hours. While she watched him, she also washed his diapers. Having him with someone I trusted put me more at ease. I also had the help of an alcoholic patient from Martinique. He carried the baby's carriage up and down the steps whenever I needed help getting Claude out for fresh air.

At my first dinner at Villejuif, I met Dr. Rogue de Fursac, a very pleasant retired physician who was drawn back into service, like me, to take care of the asylum's patients while the younger French doctors were at the front. I was very lonely, being far away from my family and my husband, and I found a badly needed friend in Dr. de Fursac. He was kind to me from the moment I joined the Villejuif house staff. I could talk to him. We both feared and hated the Germans. Dr. de Fursac listened with much sympathy to the story of my wartime experiences in Poland. "I would like to do something for you to help you forget the pain of leaving your family and losing a good life," he said in a soft tone of voice.

"When is your day off, Madame?" he asked me the next day. "Let me show you Paris," he added.

I was thrilled by his suggestion. This would be my first opportunity to have company and to get away from the asylum and to have some real enjoyment.

A few days later, Dr. de Fursac drove me to Paris. I enjoyed seeing again the familiar landmarks such as the Arc de Triomphe, Place de la Concorde, Tuilleries, and other well known, special places in Paris.

He took me to the Galleries Lafayette, an elegant French kind of department store, and bought me a large bottle of cologne scented with fern, my favorite fragrance. I enjoyed his company, his attention, and his concern for my happiness, and I very much looked forward to another outing with him. But unknown to me at the time, my life at Villejuif was to be cut short and would last only a few days longer. So that was our only escapade.

When I returned to Villejuif after sightseeing in Paris with Dr. de Fursac, Claude was soundly asleep. I sat on my bed in my small room and began thinking about the striking differences between Hilary's easy life in Rome and my own harried and often unpleasant existence in Villejuif. Although I was glad Hilary was safe, and I was proud of his achievements, I was also jealous of the pampered life he led while I was struggling for survival in a country threatened by

German invasion. That these feelings came to the surface after my trip with Dr. de Fursac was of course no coincidence. I was a young, newly married woman. I had just given birth to a healthy baby boy. Yet, for a very long time Hilary had failed to show me anything like the concern for my welfare, pleasure, and happiness that I had experienced that afternoon.

It made me wonder, as I had before, what kind of marriage this was. Hilary was advancing his musical education to the extent that he graduated as a pianist from the Santa Cecilia Conservatory in Rome. Evenings he spent at cafés in the company of his mother, meeting friends, and chatting with acquaintances. My days were spent force-feeding lunatics while running to my room every three hours to feed Claude, and my evenings were spent alone, locked up in my room with our baby. It is true that the decision for him to stay in Italy and for me to go to France was made in our best interests, but I didn't feel that Hilary cared about the differences in our lives or my difficulties. Nor did I feel that he longed to be with me and give me or share the happiness I so longed for.

But I didn't remain in the doldrums. My thoughts turned to my pleasant outing with Dr. de Fursac, and I stopped feeling sorry for myself. I undressed and sprayed myself with the fern-scented perfume he had bought for me, and then I went to bed.

This was the spring of 1940. These were the last days before France would be invaded by Germany. It came like a jolt, even though many of us felt sure it would occur in a matter of time. But all of a sudden, everything seemed to be happening at an incredible speed. One morning, as I entered the patients' ward, I heard that the Germans had bombed an airfield eight miles from where the asylum was. Listening to the sounds of German bombs, I was frightened by what might happen to Claude and me.

A few hours later, my father-in-law, who wouldn't leave Claude and me in France when he went to England—his ultimate destination,— arrived from Paris. "Irena, Italy has just entered the war," he said, "and Hilary is leaving Rome." He handed me the telegram he had received from Italy: "Going to Spain. Meet me and Mother in Barcelona, Grand Hotel Valparaiso." It was signed with Hilary's name. This was the first indication I had that circumstances were going to reunite us. Up until that point I had no idea when or how

we would be able to get together again. The events were too scary
and demanding for me to analyze my mixed feelings—great excitement about being back with Hilary and having him see his son for
the first time, yet worry about the nature of my relationship with my
husband. As distant as the latter appeared to have become during our
separation, I would have never allowed myself to doubt whether I
should join him or not. Being with Claude and with Hilary's father,
I just had no chance to even think about it. The first question that
entered my mind was how such a reunion could be accomplished with
German bombs falling everywhere.

Later I learned that Hilary didn't have such an easy time leaving
Italy. The Polish consulate in Rome apparently had an agreement
with Brazilian authorities that, in the event of a war, the consular staff
would be issued visas to Brazil as means to get away from Italy. This
helped Hilary and his mother obtain them as well, along with the
Spanish transit visas that were needed to cross that country on the
way to Portugal, from where boats were departing for Brazil. But
when they boarded the ship for Spain, an Italian official attempted
to remove Hilary from the boat and have him put in a camp for enemy
aliens because he was of military age. The official feared that, once
out of Italy, Hilary would go to France to fight against Germany and
Italy. His mother began to cry. Then, in a single dramatic gesture,
she tore from his passport the page with the French visa, which I
didn't even know he had, scattering bits of the paper into the Medi-
terranean. The Italian official very likely interpreted it as a sign that
her son wouldn't go to France to fight Italians, and that was clearly
in Hilary's favor. Besides, it was lunchtime. The official was probably
hungry, and he most likely couldn't bear to see a woman's tears.
Whatever the reason, he allowed Hilary to stay on the boat and Hilary
and his mother were able to continue on to Barcelona where, as per
the telegram, they had instructed us to join them.

I had barely finished reading that telegram when I was summoned
by the director of the asylum to his office. "Your routine ward visits
and new admissions are to be discontinued, effective immediately,
Madame. You are now assigned to help with the evacuation of our
patients to a bomb shelter," he told me.

I was stunned by his order, and I told him so. Although I was
able all along to carry on my responsibilities to my patients in the

wards and take care of my baby, this was possible only because of the regular hours of my activities. Such would not be the case during evacuation of the patients. My pleas to be excused because I was nursing a baby were to no avail.

"When I left Poland, my country was already under German occupation," I told him. "I would be at great risk of falling into the hands of the Germans with my Polish passport. I want to leave the hospital and go to Spain to rejoin my husband, Monsieur Directeur."

"Villejuif is already under military orders, which you must obey, Madame," he replied coldly. "Your name will be given to the military police if you leave."

I didn't obey him. I asked my father-in-law to stay with Claude in my room while I went to see Dr. de Fursac to ask his advice.

"The director of the asylum is a collaborationist, Madame. You should ignore his orders," Dr. de Fursac advised me without a moment's hesitation. "Don't be afraid. Go immediately through the asylum back door to the nearest police station, and ask them for a permit to evacuate yourself and the baby to the Spanish border."

I followed his advice, and within only a few minutes I had the necessary documents. But when I left the police station, I heard the sound of the bombs close by. Claude was with his grandfather in my room, and I felt paralyzed with fear that something might have happened to them. However, instead of running to the room to find them, I stopped in front of the entrance to the asylum. My near-hysteria about them and my fear of the asylum being bombed kept me from doing what I should have done —rush inside to find and rescue them. Many people were standing at the entrance to the asylum.

"My child is inside!" I cried helplessly.

"Don't just stand here. Go to your child!" somebody called.

These words filled me with shame and self-rage. I couldn't believe that I had hesitated and put my fear ahead of my duty to my child, that I had relied on others to tell me what to do. I entered the asylum and ran to Claude as fast as I could. None of the buildings were damaged, and I found my little boy safe with his grandfather. I have always been haunted by that as an example of incredible selfishness and lack of maternal responsibility. I never forgot that for a brief moment I hesitated between the urge to save my child and the desire to save myself. I don't know to this day if I have ever truly forgiven myself, although as I write about it after years of being a mother and having much more life experience, I am a bit more forgiving. But this is not a memory I live comfortably with, and today I am thankful still that, despite my initial hesitation, Claude and his grandfather were unharmed.

"Let's leave the asylum and go to Barcelona," I said to Hilary's father as soon as I entered my room.

We walked out with Claude, carrying two suitcases—one with my clothes, the other with diapers and milk for the baby's formula. Then we stopped in front of the asylum, wondering about our next step. We were at least ten miles from Paris and had no car. Public transportation appeared to be already disrupted. My father-in-law had come from Paris to the asylum by taxi, but there were no taxis to hire in Villejuif.

Suddenly I noticed a man fixing his car across the street. Gathering up the courage to approach this stranger, I asked him if, by chance, he would be heading for Paris once his car was fixed. He agreed to take us to the Gare de Lyon train station where we could get a train to the Spanish border. It was late at night when he brought us to our destination. Once there, we found huge crowds of people blocking the entrance to the station because, as the Germans approached Paris, the city was being deserted by its fleeing inhabitants.

The chaos that evening at the Gare de Lyon defies imagination. In the darkness of the night, the lights illuminating the human forms struggling to enter the station were blinding. Huge waves of people tried to force their way in simultaneously. They crowded into spaces that almost didn't exist. It was mayhem. This took place to the accompaniment of police sirens, honking cars, human shouts and screams, and the sounds of departing trains. Pandemonium reigned. People were packed together like sardines, resisting the entry of any newcomers. The overpowering smell of car exhausts, mixed with the odor of human sweat and wine, was suffocating. We made several unsuccessful attempts to break through the crowds and enter the station, but finally we had to accept the fact that we stood no chance. Our driver offered to take us to the small apartment my father-in-law had moved to while I was working at the asylum. There we would be able to rest for a few hours, and then try again the next day. Our friendly driver promised to return at five o'clock in the morning and help us once more to get to the station and gain entry so that we could board a train to Spain.

I spent a sleepless night. Several air raids forced me to go with Claude to the basement shelter. My father-in-law wanted to sleep and remained in bed during these air raids.

The next morning, as we wondered what was going to happen to us, he suddenly turned to me and asked, "Irena, when is your birthday?"

"Next week, May twelfth," I replied.

"As soon as life becomes more normal, please remind me that I owe you a birthday present. I want to buy you a nice pocketbook in Spain."

At first I was almost startled that at a time like this he would be speaking of a birthday present for me. But I was touched by his thoughtfulness and felt it was his way of helping to distract me from my worries and bring a little happiness into a terrifying situation.

At five in the morning, our benefactor of the previous night, our incredibly loyal and reliable driver, arrived and was ready to take us to the station again. This time we managed to get close to one of the entrances. The driver stopped the car and helped me get out with Claude. He picked up the suitcase with Claude's diapers and asked my father-in-law to wait in the car for his return. Everybody was running for their lives from Paris. In this completely chaotic situation, nobody was purchasing tickets. The driver and I pushed our way through the crowds to one of the last evacuation trains headed for Biarritz.

He assisted me, with Claude in my arms, up the steps of the train which was about to start moving. He threw my suitcase behind me, and ran back for my father-in-law. But the train had already started moving away from the station. The bottle of cologne, my treasured gift from Dr. de Fursac, which was wrapped in the diapers, broke when my suitcase was thrown onto the train, and all of a sudden in the midst of the tumult and worry, I caught a whiff of the fern. The lining of my suitcase became impregnated with this scent, and it accompanied me for years, whenever I traveled. It became a symbol of my war-time experiences, as well as a remembrance of the kindness of that man who had so lifted my spirits.

My father-in-law was left behind at the station, along with his luggage and the suitcase with my clothes. Separated from him, worried about him, with no money or clothes, my future seemed utterly bleak. I had no idea what to do or what was ahead of me.

There were several gloomy French women and old men in my train compartment. Terrified by the German occupation of France, they worried about their future and about relatives and friends in the army. United by their sad fate, they exchanged information about the latest radio reports they had heard before boarding the train. I was so worried about my own future and what was going to happen to me that I kept silent. But after a while I joined the conversation and told them about my predicament.

"When we get to Biarritz we'll show you a convent that has a day care center," an elderly woman said.

This friendly suggestion helped me overcome some of my despair. I began to hope that, even without my father-in-law and with virtually no money or clothes beyond what was on my back, I might be able to fend for myself.

When the train stopped in Biarritz, I got off carrying Claude and his suitcase and headed directly for the day care center at the convent. I left Claude there with the nuns for the rest of the day. Then I used the modest amount of money that remained from my last paycheck to buy a clean blouse and have my hair shampooed and set. Thus refreshed, I went to one of the elegant Biarritz hotels because my father-in-law had told me that a friend of his was staying there. Luckily, I remembered the man's name and was able to locate him. To my delight, he invited me to tea. I told him how my train left Paris before Hilary's father had a chance to board it, and I was thus in Biarritz alone, worried about how I would cope.

"Your father-in-law may be coming here by the next train," he said. "Keep in touch. He will probably contact me when he arrives, and that's how the two of you will be reunited."

Although I was glad to have made this contact, I quite frankly was disappointed that he didn't ask me if I needed any other help.

On my way back to the day care center, I remembered the Pension Nartus in Biarritz where, as a child, I had spent a long summer vacation with my family and our governess, Miss Waclawa. I stopped there and asked if they could accommodate me for the night, but they were full. Their refusal made me feel terribly lonely. When I stayed there as a child, the owners of this pension had treated me royally and anticipated all my wishes. Now I was twenty-three and in very different circumstances. And although I needed their help far more than I had as a child, they were completely indifferent to my fate. I realized what a difference having money made.

When I went back to the day care center to pick up Claude, I still had no idea where we would sleep that night since there were no overnight facilities at the convent. Fortunately, the good sisters had it all planned out for me. They introduced me to Mme. Lambert, a young washerwoman, whose two-and-a-half year old daughter was looked after by the nuns during the day. She agreed to take Claude and me to her place in Chambre d'Amour on the outskirts of Biarritz, where we were fed and given a place to sleep. Mme. Lambert's husband was at the front. Tears ran from her eyes as she listened to the radio about the advancing German forces. Because of my own fears and misery, my heart went out to her in her despair.

When I woke the next morning, the sun was high. Through the window I could see my son's snow white diapers drying on the line. Mme. Lambert had washed them for me before she left to make her first set of rounds of people for whom she did laundry. Soon afterward she was back, loaded down with the dirty wash and a bundle of dresses for me. She had told everyone at whose home she had stopped that she had a refugee in her house who had no clothes. I was overwhelmed with gratitude for her thoughtfulness and the generosity of the people who donated them.

I selected one of the dresses and fixed myself up as well as I could. Then I took Claude back to the nuns, and went to the hotels that had been turned into hospitals in order to get work as a physician.

However, these hospitals were militarized and, as a foreigner, I couldn't get work there.

When I brought Claude back to Mme. Lambert that night, I told her that I had no money to pay for my room and board because I hadn't been able to find a job. "You can knit socks for the Red Cross. That would pay for your food," she suggested. It had not occurred to me thus far to look for any job other than practicing medicine, but I felt a tremendous relief at her practical suggestion, which also would offer me her companionship.

After dinner, she made coffee and we started knitting. She had to show me how to knit the heels. The following day I again went to see my father-in-law's acquaintance. To my incredible joy, Hilary's father had just arrived. I was beside myself with joy and relief as we hugged at the outdoor café at the hotel where he sat with his acquaintance. He wanted me to come and stay at the same elegant hotel where they were staying. But I asked him instead to give me some money so I could pay Mme. Lambert for the time I had already spent at her place and to allow me to remain with her for a little while longer. Although part of me longed to stay in such a beautiful hotel, I felt shabby-looking and knew I would have been uncomfortable there without elegant clothes. I also felt somewhat reluctant to leave Mme. Lambert so abruptly, given her extreme kindness and the difficulty of her situation, from which she had no promise of escape.

Happy to be reunited, my father-in-law and I began to plan our next move. But first he went out and bought a new carriage for his grandson. "I'll take care of Claude, Irena, so you can take our passports to the nearest Spanish Consulate and get us visas so that we'll be able to get to Spain." The nearest consulate was in Bayonne, a nearby maritime city.

I was impressed by his ability to think so clearly about our situation and to organize a practical plan of action. I felt that I, myself, wouldn't have been able to figure out what to do next, but I knew I was equal to the task of carrying out what he proposed. Thinking back on all this, I realize that I was underestimating myself, as I had shown a good bit of resourcefulness in those difficult and unusual circumstances. But I hadn't ever thought of myself as being competent in such matters, and it hadn't sunk in yet that I had already demonstrated more competence than I had believed I was capable of. Besides, it was such a relief to have someone to lean on after having to fend for myself for those few days.

In Bayonne the next morning, I found myself in the midst of huge crowds of people chaotically moving in all directions. The local population of this maritime port was significantly augmented by new arrivals from all parts of German-occupied Europe. All of a sudden, among all these unfamiliar faces, I was surprised and delighted to find myself in the arms of two good friends. One was my classmate from medical school, Stanislaw Kryszek, whom my father-in-law had recognized on the streets of Paris and had brought to our hotel to visit me. Stanislaw was now about to board a boat bound for England. The other friend was Dr. Anastazy Landau, my professor of internal medicine from Warsaw Medical School. He pointed out that I stood no chance of getting a visitor's visa to Spain as long as Franco was in power. I could only get a Spanish transit visa, and that required me to have a visitor's visa to another destination. Such evidence was required as proof that I wasn't planning to remain in Spain, but would only pass through Spain on my way to Portugal, from where boats were going to Brazil. He thus suggested that I first go to the Portuguese consulate to get a visa for Portugal before applying for a transit visa to Spain.

Following his advice, I rushed to the Portuguese consulate. The line of people waiting to enter the third floor office of that building extended down the street and around the corner. I took a place at the end of the line and awaited my turn. When it came a few hours later, I was asked if I had tickets and visas to an overseas destination, as well as three photographs of myself and enough money for a Portuguese visa. Since I had none of these things, I was ready to leave empty-handed and in despair.

Without warning, a heavy downpour began just as I was leaving the consulate. Having no umbrella, I sought shelter in the building. When the rain stopped, I heard sounds of excited voices coming from the third floor. Driven by some unexplainable force, I continued waiting in the building until the reason for this excitement became clear to me. Apparently, orders had just been received from Lisbon to issue Portuguese visas to all the applicants—the requirements for overseas destination, fees, and photographs had been waived, effective immediately. Moving automatically, as if I were a sleepwalker, I once more occupied my place at the end of the line. The result was that I obtained the last two Portuguese visas issued on that day—one for Hilary's father and one for myself. Our baby required no visa, passport, or exit permit.

During the long hours I spent in line at the Portuguese consulate, I became acquainted with the woman just ahead of me who, like myself, held a Polish passport in her hand. She too wanted to go to Spain and told me that even with a Portuguese visa it might not be possible to get a Spanish transit visa in Bayonne because the crowds applying for visas there were enormous and, with Franco's government being pro-German, the Spanish consulate was very hostile to applicants fleeing from the Germans. But she felt that since only a few people had thought of applying for visas at the Spanish Consulate in Hendaye, a small border town, they might be more sympathetic to applicants and we'd have a better chance. She then invited me to go with her the next morning to Hendaye. It turned out to be an excellent idea. We went to Hendaye in her car and quickly obtained visas. While there, a French intelligence officer advised us to cross the Spanish border within the next twenty-four hours because it would soon be closed by the approaching Germans. I returned immediately to Bayonne to obtain an official exit permit to leave France. After all the machinations of getting the visas, this proved to be the most difficult of my tasks.

As I stood for about an hour at the end of the line in front of the municipal building on a big square in Bayonne, I realized the hopelessness of the situation. Whenever city employees from the adjoining buildings approached the main entrance, the French guards, who stood in front, used the butts of their guns to push the people who were closest to the door back in line. When the crowd became disorderly, only the strongest people could remain in front. After I was pushed back twice, I understood my predicament. To remain there was futile. So I moved away from the main building and stood in the shade of a tree trying to figure out what to do next.

There had to be a way of getting permission to leave France. I recalled Lotta and her scheme to get Italian visas. But now I had to devise my own scheme, and I knew that I must act promptly. I watched the events on the big square, noticing several times that municipal employees from a small building located very close to where

I stood would walk across the square to the main entrance. Whenever they approached, the guards pushed the crowds away from the door to let the employees enter. I waited until the next group of employees was passing by my tree and, without any hesitation, joined them. I grasped the hand of a young woman in the group and started speaking in French very rapidly. I told her that I left a small baby in Biarritz to seek permission to leave the country. Now I needed to travel to Spain to join my husband. There was no way I could fight my way through the crowds to enter the building where permits to leave the country were issued. Would she help me? Making no reply, she took my hand firmly and led me past the guards into the building. She accompanied me to an office on an upper floor. A few minutes later I left, holding exit permits for me and for Hilary's father. This time I felt very proud of myself.

When I returned to Biarritz, my father-in-law was already aware of the deadline for crossing the Spanish border. But his attempts to arrange transportation for us to the border crossing point had been unsuccessful. Neither the trains nor the buses were running, and taxi drivers were demanding a fortune for taking refugees to the Spanish border. I went to say my good-byes to Mme. Lambert and told her about our problem. And again, it was she who came to the rescue.

Her semi-invalid brother-in-law was a cab driver, and he would take us to the crossing point for the price of the gasoline. Thanks to the efforts of these very good people, my father-in-law, Claude, and I found ourselves on a train to Barcelona before the border was closed.

Although my relief was enormous, I suddenly became aware that, shortly, I would be seeing Hilary and that he would see me looking very unattractive. Thus, as old anxieties faded, new ones took their place. I was still wearing the hand-me-down dresses collected by Mme. Lambert, and my hair was long and straggly, and pulled away from my face, which was not a style I felt was very flattering to me.

In those days, trains in Europe still used coal-fired locomotives. Carriages were divided into compartments, each containing eight seats. Air-conditioning was still practically unknown. The only way to have any fresh air in the inside of a compartment was to lower the window panes. But then the smoke from the locomotive would get inside. The alternative, on a hot day, was to suffocate.

The slow-moving train was full of Spanish-speaking people who could not understand French. I didn't speak Spanish, but I realized that my fellow passengers were talking about the incredible sufferings of the people jailed by General Franco. I was aware of their fate and horrified by what I knew. Many of the passengers were carrying small hampers of food that they generously shared. The train often stopped at small unscheduled stations where General Franco's gendarmerie suspiciously viewed the passengers.

After some hours of the ride, little Claude became visibly and vociferously hungry. It was time for his meal, but I did not have hot water to prepare his formula. In principle, there should have been some water in the toilets in the carriage, but what with the crowd and disorganization, the reservoirs were empty. There was probably water to find at the little stations at which the train occasionally stopped, but I feared that the gendarmes who walked the platforms might stop me and that the train would meanwhile leave.

The baby was crying and the kind Spaniards in my compartment were showing sympathy but not much comprehension of the situation and could not understand my attempt to explain it in French. They understood that the baby was hungry, that an amicable peasant woman offered me some liquid from a part of her hamper lunch, and that I had a great trouble refusing her for fear of hurting her feelings. I finally managed to convey my need for hot water to dilute the formula. A young man, wearing a railway employee's uniform, who traveled in our compartment and observed me and my baby with sympathy, left the compartment at a small stop and soon returned with a canteen full of hot water. How grateful I was! At the next stop my benefactor left the train. A few minutes later Claude was fed and did not start yelling again until we were near our destination—the large station of Barcelona.

As we approached Barcelona we found a passenger who knew some French. He revealed that the hot water given to me to feed Claude came from the tank of the locomotive engine!

When we arrived at the hotel in Barcelona, my mother-in-law greeted us. "Where's Hilary?" she asked us. We were stunned.

"We thought he was with you," I said.

While waiting for us in Barcelona, Hilary and his mother had been sitting in their hotel lobby talking about the problems they feared we were having getting out of France. France was by then totally occupied by Germans. Apparently, they were overheard by a man who approached them, claiming that he could get anybody safely out of France to Spain for a fee. In response to this, my mother-in-law sold her emerald pendant and gave him the money. In return, the man offered to accompany Hilary to a location at the French border, which he said was the place we would be entering Spain. As soon as they got to the alleged place, the man disappeared, leaving Hilary alone to watch for us. After hours of waiting, Hilary called his mother to tell her that he still hadn't found us. Fortunately, by then, we were already in Barcelona. Hearing this news, he made his way back.

Later that night, with hugs and tears of joy, I presented four-and-a-half month old Claude to his father. While Hilary looked with curiosity at his son, the shameless infant got very red-faced and, with a loud noise, eliminated a considerable amount of his intestinal contents into his diapers, after which he was soon fast asleep. Hilary stood watching Claude for a long time. I wondered what he was feeling and, although he never said what he felt, I could observe on his face all the curiosity and tenderness you'd expect of a new father seeing his infant son for the first time. All of us talked late into the night until we were too exhausted to talk anymore, and we then fell asleep.

It was a tremendous relief to finally be reunited with Hilary. But after living different lives for nearly half a year, we needed time to adjust to each other, and this was slow in coming. We needed to be alone to restore our romance, yet we were constantly with Hilary's parents. And a new source of difficulty appeared now—Hilary's mother immediately began to interfere with my authority over Claude's care.

In addition to these personal family tensions, during the next ten days our life in Barcelona wasn't very pleasant for other reasons as well. The hotel was full of refugees from all over Europe. The wartime atmosphere made it difficult for us to relax. We had to report to the police daily to explain why my father-in-law and I, having only forty-eight hour transit visas, still remained in Spain beyond the time we were granted. The reason was that, as soon as Italy entered the war on the side of Germany, Hilary and his mother had obtained visas to Brazil, our ultimate destination. On that basis they had been issued

Spanish transit visas. Since the boats to Brazil were leaving from Portugal, Hilary and his mother still needed Portuguese visas, which his father and I already had obtained in France. Therefore, we over-stayed the forty-eight hour limit of our transit visas waiting until Hilary and his mother could obtain their Portuguese visas. Portugal is a small country for which the sudden influx of refugees fleeing from Europe created a problem. Obtaining Portuguese visas in Barcelona was difficult and required bribery.

"Your passport isn't in order!" became the standard reply to the applicants for Portuguese visas. Hilary became exasperated hearing these same words every day at the Portuguese consulate.

One day he told another hotel guest about his frustrations. His listener, an older and a more experienced man, suggested inserting a folded ten dollar-bill into the passport. Uncomfortable with bribery, yet seeing no alternative, Hilary followed the suggestion. This time the consular official took the passport to another room, and when he returned, the visa was in it. Fortunately, I had better luck securing the Brazilian visa I still needed, and I got it with unusual ease.

With all these formalities concluded, we were glad to leave Spain, where the strong pro-German sympathies of Franco's government became increasingly ugly to us.

We went to Estoril, a small resort in Portugal, where we had to wait a month for a ship to Brazil. This town was crowded with foreigners, all of whom were seeking refuge in South America. I spent most of the time taking care of Claude, while Hilary and his mother made the acquaintance of many people, all waiting for their ships. These people had many interesting stories to tell, and Hilary enjoyed spending time with them. Hilary's father kept other com-pany and was never with them. I felt lonely when Hilary was out and about with his mother, leaving me at the hotel to take care of the baby. I got a few more hand-me-downs from strangers, but still had no money to buy a new dress or to go to the hairdresser. I felt ill at ease without my own clothes, and without being able to have my hair done. It simply didn't occur to me that my concern about my appearance may have been excessive, given the circumstances. But I was unhappy—the war was frightening. I missed my family and, although reunited, Hilary and I continued to live each in our own world.

My father-in-law, who never intended to go to Brazil, decided to fly from Portugal to England. He had planned to go there from the time we left Poland because he had business connections there and would be able to work, support himself, and send us money in Brazil, which he felt very committed to do. In spite of problems in his marriage, he was very much a loyal, family man. But I think it was also a convenient way to separate from his wife.

Before Hilary's father left, he gave me a beautiful leather pocketbook, that birthday gift he had promised me the night that the German bombs were falling all around us in France. What a lovely man he was. I still had and treasured the cameo brooch he gave me when I married Hilary. I was sad to see him go, but I knew that he couldn't wait to get back to his textile business in England. Even though his position as a representative of British shirting materials in Poland had been interrupted by the war, his contacts could be depended upon for making a livelihood there. He promised to send us money to start our new life in Rio de Janeiro.

There was never any question of my mother-in-law going with her husband. They were estranged, and in any event she wouldn't leave Hilary. She realized, too, better than I did, how much we were going to need her help in taking care of Claude. We were war refugees who, at this particular time, had no place to go except for Brazil. In spite of my extraordinary success in working for a while as a physician in France, I had remained an immature and helpless human being when it came to dealing with my husband and his mother. I had no idea if and when I would be able to begin to work in Brazil and, if so, what my professional position would be there. In spite of my resentment of Hilary's mother, I couldn't think of a way we could arrange for Claude's care without her.

I knew that Hilary was going to miss his father, although he played down even this emotion. Hilary's love for his father was deep and genuine in spite of his father's strained relationship with his mother. His failure to exhibit affection toward others in the presence of his mother may well have been to avoid provoking her jealousy. Later in our life, I had many opportunities to realize how strong the ties were which bound Hilary to his father. Hilary's father remained with us until just before we left Portugal. He then flew to London, where he remained through the end of the war.

Going to the New World

In July of 1940 we left Lisbon on the S.S. *Serpa Pinto*, slowly making our way to Rio de Janeiro. The ship was full of refugees exchanging their tales of woe. After two of the four weeks of travel, the ship docked at Madeira for a brief lay over. Madeira is the largest of a group of islands in the North Atlantic Ocean that belong to Portugal. It is about 360 miles from the coast of Africa and 535 miles from Lisbon. Its mountainous peaks and the sea coast line create scenery of exquisite beauty. Madeira wine is world famous.

My mother-in-law asked Hilary to accompany her to the shore. "What a great opportunity to visit this island, Hilary," she said. "Too bad Irena has to remain on board! Of course she can't leave Claude alone." Unlike what many grandmothers would have done, she never suggested that she stay with Claude so that Hilary and I might enjoy seeing Madeira together, especially since we had been apart for so long.

As soon as we docked, Sofia Semeonovna motioned Hilary to follow her, which he did. I was furious. How could they leave me alone to take care of Claude, after those long months in France when his care had been my sole responsibility under very strenuous circumstances. Their selfishness appalled me. I could feel my resentment and anger increasing every instant. Once they took off, I was determined to visit Madeira by myself if I couldn't see the island together with Hilary. The problem was Claude. I hated to leave him alone, but I felt that if I surrounded his berth with pillows, he would be in no danger of hurting himself in the event he might fall. The pillows would protect him, and I used all four of them for his safety. Once that was accomplished, and he seemed quite snug, I locked the cabin and went ashore.

I only went for a short walk on the island, but Hilary and his mother were already back in our stateroom when I returned. "You're a degenerate mother," declared my mother-in-law. Claude indeed had tumbled onto the pillows, which is where she and Hilary had discovered him, but just as I suspected, he was utterly unscathed. Hilary didn't say anything, but I could see by the way he looked at me that he didn't approve of my leaving Claude alone in the cabin.

"I'll do it again each time I'm left alone to mind the baby. I too would like to have some fun, just like everybody else," I said hotly, making my resentment apparent. Blinded by my anger and despair, I completely failed to realize that I had acted in a totally irresponsible manner. I had tried to punish Sofia by abandoning her grandson, forgetting that I was hurting myself, too, by neglecting my own baby.

Hilary still didn't say a word. It was becoming quite clear that, although Hilary wasn't about to oppose his mother when she usurped my marital prerogatives or just simply interfered with our relationship, he wouldn't oppose me when I stood up to her. If there was any struggle, the two women would have to fight it out with each other. It was the easy way out.

A gala farewell evening was the main social event on the ship. My mother-in-law put on a black lace cocktail dress, a false pearl necklace, and her emerald ring. Although he was still a bit plump, Hilary with his blond hair looked handsome in a dark suit. "Let's go on deck," Hilary's mother said. Then both of them looked at me.

"I can't go like this," I said with tears in my eyes, pointing to my hand-me-down from Mme. Lambert—an everyday, short-sleeved polka dot dress. Although my lack of evening clothes was amply justified by my war-time experiences, I just couldn't see myself appearing at a gala evening without a suitable dress. I also was painfully aware that I wouldn't look attractive unless I had my hair cut and set at a beauty salon, and I had no money for a hairdresser. I did not want to appear shabbily dressed in the company of my good-looking husband and my mother-in-law. Although I liked to look attractive as much as most women do, I might have been able to ignore my appearance had I felt that I was loved. But as it was, I felt insecure and lacking in self-confidence.

"Go upstairs on deck, Mother, and I'll stay with Irena," Hilary said.

"All right, I'll be there," his mother replied. In the mirror I saw her wink at Hilary behind my back.

She left, and Hilary sat down next to me on the edge of the berth. For a while we were silent, listening to the sounds of music. Claude was asleep. I undressed and crawled into my berth and under the covers. "I'll stay with you until you're asleep," Hilary said.

A few minutes later, when I had my eyes closed and pretended to be asleep, I heard a slight movement as Hilary tiptoed out of the cabin, quietly closing the door behind him. Lonely and unhappy, I burst into loud sobs. I missed my father and Bronislawa. I couldn't sleep for a long time as I listened to the sounds of music and laughter long into the night. My pillow was soaking wet and tasted salty when I finally fell asleep, totally exhausted. There was still no trace of Hilary.

At last, the day following the gala evening, we arrived at Rio de Janeiro where we planned to establish our new life. Hilary and I were twenty-three years old, Hilary's mother was in her fifties, and Claude was six months old. We checked into an inexpensive hotel. Because Hilary's mother insisted on it, we all shared one large hotel room. She justified this by saying that it saved us money and gave us all a chance to keep an eye on Claude. Hilary and I in this set-up, of course, had no privacy, no chance at all to be alone. I remember the room very well. It was square. The headboard of a large matrimonial bed was placed against one wall, and a twin-size bed in which Hilary's mother slept stood lengthwise against the opposite wall. Next to her bed was a door to the entrance hall. Claude's crib was placed in the middle of the room, close to the foot of our bed. One of the two remaining walls had two large windows. A large wardrobe and two chests of drawers stood against the fourth wall.

One night Claude woke up crying, needing his diapers changed. I was sleepy and Hilary got up to change his diapers. His mother woke up and shouted, "Don't you dare! Changing diapers is the mother's job!" I didn't want a scene in the middle of the night, so I got up to take care of Claude. After that, Hilary never offered to change diapers again. It was awful that even when his instincts were good, he would let his mother undermine them. Only her hostility toward me could explain why she, a professional woman from a country where women professionals were treated as equals of men, insisted so upon my performing "motherly" responsibilities to the exclusion of any help from my husband. She simply couldn't tolerate Hilary helping me in any way.

"You and Hilary should pay no attention to my being in the same room. Behave as if nobody else were here!" Hilary's mother said to me one morning when we were alone. I couldn't believe that she would say that or think it would be possible for us to ignore her presence. It seemed as if she would say almost anything to try to make her outlandish intrusion into our marriage seem normal.

The next morning she wasn't feeling well and remained in her bed longer than usual. When Hilary went out and she and I were alone in the room, she called me to her side: "Don't you think, Irena, how strange it is that an adorable child comes to this world as a result of a dirty act men and women perform in bed?"

In spite of my prudish upbringing, I didn't consider my sex life dirty. In any case, I would not discuss my views about sex with Hilary's mother. "I don't think what men and women do in bed is dirty," I replied. And with that I walked out of the room.

"Oh, that's something new to me," I heard her call after me.

The whole situation was becoming more and more intolerable. There were nights when I longed for Hilary, to be in his arms, to have him to myself, to talk, to be close, but I didn't make my feelings known to him. Her presence and his toleration of the situation intimidated me and made me feel it would be useless to say anything to him.

One day I finally had enough and threatened Hilary that I would sleep on the beach unless we got a bedroom to ourselves. I felt that my need for privacy and our need to be alone as a couple had to be made an imperative. Hilary told me that something would be done about it, which led me to believe that as soon as two suitable rooms became available and their price was acceptable we would have separate accommodations.

Looking back on all this, I realize that being a refugee was very much a factor at that dreadful moment in my life. The loss of family, country, home, and money deprives you of options you normally have. Had I been in Poland, with family and friends to turn to and connections to find work, I very likely would not have continued to tolerate such a miserable situation. But now, in Brazil, I felt terribly alone and unable to envision coping on my own. I had no one to turn to for advice or comfort, and I couldn't imagine how I would have managed to support myself and take care of Claude, or that I would be given a chance to take him away with me.

Although Hilary did not tell me how long it might take before we would have a room of our own, and his mother did not discuss this matter with me, within a day an unexpected outside intervention brought about the change I so wanted. We had already begun to develop friendships within the community of Polish refugees, many of whom my mother-in-law had met aboard ship. In fact, she was well liked and regarded by many people as a sociable and vivacious person. But when one of the Polish ladies, a refugee like ourselves, became aware of our abnormal living circumstances, she let Hilary's mother know exactly how she felt.

"What are you doing in the same bedroom with your children?" she had said to my mother-in-law, apparently in a rather disapproving tone of voice. "Only among poor peasants does the whole family sleep together. You and I haven't been raised that way. You're ruining the marriage of your children."

This lady never told me what my mother-in-law had replied. But faced with my rebellion, my threat to sleep on the beach, and now, happily, some "public opinion," my mother-in-law gave in, and we got a separate room sooner than I had expected, within a day after voicing my demand.

"Do you still love your husband?" the same friendly lady asked me the next day when she saw me taking Claude out for some fresh air.

"I don't know myself," I replied truthfully.

In spite of allowing us to sleep in a room by ourselves, my mother-in-law found plenty of other ways to interfere with our marriage, primarily finding constant reasons to demand his company on her errands or social occasions. With all this still going on, it was virtually impossible for Hilary and me to learn more about each other and to work out the inevitable problems and differences that exist between marital partners. Such problems were magnified in the case of those of us who had been separated by the war. We needed time together so that we could build up a storehouse of intimacy, happy times, and experience in working out differences—all of which are necessary for developing a solid, loving marriage based on trust and understanding. Instead, annoyed and frustrated by this triangle in which I had to share my husband, I often didn't even feel part of a couple. As a result, I could never be sure of Hilary's real feelings for me.

As soon as my father-in-law sent us money from England, we moved out of the hotel and rented an apartment on Santa Clara Street, a short walk from Copacabana beach. It was a third-floor walk-up with three bedrooms, a dining room, kitchen, and bathroom. We furnished it with cheap second-hand furniture. Because the money was her husband's, my mother-in-law held the purse strings. Hilary and I did not participate in any decisions about what was most needed. Since only one set of bed linens had been purchased, I had to wash all our sheets by hand every Sunday morning and dry them in the sun on the roof. There were no laundromats in those days in Brazil, and I had no money for a laundress.

During the day we kept the apartment windows closed to keep the heat out. At night, when we opened them to get the cooler air, roaches would fly in and settle on the floor. We would see them whenever we turned on the lights, as they scurried for the darkness under the furniture. Often, after a day of caring for Claude, I would be too tired to wash out my underthings and, instead, put them down on the chair to be washed in the morning. I would find big holes in them, seemingly eaten up by the variety of roaches we had there.

We were so poor that, except for the second-hand clothes from Mme. Lambert, I still owned only one cotton dress, which I had made in Rio and washed and ironed daily. You couldn't buy ready-to-wear dresses in Rio, and although having them made was quite inexpensive, I couldn't afford a second dress as yet. We didn't have many possessions; the few pieces of cutlery that we used were donated by Mrs. Luz, an English lady who was very compassionate and became quite moved listening to our wartime experiences.

Hilary and I began looking for jobs within a month of our arrival in Brazil. Finding jobs wasn't easy, by any means. Although we were physicians, we didn't have licenses to practice medicine in Brazil. Such licenses required graduation from a Brazilian medical school, a situation unlike that in the United States where a foreign graduate can take a licensure examination. On the other hand, unlike France, there was no shortage of doctors in Rio due to the war, so they weren't hiring unlicensed foreign physicians anyway. That's why the only work related to medicine I was allowed to perform was practical nursing duties, which even included babysitting jobs. So, although it was humiliating to me, I took a job as a practical nurse, mostly providing nursing care to private patients at Strangers Hospital in Rio de Janeiro. I was actually lucky to get this job, since at the time I spoke neither English nor Portuguese, having just begun to take lessons in the latter. But without any nursing education, I lacked the skills I needed for this work. A sympathetic English-trained nurse, Julia Pyles, understood my predicament, and she patiently instructed me so that I could carry out the duties I was assigned.

Once I had an American patient, probably the first American I ever met, who requested a private night nurse following his appendectomy. When he realized that I didn't speak English and that I kept falling asleep in my chair, he gave me an Agatha Christie detective story to read. Reading this book would help my English, he explained. Although it did not help much, I appreciated his kindness, which did not stop there. When he was well, he went to the trouble of discovering my address. One day he turned up with a small suitcase, and he offered it to me as a way of thanking me for taking good care of him.

My mother-in-law opened the door to let him in. Observing his constant glances at my bosom, she remained in the room and found a way to bring his visit to an abrupt conclusion. With obvious satisfaction, she banged the door behind him. Though I might have done the same in response to his apparent fascination with me, I again found it annoying that my mother-in-law interfered in my relationships and took it upon herself to make decisions that should have been mine and not hers.

During January and February, which are the hottest months of the year in Brazil, Hilary's mother took Claude to Itaipava, a lovely mountain resort. Hilary and I visited them on weekends. The coolness of the hills was marvelous, but returning to Rio was awful, for the humid heat there was enough to make you feel nauseated.

Despite my unhappiness with my mother-in-law and the general difficulties of our entire situation, I was not so down on her that I didn't value her relationship with Claude. One day when Claude was one year old, I walked in on them when she was giving him a piggy-back ride. With Claude's lovely, big blue-green eyes framed against the shoulder of this strong, stocky, blond woman in her late fifties in a blue flowered dress, I had to admit that they were a pretty picture indeed.

Once I was offered a babysitting job through the hospital, which meant working in a private home. Whenever this baby boy cried, I would spank him, causing him to scream all the more. I was angry that I couldn't work as a physician and that I instead had to take care of someone else's infant. I hated this job and was relieved when it ended. On another occasion, I took on the terminal home care of Mrs. Pullens, a very old and rich English lady dying of ovarian cancer. I wasn't happy taking care of her, either. But Mrs. Pullens' daughters appreciated my services and invited me to spend a few days at their unoccupied country home after their mother's death.

I hadn't had a vacation for three years, and Hilary insisted that I shouldn't miss the chance to leave the city. At the time, Claude was away with my mother-in-law in Itaipava, and I accepted the Pullens' invitation. Hilary, because he had begun earning money giving piano lessons and couldn't afford to miss them, was unable to accompany me. Unwilling to go there alone, I asked a friend, Stefa F., a Polish refugee like myself, to come with me. We stayed for one week in the Pullens' bungalow. It adjoined the Brazilian jungle and had two bedrooms, a bathroom, kitchen, and a dining/living room. There was a small garden in front. The Pullens had ordered for us the delivery of meat, eggs, bread, and milk from the village nearby. But I missed my mother-in-law's cooking because I didn't know how to cook. I not only regretted having no domestic skills, but I felt sorry for myself. I once again became keenly aware that, had I remained in Poland and had the Germans not invaded, I would have had a cook, a maid, and a nanny. In retrospect I realize that I was being a bit immature. There is no way around it—knowing how to cook is not only a veritable necessity, it often is a source of great pleasure and true independence. But I didn't understand that then.

Stefa, my friend, was not a great cook herself. But she taught me how to scramble eggs. She would first beat the eggs well with a little cream, salt, and pepper. Then she added this egg mixture to finely chopped scallions, which she had sautéed in butter. The success of her dish depended upon the slow and constant stirring of the eggs over a low flame. I paid close attention and, for many years to come, scrambled eggs comprised the extent of my culinary skills.

One afternoon, while Stefa napped, I restlessly ventured on my own into the jungle. At first I was thrilled to be surrounded by lush vegetation and to hear the sound of birds. Then, suddenly, I saw a long, narrow snake suspended from a tree branch above the path where I walked. I immediately stopped in my tracks. My fear was overwhelming. It took all my willpower to move ahead past the snake and out of the range of its attack. This was the first and last time I dared to go into the jungle by myself.

When I returned to Rio, my mother-in-law was still away with Claude, and Hilary was alone in our Santa Clara Street apartment. Feeling uninhibited in her absence, he was ecstatic to be with me again. Hilary decided he would prepare a meal for both of us. But since, like me, he also didn't know how to cook, plain chopped spinach was our main course. To make the occasion more festive, he had bought new stainless demitasse spoons, which we considered a great luxury. This sort of moment was quite rare at that point in our lives, and I savored it, for it made me feel loved and very happy.

Municipal Functionary

During the first year Hilary and I lived in Rio de Janeiro, we held jobs only sporadically. I worked at times as a nurse's aid and babysitter, and he gave piano lessons. We also had a short-lived job in a private medical laboratory owned by a man named Paulo Proença.

My job in this lab required more experience in microbiological techniques than I had acquired in medical school, and I didn't have an opportunity to improve my skills. I had to work close to a Bunsen burner in the unbearable heat of a tropical summer, and I hated it. One day, unable to withstand this discomfort, I sneaked away from the laboratory into a shower to refresh myself. Although I wasn't aware of it, this happened to be Proença's private facility. I was fired because I used it. As soon as I told Hilary about it, and without saying a word to me, Hilary went to Proença to express his indignation. He resigned on the spot. I was surprised that Hilary had given up his job because of me. Although I was enormously pleased and relieved by his loyalty, I worried that now both of us were unemployed. When Hilary's mother discovered what had happened, she upbraided him for having agreed to work with me in the first place.

Thus far I had not succeeded in getting a job that would give me the opportunity to utilize my training in medicine. Then one evening, after losing my job at Proença's lab, I met a prominent Brazilian pathologist named Oswino Penna at a cocktail party. Dr. Oswino held a leading position in the administration of the Rio de Janeiro city hospitals. Having built new marble morgues in all of these hospitals, he needed pathologists to perform autopsies. I had performed about one hundred autopsies in

Poland when I was a voluntary assistant in the Department of Pathology as a third-year medical student, and it was one of the few things in the field of medicine I knew how to do well. After I described to Dr. Oswino how we had been required at Warsaw University Medical School to write complete and detailed autopsy protocols, including lengthy Latin diagnoses, he asked me to meet him the following day. I re-created for him from memory the autopsy protocol forms that were used at the Warsaw University Hospital. He thought these were excellent, and had the protocol translated into Portuguese and reproduced for use in all the hospitals in Rio. We then went together to a surgical supply store to buy autopsy instruments for me to use in my work: a skull holder, a bone saw, and all the knives, forceps, scissors, and probes I suggested.

A few days later, I was officially hired and became a Rio de Janeiro city employee with an identification card. As a non-licensed physician, I couldn't be hired officially as a pathologist, so my title was "extranumerary contractual laboratory technician." However, I was ecstatic because my responsibilities would be the same as those of a licensed physician and I would be working in the capacity of an assistant pathologist at the Hospital Miguel Couto. After months of humiliating work as a nanny and a nurse's aid, as well as in other uninteresting jobs for which I wasn't particularly well trained, I finally had an opportunity to use my medical school training and do work I liked and felt competent to do. This did a lot for my self-respect, and it also restored my confidence in my professional future. Not surprisingly, I discovered that it also carried over to my personal life and gave me some strength in dealing with my mother-in-law. (But more about this later.)

The morgue in which I worked was the fanciest and best-staffed I had ever seen. The autopsy tables and even the typewriter stands were carved out of green marble. A young man, who was assigned to be my secretary, was responsible for typing the protocols. I don't know how we would have managed if I hadn't had such an eager-to-learn secretary, for my knowledge of Portuguese was virtually nil. While I was dissecting the organs, I dictated my observations in Latin. Since the roots of words in Portuguese medical terminology are Latin, he recognized their similarity and began to change the endings of the Latin words, translating them into Portuguese. Thanks to his ingenuity, I ended up with typed Portuguese protocols. In addition to this excellent secretary, I also had a morgue attendant at my disposal to saw the skull and wash the body.

Like many other city employees in Rio and other Brazilians, I had only a part-time job from eight o'clock in the morning to twelve noon. At that time in Brazilian hospitals, full-time jobs were not yet customary and were considered characteristic of employment in the United States. A good, free, hot lunch was available in the physicians' dining room before we all dispersed to go home. It included steak, fried egg, rice with black beans, and a banana, all of which were sprinkled with *farina de mandioca* — a tasty cereal flour.

Dr. José Norberto Bica, my superior, was a surgical pathologist. He also was a good chess player, an avid reader, and a charming man. Being a surgical pathologist, he never actually performed autopsies. In fact, he would have been reluctant to perform autopsies under any circumstances because a large number of the corpses were those of people who had died of tuberculosis. Having had this very disease in the past, he feared getting reinfected. Needless to say, he was delighted when I became available for this service. I considered myself immune because of the mild episode of TB infection I'd suffered in my teens. Also, I needed this job and decided not to worry about the possibility of my own reinfection.

In Brazil, tuberculosis carried with it considerable social stigma, very much the way that syphilis did and still does in the U.S. and in Europe. People didn't like to admit the existence of tuberculosis in their family and referred to it only in whispers. This stigma reduced the likelihood that a doctor would indicate on a death certificate that someone had died from this disease. Another reason why many death certificates did not indicate that the deceased had tuberculosis until autopsy proved its presence was that many people in poor families died without clinical diagnosis, perhaps not ever having been seen by a doctor.

I was responsible for doing all the autopsies at the Miguel Couto Hospital and performed about four hundred of them during the next three years. I was a fast worker, and since I had a morgue attendant to help me, some mornings I managed to do three autopsies in a row before lunch. Every hour on the hour I would have an autopsy completed, along with its report typed in Portuguese.

As I would read back over my autopsy reports to make sure they were correct and complete, the Portuguese words gradually became familiar to me. After some time, my growing familiarity with Portuguese medical terms helped me to master the rest of the Portuguese language. Within a year or two I could speak, read, and write Portuguese with complete ease.

Aside from helping me to learn the Portuguese language, my autopsy protocols provided documentation of hundreds of cases of tuberculosis that had previously gone undetected. Close to one-fourth of the autopsies I performed revealed cases of unsuspected tuberculosis. This indicated that this disease was far more widespread in the population than had been assumed and was of epidemiological significance. Because of their importance, my autopsy protocols were included in a dissertation on this subject submitted by a candidate for an associate professorship of pathology at the University of Rio de Janeiro.

One day Dr. Bica entered the laboratory very excited. "There's a Greek doctor in New York who can diagnose cancer of the uterus by looking at single cancer cells in smears from the vaginal secretions of women!" he exclaimed. "He's invented a special stain for this purpose. I'd like to try it." He immediately proceeded to mix some dyes and chemicals. At the time I had no way of knowing what importance this Greek doctor with the long name (Papanicolaou) would later play in my life.

Dr. Bica was a pleasant man to work with, and he always treated me with respect. I admired him and never had any problems working with him. Before long, he invited me and Hilary to his house to meet his wife and children. We then became friends.

I could always depend on Dr. Bica's help when I had problems with the morgue attendant. The latter was a very colorful character who, wearing custom-made suits of imported British linen and alligator shoes, was a bit of a dandy and looked out of place in the hospital environment. Whenever he wasn't busy in the morgue, he worked as an ambulance attendant, alerting undertakers about any approaching funerals and undoubtedly being well compensated for these services. This wasn't the only way he showed himself to be resourceful in finding additional sources of income. One time I noticed that the tissues from the autopsy specimens didn't appear to be properly dehydrated in alcohol. Using a special instrument to check this—a densitometer—I discovered that the alcohol supplied by this man had been highly diluted. I never found out what he did with the stolen alcohol, whether he drank it or sold it. But Dr. Bica made him realize that we knew he was stealing laboratory alcohol.

As a rule autopsies were performed on every patient dying at the hospital. No family permission was necessary, as it is in the United States. One day when I was about to start an autopsy, the outraged family of the deceased confronted me, insisting that they had paid money *not* to have an autopsy performed on their relative. Because the morgue assistant had been accepting bribes, Dr. Bica finally fired him. Yet since we couldn't find a replacement, in the end he had to be rehired.

My experience in doing autopsies was now well established. Oswino Penna then asked me to teach autopsy techniques to pathologists at Santa Casa de Misericordia, where he was the chief of pathology.

After I had worked for some time at the Hospital Miguel Couto, I became acquainted with Dr. Lourenço Jorge, head of the Department of Medicine. One day, when my mother-in-law became ill, I asked him to come see her as a patient. Sofia Semeonovna received Dr. Lourenço in our Santa Clara apartment, where she was lying down on a small sofa in the otherwise unfurnished, tiny spare room. She wore her long blue, flowered cotton dress. Without raising herself, she stretched her hand to him. Then in response to his question about how she felt, she listed her complaints, shedding an occasional tear. He examined her and humored her. In response, she appeared to forget her ills and aches, and she became very animated. Laughing, she told him that in spite of her age and past medical history, she felt full of life.

After examining her, he told her what would have relieved the anxiety of any Brazilian woman. "Don't worry, it isn't tuberculosis, flu or anything serious. It's probably just your old syphilis," he said, as he patted her on the cheek.

"This man is a complete imbecile; an aging married European woman dentist would be the last person to have syphilis," she declared. Of course she had never had syphilis, but Hilary and I had a good laugh at the mistake made by Dr. Lourenço and at Sofia's resulting indignation.

The fact that syphilis ran such a mild course in Brazil in contrast to Europe and the U.S. where it always was a severe disease may be related to its lack of a social stigma manifested in a rather amusing way among the upper-class Brazilians. Elegant ladies, while on their way to or from the pharmacy, greeted each other in the street, freely exchanging information about going to get or already having had their injection against syphilis. Young men were proud to tell each other they had gotten syphilis as a proof of their manhood. The disease Brazilians were ashamed to have and did not talk about was tuberculosis, which has no stigma attached to it in Europe or the U.S.

Working at Miguel Couto Hospital and teaching pathologists at Santa Casa de Misericordia, I had little time to care for my growing son. He was three years old and a beautiful child. In addition to his wonderful big blue-green eyes, he had begun to develop a charming smile.

I was constantly torn by conflicting emotions about leaving Claude every day for half a day when I went to work. We needed my income, and I also wanted to practice medicine. Yet I loved my little boy, and nothing made me happier than seeing a smile on his face. I felt guilty spending so little time with him. I also feared the consequences of constantly letting his grandmother exercise her authority over him. I realized that my partial abdication of maternal duties involved giving up some of its associated rights and privileges—that this was the price I had to pay for having a career. But I knew that it wouldn't have had such unpleasant consequences if my mother-in-law had been more supportive of my role as Claude's mother. Sometimes what she did to undermine my position was extremely disturbing, so much so that it would lead to an argument.

Once, in response to my disregard of her mandate that Claude wear clothes chosen by her and not me, she became very angry, screamed, and tried to hit me. At that moment, Hilary arrived. I left him alone with his mother and went out with Claude. But when Hilary and I discussed the incident later, he minimized the seriousness of his mother's attempt to hurt me physically.

"How hard could an old, sick woman hit you?" he asked. "You overreacted to her crazy behavior." In retrospect I realize that he was right.

When Claude had chicken pox, I was able to spend afternoons reading him "Juca e Chico," the Brazilian counterpart of a famous

German fable, "Max und Moritz," about two mischievous boys. By the time he recovered, I knew this story by heart.

Sofia Semeonovna continued to make my life miserable. Once by accident I overheard her critical remarks about me in the course of a conversation she had with another Polish lady. She continued talking about how wonderful her son was and to what extent I was an unsuitable wife for him. It bothered me so much that several days later I asked Hilary, "Am I really such an ill-chosen mate for you, Hilary?"

Without giving him the opportunity to reply, I went on. "Even assuming this to be the case, should your mother say that to other people?"

"What do you mean by your questions, Irena? What are you talking about? What happened?" He seemed to be upset.

When I quoted his mother's words, he looked shocked. "You may rest assured that I'll put a stop to her unrestrained tongue," he said.

This was the first time I had ever heard Hilary criticize his mother, especially on my behalf. Hilary was changing with the passage of time. He was becoming more mature and experienced, and he was gaining respect for my career advancements. I was thrilled that he offered to stand up for me. But knowing how much she dominated him, I doubted he would actually accomplish much with her. The next day he told me about their confrontation.

"Your wife hates me," his mother had complained. By saying that to him, she succeeded in defusing his anger. His previous indignation at her behavior was nowhere to be seen. And while his mere annoyance that Sofia Semeonovna had behaved so badly towards me was certainly better than his former indifference to this problem, it still was far from satisfactory. I again realized that Hilary would continue to try to pacify both me and his mother, or to ignore the situation altogether.

So despite this very small sign of progress on his part, nothing much came of it, and we continued to live in a tense atmosphere. Sometimes I could hear Hilary and his mother speaking Russian in another room. Once they sounded as if they were arguing about me. I blamed Hilary for placing me in this situation—of having to live with a mother-in-law who was dismissive and disrespectful. But I must admit, I was beginning to get the impression that Hilary's mother was sensing that the balance of power was changing. I was rather sure she knew that, although she had succeeded in hurting my feelings and causing a lot of tension, she had failed to achieve my submission to her or to convince Hilary that I was a worthless nitwit. Her realization of this came partly from my standing up to her but, more importantly, instead of always following her demands without reservations, Hilary had begun to argue with her. By then, Hilary had begun earning money, which contributed to his growing self-confidence.

As long as the war lasted, our status as refugees remained unchanged in Brazil. We felt fortunate to be far away from the European theater of war, but uncertain of our future. And while all the personal difficulties we went through since we left Poland had taken their toll, the hot summer months when my mother-in-law took Claude on vacation gave Hilary and me some respite, and an opportunity to mend the delicate fabric of our marriage.

Bad News from Poland

When we first arrived in Brazil, Hilary was uncertain whether he would have an opportunity to establish his career in medicine. In the meantime, he managed to earn a modest if sporadic income by giving piano lessons. On one occasion, he was even asked to accompany a well-known Polish dancer named Ruth Sorel when she performed at a recital in Rio de Janeiro, but I don't remember whether he was actually paid for it.

Then one day, walking down Avenida Atlantica, Hilary suddenly was stopped by Luty Kosobudzki, whose family was long established in Brazil but sent their son to Gymnasium Mikolaj Rej in Warsaw where Hilary had been a student. After graduation Luty had returned to Brazil, where he had studied medicine and was now in practice. Thanks to this accidental street encounter and Luty's professional contacts, Hilary got a research position at the Rockefeller Foundation Laboratories in Rio de Janeiro, where he began working on a vaccine that was being developed for yellow fever.

Hilary was thrilled to get involved in medical research, which already had appealed to him in medical school. At the same time, this job relieved him from his financial worries. He did not have to depend on sporadic piano lessons and his father's support. He did not have much opportunity to further his musical career while in Brazil because no piano would fit into our small apartment. But he had advanced his experience in virus research and, in just a few years, he became recognized as an outstanding virologist, having published papers in prestigious scientific journals in the United States.

Several months after Hilary began his work at the Rockefeller Foundation, he developed an acute illness with a very high fever. Still, he insisted on going to work. Hilary's mother made me call the head of his laboratory and request that he order Hilary to remain at home. I felt he should also be examined by a physician, so I called an elderly unlicensed refugee physician on whose judgment members of the Polish community in Rio de Janeiro depended. Although I could communicate more easily with him than with Brazilian doctors, he wasn't of much help. He just shook his head and said that Hilary had some kind of Asiatic flu, for he remembered seeing similar infections during the First World War in Poland.

In the meantime, Hilary had managed to sneak out of the house to the laboratory, where he collected his own throat washings and inoculated mice with them. Within a few days these mice showed evidence that they were infected with the Venezuelan Equine Encephalitis virus, with which Hilary was working at the time. Since this virus had been known to occur only in horses and Hilary had used new, healthy mice to infect with his throat washings, their sickness must have been caused by the virus isolated from Hilary's throat. There was no treatment for this infection, and Hilary was fortunate that it resolved itself and he recovered. However, his illness was the first known instance of a laboratory contamination with this virus. Naturally Hilary was eager to report his findings to the scientific community. Because of the risk he took running around with a high fever, he got an original publication out of it and also extended the knowledge that this virus could be transmitted to humans.

Aside from giving him great satisfaction, Hilary's job now brought us a steady and decent income. So after living for nearly two years on Santa Clara Street, we now were able to move to a nicer apartment, one on Barao de Ipanema in a building with an elevator.

During this period, my mind frequently wandered to my former life in Poland. I was very worried about the silence from my own family since our arrival in Brazil. In a recurrent nightmare, I saw my father in a large crowd of people moving away from me. I called to him, but he didn't hear me.

I was alone in our apartment one day when the telephone rang. "There's a telegram for you from the International Red Cross office in Geneva, Doutora Irene. They'll deliver it," said the operator.

"Can you read it to me over the telephone, please?" I asked.

"There's bad news," the operator replied.

"Please read it to me," I insisted.

"Henryk Grasberg died."

I had thought many times about what it would be like if my father died before I had a chance to see him again, and I dreaded that possibility. But now it had happened. I hung up the phone and sat without crying, incapable of doing anything except listening to the violent beating of my heart. When Hilary returned home, he found me sitting immobile and could tell something terrible had happened. We were alone; his mother and Claude were in Itaipava. Seeing Hilary, I began to cry. Through my sobs I told him the news, and he held me, trying to calm me down. Finally I grew quiet, and for a while could neither talk nor cry. In virtual silence we had our evening meal and went to bed. But I woke up repeatedly, crying again. Grieved and disturbed as I was, the comfort that Hilary gave me that night made me feel much closer to him than I had ever felt before.

The next day the telegram itself was delivered. Now it was in writing. My father, the only person I truly loved and felt loved by unconditionally, was gone. I now wondered if Hilary could ever replace him in my life, if he could ever provide me with anything like the depth and reliability of love that my father had given me—a kind of love I treasured, wanted, and felt that I needed.

A few weeks after the telegram about my father's death reached me, I had my first asthmatic attack. I was tested and shown to be allergic to a number of substances. But even when I avoided them, I still had these attacks, which continued for as long as we lived in Brazil. At night I would get out of bed and sit in a chair, breathing with difficulty and wheezing. I can list several reasons to explain what had caused this. An all too facile psychological explanation would be that it was my way of repossessing or bringing me closer to my lost father, who had such bad bronchial asthma. But perhaps these attacks were simply brought on by the stress of his death. There also were other probable reasons. I was hypersensitive to tubercle bacilli as a result of the large number of tubercular patients I had performed autopsies on. Asthma is a common manifestation of hypersensitivity. In addition, I was constantly exposed to the dust from the construction of a new building adjoining our apartment house. Each of these factors may cause asthma. In spite of my asthmatic attacks, which I suffered mainly at night, I continued working.

Among the friends we made in the Polish refugee community was an attractive young woman named Elzunia Adamowska, who made her living as a beautician. She had left her husband in Europe and had come alone to Brazil. When she would come to our apartment to wax my legs, Hilary enjoyed drawing Elzunia into conversation

"Elzunia, please tell us why you left your husband in England and came by yourself to Brazil," Hilary asked her more than once. He was sitting on a chair close to the couch where Elzunia was waxing my legs.

"My husband and I had been married only for two years when he brought other women home," she said, blushing. "He wanted me to go out and leave him alone with them. After it happened several times, I just couldn't take it anymore," she raised her voice, then sighed. I noticed that Elzunia's sheer summer dress was transparent and that Hilary's eyes slid up and down her attractive, shapely body. I felt pangs of jealousy seeing the way Hilary looked at her.

"Now, your legs are all smooth," she said, turning to me at last. She also smiled at Hilary, as if to let him know that she was flattered by his attention.

"I saw you staring at Elzunia when she was bending over me in that transparent dress," I confronted Hilary as soon as she was gone. "You've never looked at me like that."

"It would be a sad day for you, Irena, if I ceased to respond to the sight of a beautiful woman," Hilary replied.

Shortly after her visit to our apartment, Elzunia broke up with Stanislaw P., her lover at the time, and told him about her plans to marry another man. Once Elzunia was out of his life, Stanislaw P., who knew Hilary and me and who used to live in my father's apartment house in Warsaw, felt lonely and began to see us more often.

One day he failed to arrive at a party to which all of us had been invited. Prompted by a strange premonition, Hilary and I left the party and broke into his apartment where we found him unconscious. His suicide attempt was unsuccessful because the large amount of alcohol he had drunk made him vomit the lethal dose of sleeping pills he had taken. Sharing the satisfaction of saving the life of our friend brought Hilary and me closer. I remembered his tenderness to me after my father's death, which also had reinforced our ties. It seemed that living together through such dramatic experiences had become an important part of our marital life and that such events overshadowed the torments I felt watching Hilary's attraction to beautiful women.

Besides Stefa, with whom I went on vacation, and Elzunia Adamowska, we maintained contact with other Poles in Rio de Janeiro. We often spent Sunday evenings with other members of the Polish community in Norbert Krautman's house. Norbert was born in Czechoslovakia and educated in Poland and in Germany, where he graduated from a medical school but never established a medical practice. He used to tell us how he made a living as a gas station attendant and admitted that his charges for car repairs were totally unrelated to the amount of time and effort it took to perform the job. They were strictly dependent upon his plans for the evening. Was he going to go to sleep, take a girl out to dinner, or buy her a piece of jewelry?

In Brazil, Norbert initially traded in semi-precious stones and later became involved in an import-export business that, after the war, exported Polish cement to Brazil. He made a big fortune and acquired an enormous amount of land in Mato Grosso Brazil, the extent of which had to be surveyed by plane. Many years later, after our immigration to the U.S., Norbert used to visit us there and be our house guest. He spent much time writing, but although he knew several languages, he couldn't write grammatically in any one of them.

Although we were part of the Polish community, we also became eager to befriend Brazilian people and to gain a better understanding of the country that was now our home. Brazil was a two-class society, with a small group of fabulously rich people on top and a majority of poor at the bottom. The slopes of the hills on the periphery of Rio de Janeiro were covered by *favelas*—dilapidated wooden shacks where the poor population lived, often together with goats or other animals. The middle class hardly existed. We established social contacts with several members of the intelligentsia, mainly professional people: physicians, lawyers, writers, teachers, and intellectuals.

Our first Brazilian friend was Helio de Almeida, the son of a wealthy family and president of the students' union at the University of Rio de Janeiro. Intellectuals like Helio and his friends, especially Odila da Silva Jardin, resented the contrast between the luxurious living of the rich and the extreme poverty of the poor in Brazil. Their concern about social injustice attracted them to liberal and, in some cases, left-wing political ideas. I understood their idealistic motivation and respected their feelings, but it was unthinkable to me that I, as a war refugee and a foreigner, should become involved in Brazilian politics.

One day Helio took us to a dinner party at the house of Antonio Batista, the son-in-law of Louis Barbosa, a politician, lawyer, and writer. The lively conversation that took place that evening allowed us to learn about some of the finest Brazilian writers—Machado de Assiz, Olavio Bilac, Jorge Amado, and the poets Carlos de Andrade and Manuel Bandeira. At this party we also sampled a Brazilian food called *watapa*, which was so spicy that you could swallow it only by feeding yourself coconut fat between spoonfuls.

Helio's friend, Odila da Silva Jardin, was having an affair with a Dutchman, Julius van Soesten. One day, after the end of their affair, Julius came to see Hilary when I happened to be alone at home. Speaking to me about the end of his relationship with Odila, he admitted he had abandoned her for another woman. "Irena, men are polygamists by nature; neither Hilary nor I were born to be monogamists," Julius said.

These words reminded me of my own father's reaction when I complained to him about Hilary taking another girl instead of me to a dance. I could feel my face getting red but I didn't reply, for I felt as if the ground were moving under my feet. The feelings I had in reaction to the way Hilary behaved in the presence of Elzunia returned. Was Hilary deceiving me or merely bragging in the company of other men? I would never know the truth. Unfortunately, these doubts and my jealousy would remain with me much of my life.

By 1944, with no end to the war in sight, the possibility of return to our pre-war life in Poland was unlikely. Hilary now was encouraged by members of the Rockefeller Foundation to pursue his scientific career as a virologist in the United States.

My situation differed from Hilary's. I had just been offered an assistant professorship at the University of Rio de Janeiro Medical School. My acceptance of this offer would provide me with an academic position, professional status, a secure job, and significant career advancement. I feared having to begin my medical career all over

Irena teaching autopsy techniques to Brazilian pathologists at the morgue
of Santa Casa de Misericordia Hospital in Rio de Janeiro (1943)

again in another country. But I was not about to stand in the way of
Hilary's future; there was absolutely no question about my accompanying Hilary to the United States, even though I regretted relinquishing my own opportunities in Brazil. Also, I had come to feel at home
in Brazil; I spoke Portuguese, had made friends, loved the sounds of
the samba, and would miss it all very much.

On my departure, the Brazilian pathologists to whom I had taught
autopsy techniques gave me an album with photographs of the beautiful
façade of Santa Casa de Misericordia Hospital, its laboratories, and the
morgue. In one of these photographs, I appear bent over a dead body,
with a long knife in my hand. Years later, when my son Claude became
a crime reporter at *The Washington Post*, he framed this picture and hung
it in his office as living proof of his family's criminal background!

Among the many friends who saw us off when we were leaving
for the United States were my boss, José Norberto Bica, and two
other friends, Norbert Krautman and Stanislaw P. As I looked at
them for the last time, I felt my heart overflowing with emotion.
Norbert knew I still had only one change of bed linens. By then it
wasn't anymore a lack of money but, rather, because I usually was

too busy with my professional responsibilities to think about domestic purchases. So Norbert bought us material for sheets as his farewell gift. Stanislaw P., always elegant, came with a bouquet of roses.

Even though the war was still raging in Europe, Hilary and I had succeeded in establishing a reasonably normal existence for ourselves in Rio de Janeiro—Brazil had begun to feel like home.

Although our roots in Brazil were young and fragile, we had established them, we loved the country, and we had become reasonably successful there. In spite of being unlicensed physicians both of us were actively involved in medicine and made our livings this way. The fate of other Polish refugees varied. Some of them, like Norbert Krautman, made great fortunes but never utilized their professional background. Others, like Stanislaw P., made a modest living, felt lonely and uprooted, and never adjusted to Brazil.

We knew, however, that this move to the United States offered some real hope for a better life. But once again we had to leave the familiar and head for the unknown. Hilary's father was still in England and continued sending us money so that we were reasonably well-provided for financially. He didn't write much and whenever he did it would have been to Hilary or to Sofia Semeonovna. I don't recall if, when, and how Hilary or his mother wrote him about our going to the United States, but he knew about it.

We were the only passengers on the *S.S. Cantuaria,* a merchant marine ship that sailed from Rio de Janeiro to New York in November of 1944. The ship was in a convoy in a complete blackout because of the danger from German submarines. So despite the improvements in our overall situation in comparison to our previous journeys, this one was still touched by the war, although much less fearsomely. In spite of the blackout, this crossing was more sedate.

I used my free time to cut the linen that Norbert Krautman had given us, and I made it into bed sheets. With some pride and lots of patience, I hand-sewed all the hems. Hilary and I befriended the captain and the crew, who entertained us with strange tales. One was about an unbalanced woman passenger who had thrown her child out of a cabin window on their previous trip. Although Hilary and his mother were captivated by these stories, I was too distracted to really pay attention to them, for I was preoccupied with the uncertainties of our future in America.

It was true that Hilary, as a scientist, would have greater opportunities in the United States than in Brazil. But what was awaiting me? Even though I had succeeded in beginning my professional career twice, first in France and then again in Brazil, I quite naturally felt some anxiety about having to do this a third time in America. I would have to depend upon Hilary's friends from the Rockefeller Foundation to help me explore my professional opportunities. At the same time, I feared establishing a new home and anticipated the stresses created by continuing to live with Hilary's mother.

Despite all these preoccupations and worries, I was well aware that Hilary and I had solidified our marriage a great deal during our time in Rio de Janeiro. In addition I had the joy of watching our son Claude develop into a lovely little child, and the situation with my mother-in-law, though it still left a great deal to be desired, had improved. Knowing all this made my anxieties easier to bear as we sailed toward the United States to start a new life.

A New Homeland

We docked in Brooklyn on a late November evening in 1944, one month after leaving Brazil. An F.B.I. agent, who boarded the ship before we were allowed to go ashore, subjected us to a long interrogation. We found his final question—"Do you like Stalin?"—naive and offensive. We wondered what prompted him to ask this. Maybe it was our accents or that our names sounded Russian to him, and he then leapt to the conclusion that we could be communists. Or he could have harbored some resentment of immigrants, especially if he felt they had more money or status than he did. I'll never know. But we hastened to assure him of the truth—that we didn't support Stalin. We were tired. We were in a strange country, and the last thing we wanted was trouble or a delay.

By the time we left the ship it was late and we were exhausted. We were too tired to be curious about our new and legendary country. We wanted to sleep. I don't recall who recommended a nearby hotel in Brooklyn, but the four of us spent the night at the St. George Hotel. There the sight of a drunken sailor on the floor of the hotel lobby scared Claude, now four-and-a-half.

The next morning Hilary called John P. Fox, with whom he had worked in Brazil. He was one of our sponsors in the United States, and he advised us to come to Mamaroneck, New York, a Westchester County suburb where he lived and where he had made arrangements for us to stay. During the next several weeks we lived in the attic of a small house belonging to an elderly couple. It was very dusty there. The cold weather and the dust didn't agree with me; I developed bronchitis and suffered from asthmatic attacks similar to those I'd had in Brazil. After my bronchitis resolved, these attacks ceased and I remained free of them for years. During these several weeks when we lived in Mamaroneck, John P. Fox arranged several job interviews for Hilary.

On Christmas morning our landlords set up an electric train in front of their Christmas tree. We watched the expression of amazement and happiness on Claude's face as he stood at the top of the staircase, clasping his little hands together before he walked down the steps towards the train. Ever since this Christmas morning, we promised ourselves we would create a similar happiness for Claude in our home.

Soon after the New Year, through the help of John P. Fox, Hilary found a job in Pearl River, New York, about forty miles from New York City. He became a member of the staff of the Viral and Rickettsial Section of Lederle Laboratories—a division of the American Cyanamid Company. A year later, he was promoted to assistant director of that section. His work involved basic viral research, as well as the development of viral vaccines.

When we moved to Pearl River, we first lived in a boarding house that was clean and well heated, unlike our Mamaroneck quarters. There was no dust, dirt, and dampness to trigger an asthma attack. With Hilary working, much of our anxiety about money was eliminated, and a month later we were able to rent a house in Pearl River. Unfortunately, the house had dirty walls, and the floors were in miserable condition. We still couldn't afford to have it cleaned professionally and had to do most of this ourselves. We even tried to sand the floor but, afraid that dust would cause my asthma to return, we hired a man to finish up this job. We bought second-hand furniture, and this house became our home for the next several years.

Claude went to a local public school. He stopped speaking Polish and Portuguese, and soon spoke only English. He rejected the white rabbit fur coat that his grandmother had bought him in Brazil in favor of a snowsuit, more typical of what the children around him were wearing. When Claude came home from school at three o'clock, usually I was out job hunting. Hilary was still at work at Lederle. So my mother-in-law would greet Claude and take care of him after school. She also prepared our dinners. But whenever she didn't feel well, she'd lie down, call Claude to her side, and give him step-by-step instructions on how to cook a meal. "Claude, scrape a couple of carrots, peel an onion, then put them in the pot and cover with water," she'd say. Claude never seemed to mind this; in fact he rather liked it, which is why I'm quite certain that his experience of cooking under his grandmother's supervision played a central role in his later love of the culinary arts.

Several weeks after we settled in Pearl River, and realizing how I felt, Hilary reminded John P. Fox that I was a physician and needed to develop my professional career in this country. I needed training at a good medical institution to improve my knowledge and skills, and to establish contacts necessary for my professional future. Through John's contacts I became a voluntary assistant in the Department of Pathology headed by John G. Kidd at Cornell University Medical College in New York. This meant a long and strenuous commute from Pearl River to Manhattan by bus and two subways. Traveling this way was new for me, and I found it very unpleasant. Whenever passengers entered an already full train, people's elbows would dig into my back. I sometimes felt I could hardly breathe. At times I felt bitter at having to put up with this discomfort, especially when I remembered the ease of my privileged past. This type of commuting was a striking contrast to my pre-war manner of being transported in Warsaw by a horse-drawn carriage. But I was determined to succeed and wasn't about to let these recollections stand in my way.

Having a full-time job, plus a three-hour commute, I spent less time at home than I had in Brazil. But this was the only way to develop my professional career, and Hilary fully supported my efforts.

Then, in July 1945, my status was elevated from voluntary assistant to research fellow in the Department of Pathology. This was a more prestigious appointment and one for which I was paid—although the stipend was modest, just $1,200 per year. My position involved assisting Dr. Kidd in his experiments with transplantation of malignant tumors in rabbits and mice. Dr. Kidd, an immunologist, was attempting to arrest the growth of cancer in these animals by stimulating their natural defense mechanisms.

Dr. Kidd had been appointed chairman of the department only a year before I came to work for him. Even though his special interest in immunology and limited experience in pathological anatomy would probably have precluded his appointment to the chairmanship of pathology in a community hospital, his research was quite valued in such top medical schools as Cornell University Medical College. Before coming to Cornell, he worked at the Rockefeller Institute for Medical Research with Dr. Peyton Rous, a Nobel Prize laureate who had discovered a chicken sarcoma virus. Dr. Rous was a strict disciplinarian who called his assistants by their last names and expected them to respond immediately. Once, when Dr. Kidd was in the toilet, he heard Dr. Rous calling for him in his usual, highly demanding way. In response, Dr. Kidd came running out with his pants down, shouting, "Coming, Dr. Rous, coming immediately!"

This incident amused his colleagues enormously, and the story followed Kidd for a long time. Having disliked that sort of treatment, he made up his mind to be more respectful in dealing with his own assistants, and he was.

"Why don't you stay home and look after your son, Dr. Koprowska?" he asked me shortly after I began working in his department. He was surprised that I was determined to raise my child and practice my profession at the same time. But once he realized that I was serious, he became very helpful. Whenever he sensed that I was preoccupied with a personal crisis, he was very understanding. "Dr. Koprowska, go home, take care of your problem, and come back after you've resolved it," he told me on several occasions.

Some of the problems were more important than others. In those days I was concerned not only with my son's upbringing, but also with the fate of my family in Poland. I had lost contact with my family during the war and was naturally concerned about their well-being. I took advantage of Dr. Kidd's offer to take time off so that I could better organize my search for Bronislawa and my brothers once the war was over and this had become feasible.

Until that point in my career I hadn't developed the inquisitiveness that characterizes people involved in scientific research. But in Dr. Kidd's lab, this changed. Although my work with him primarily involved providing technical assistance in animal experiments, he made certain that I understood the purpose of his research and the reasons for what he did in his work. He taught me how to go about planning an experiment, how important it was to be very clear about the questions that were to be asked and then answered, and how to design an experiment accordingly. Listening to him, as well as watching how he worked, my interest in doing research began.

He required all of his research fellows to teach medical students and attend departmental conferences. These experiences helped me to improve my command of English, which was initially quite limited.

I was very proud of being a research fellow at Cornell, although other foreign physicians were earning more money than I as clinicians in emergency rooms or in private offices, supervised by licensed physicians. They would do this kind of work until they could get sufficient command of the language and acquire the clinical experience in medicine as it was practiced in this country to pass the state licensing exam and practice medicine.[4] On the other hand, I had always aspired to the more scientifically oriented aspects of the medical profession, which did not require a licensing exam.

Due to the war, there had been so many interruptions in my career that it was as if I had lost a sense of my original interests and aims. Now that I was free to decide on what course to take, I wanted to re-evaluate my original interests, for I had grown and had many new experiences. I wanted to be absolutely sure that I wasn't making a decision based just on my past inclinations or on what was the easiest thing to do at the moment.

I eventually decided that—in contrast to Hilary and Dr. Kidd—I didn't want to be totally confined to experimental research. I also wanted more direct contact with clinical medicine which working in a hospital would offer. I already had found out that the large number of autopsies I had done in Poland and Brazil could be credited towards the requirements to become board-certified in pathologic anatomy. But before becoming eligible for board certification, I had to pass the New York licensure examination, and I worried whether my English was good enough to succeed. I also wondered if I could cope with "true" and "false" types of examinations given in the United States. As a result, despite my more clearly emerging career inclinations, I sometimes wondered if the necessary efforts would result in success.

I didn't discuss my future career plans with Dr. Kidd. His own wife didn't have a career of her own, just as most American women

---

4. American physicians were required to take national licensing exams that allowed them to practice medicine in almost any part of the United States, but doctors who received their medical degrees from a foreign medical school could take only state exams. However, they could become licensed in more than one state.

of her generation and socio-economic status were expected to remain at home to take care of their house and family. The few women scientists Dr. Kidd had known at the Rockefeller Institute were usually unmarried, or if they were married, they did not have children. I didn't fit into either category.

One summer we rented a cottage in Maine where Hilary, Sofia, Claude, and I spent our vacation. Our cottage was small and didn't give us much privacy. But one evening Hilary asked me to come with him for a walk. It was already dark, the moon was full, and the sky was studded with stars. Hilary and I became very romantic under the shining moon. Somehow this interlude helped me to return home more confident that I would be able to cope with my problems.

Within a year after the Second World War ended in 1945, my father-in-law came from England to visit us in Pearl River. It was his first visit, and from the moment he arrived, he wanted to know as much as possible about our lives. Almost immediately, he advised us to buy a house instead of renting one as we did. Also, he quickly realized the hardship involved in my commuting and insisted that the house, which he intended to help us buy, should be located halfway between Hilary's and my places of work. He put the down payment on the house Hilary and I selected (with his approval) in Englewood, New Jersey. Fortunately Hilary's mother did not interfere with our house hunting and the idea of moving. Moving was time-consuming and stressful, but just as my father-in-law had anticipated, it did improve the quality of our lives. We had a nicer home and moved to a more attractive community. There was enough room in the house for Hilary's parents to have separate bedrooms.

Hilary's father also deposited money in his and Hilary's joint name in a bank in New York. This direct financial help to Hilary led to considerable friction between Hilary's parents, who often quarreled during this visit. Most of the time I couldn't hear what they quarreled about. I just heard raised voices. Once I woke up in the middle of the night to hear my mother-in-law's deep threatening voice demanding money. Their violent argument was such a traumatic experience for me that it remained long in my memory.

In guiding and helping us to purchase our new home, Hilary's father made my life easier and far more pleasant. My commute was considerably reduced, making my day away from home shorter. My father-in-law even became instrumental in improving our social life. Our acquaintances in Pearl River had been limited to several of Hilary's co-workers at Lederle and their wives. When Hilary's father noticed our relative isolation, he introduced us to some of his New York acquaintances, who turned out to be families of people he had known before the war in Poland. Some of them, in turn, had relatives in Englewood whom we befriended.

The first couple we met were Ruth and Wolfgang Berthold, who became our lifelong friends. Well read and a very warm person, Ruth was younger than her husband, only a few years older than Hilary and I, and more interesting to talk to than he. Both loved music, and through them we met several musicians and music lovers, some of whom were physicians. Once a month we would meet at one of our homes for musical evenings, where the musicians among us would perform. These were lovely occasions, and Hilary was very much in his element. We also purchased joint subscriptions to concerts and theaters, and these evenings out on the town together made our life more pleasant and interesting.

My father-in-law also encouraged me to search more intensely for Bronislawa, Gene, and Gabriel. With his help and through his contacts, I found out that my family was alive, and that Gene was working as a radio broadcaster. As soon as I got the necessary information, I wrote to him immediately in care of the Polish radio in Warsaw. We initiated a vivid correspondence, exchanging information about our respective fates during the war and making plans for the future.

My affection for Hilary's father grew because of his concern about our well-being and his interest in my family. Thanks to him, I came to realize that once I had re-established contact with them, I had to change my role. I could no longer behave like a self-centered, spoiled child and expect them to look after me. I now knew that I had to bring my brothers and Bronislawa to America and take care of them until they became established in this country. I realized to what extent their life in Poland had deteriorated from what I remembered of our pre-war life. Taking on this new caretaking role helped me to become a more mature and responsible person. Soon I found out that Bronislawa, as my parent, would be entitled to a preference visa, enabling her to come to the United States as soon as I acquired American citizenship. But since, according to the immigration laws, brothers and sisters are not entitled to preference visas, I would have to arrange for Gene and Gabriel to come on student visas and help them to complete their education. It turned out to be easier to bring them to McGill University in Montreal, where they could live, study, and wait for the American immigration visa.

My father-in-law went still further in assisting me with this project. He helped me plan all the logistics of bringing Bronislawa, Gene, and Gabriel to the United States. With this, I realized far more than ever before what a kind person and good friend he had always been.

In preparation for leaving Poland, my family had to raise money. They asked my permission to sell the two Hoza Street apartment houses inherited by all of us from my father. Although Hilary's father thought that perhaps at some future time I could recover my inheritance, I didn't have the heart to refuse their request.

Bronislawa and my younger brother Gabriel left Poland in 1947; they went to Sweden with just a few suitcases. After my father's death, my family's wealth had dwindled to practically nothing during the war. They were able to sell the large, undamaged apartment house to Polish Air Lines (LOT) for a nominal price, barely enough to buy some clothes, luggage, and travel to Sweden. Without other resources, they had to accept menial jobs. Gabriel got a job as a gardener in Stocksund on the outskirts of Stockholm. Bronislawa worked in a jewelry factory making shell ornaments, while she eagerly awaited emigration to America. Knowing that Gabriel was looking after Bronislawa, Gene decided to remain in Warsaw for another year. A year later, when Gabriel was accepted to McGill University and went to Canada, Gene came to Stockholm to be with Bronislawa and to wait until I became an American citizen. After this finally happened, I helped Gene get into a graduate school at McGill and to come to Montreal.

XV

Becoming a Pathologist

In 1946 I completed one year of my research fellowship in pathology with Dr. Kidd at Cornell. That same year, American war veterans were returning home from Europe. Although I would have liked to continue at Cornell, it was not possible—the fellowship was no longer open to me. First preference for research fellowships and other positions was given to returning veterans. Most American women felt frustrated and disappointed if they had to give up jobs they had come to enjoy or depend on. But I believed that the veterans, having risked their lives for their country, deserved those jobs more as rewards for their sacrifices. Perhaps it was easier for me to feel this way because, as an immigrant, I considered myself less entitled to such privileged opportunities than they were. After all, I was still an outsider, new to this country and not yet a citizen.

However, I did not remain without a job. Although I lost my fellowship at Cornell, Dr. Kidd found me another, this time in applied immunology, with Dr. Jules Freund at the Public Health Research Institute of the City of New York. My new job gave me more time to study for the New York State Medical Board's licensure examination. Also, the pay was better.

Jules Freund was an outstanding immunologist, and famous for demonstrating the importance of certain substances called *adjuvants*, which enhance the effectiveness of vaccines. Unfortunately, though, despite his excellence as an immunologist, he was a very unpleasant man to work with. He never smiled, and he didn't like me any more than I liked him. I didn't know much immunology, but his

140

slightly ironic attitude toward me discouraged me from trying to learn more from him and failed to stimulate my interest in this field. Hilary's friend, George Hirst, was working at the same institution, and I enjoyed talking to him. Once I confided in him my difficulties in dealing with Jules Freund. He replied that, as far as he knew, everybody working with him had similar complaints. Freund always acted as if he held a low opinion of my intellect. Several weeks after I began working with him, I found out that he knew Hilary from immunology meetings they both attended and that he respected him very much as a scientist. I thought then that Dr. Freund may have compared my lack of knowledge of immunology to Hilary's proficiency in and contributions to this field and that this may have influenced his attitude towards me.

In spite of his lack of empathy and the unpleasant manner with which he treated me in general, Jules Freund did let me know that he greatly admired Hilary. On more than one occasion he said to me, "Your husband is a great scientist, Dr. Koprowska."

One example of how petty and indifferent he was—and only one among many—was that, in contrast to Dr. Kidd, he was utterly impersonal and uninterested in being the least bit supportive when he knew that I had a personal problem at home. The difficulties women experience in combining a career with family obligations were of no interest to him whatsoever.

"It's only five minutes before five o'clock. Too early to go home, Dr. Koprowska," he said one day, watching me prepare for my long journey from the foot of East Fifteenth Street to Englewood, New Jersey. The Public Health Research Institute was much further away from home than Cornell University Medical College, which was located relatively centrally in Manhattan.

"I didn't know that you were such a meticulous time watcher and would begrudge me these five minutes, Dr. Freund," I answered somewhat disrespectfully, considering that he was an older person for whom I was working.

"You're a time watcher, not me, Dr. Koprowska. You always leave five minutes before five o'clock."

One incident surprised and challenged Freund's opinion of me. In the midst of our work he complained that a vaccine that we had been testing in the laboratory was not effective.

"Do you have any idea what may be wrong, Dr. Koprowska?" he asked me in a tone clearly tinged with irony and skepticism. From his expression, it was clear he expected nothing in the way of an illuminating answer. It was as if he hardly expected me to give a correct or even reasonable answer, and was just going through the motions — maybe even to prove the legitimacy of his attitude toward me.

"I have no idea", I responded. "But what about adding the adjuvants and seeing what happens, Dr. Freund?" He apparently felt this idea had merit, for he decided to try it right then and there. It was obvious that he was surprised that I thought of the correct solution to the problem, and he was flattered that it involved the use of his own discovery. To this day I don't know why he had not thought of this himself.

As my one-year fellowship with him in applied immunology was approaching its end, I felt that I had learned relatively little in this field. I began to wonder what I would be doing the following year when an unexpected event occurred and provided an answer to this question. One day George Hirst, who knew of my interest in pathology, came into my laboratory very excited. "Come quick with me to Willard Parker Hospital, Irena," he said. "Their morgue is just across the street from us. They are doing an autopsy of a man who died of anthrax, which as you know is a very rare disease. You'll want to see it." I followed him, and I learned that the deceased had transported a load of hides by sea from animals that must have died of anthrax. He had become infected with their bacteria and died.

George Hirst and I were not the only people watching this autopsy with interest. Arthur Allen, a well-known pathologist who had heard of this unusual case and come to see it, was also there. He began asking me questions about who I was and what I was doing in the morgue. He smiled at me and listened carefully to my answers, and then asked me, "How would you like to have a job in pathology? My wife, Sophie Spitz, is the pathologist at the New York Infirmary. She is looking for an assistant."

I decided immediately to take advantage of this opportunity and to resume my training in pathology. Arthur Allen arranged an interview for me with his wife, and upon the completion of my fellowship in applied immunology I became assistant pathologist at the New York Infirmary for Women and Children. This was a hospital previously connected with one of the first medical schools for women established at a time when regular American medical schools did not accept women students. By the time I got a job there, the medical school had been closed because women applicants could then be accepted to regular medical schools.

That same year, 1947, I passed my state board examinations and thus became a licensed physician in New York state. My doubts concerning my professional goals had vanished. I knew now that I was moving in the right direction. As a licensed physician with two years of additional experience in pathology, I would be eligible to take the American Board of Pathology's examinations and become a board-certified pathologist. And, at a personal level, getting away from Dr. Freund was a great relief.

The first day of my employment at the infirmary was memorable for more than one reason. I was introduced to Charlotte Jones, their staff gynecologist, a heavy woman with a deep voice who wore a man's black hat on the back of her head. I was shocked by her masculine appearance because women physicians I recalled in Poland looked quite feminine. But our conversation became even more memorable than her appearance. As she began talking, she placed before me George N. Papanicolaou's 1946 monograph, "The Diagnosis of Uterine Cancer by Vaginal Smears." I did not know then the extent to which my first exposure to Papanicolaou's writing would impact my future life.

"You will need this book," she said. "Since its publication, vaginal smears have been named 'Pap' smears after its author." She opened the monograph, which was full of color illustrations. "Look at these bizarre cells," she exclaimed, pointing to one of the pictures. "These are cancer cells. Note how distorted they are in comparison to the regularly outlined normal cells illustrated on the preceding page. Can you see it? In fact, let me show you some more examples."

After this, she quizzed me to see if I had absorbed what she was trying to get across. I demonstrated to her satisfaction that I did understand, and she continued. "There are about ten thousand Pap smears collected each year at the Strang Clinic, and for several years I've examined every single one of them under my microscope at this hospital. Today is my last day. From now on the job will be yours—*you'll* have to examine them in search for cancer cells. Good luck and good bye!"

"I think that she'll do all right," I heard her say to Sophie Spitz on her way out. Charlotte Jones's farewell comments had a dizzying effect on me. I remembered the time back in Brazil when my boss, Dr. Bica, had become excited about Papanicolaou's method of diagnosing cancer of the womb. But although he had purchased the stains developed by Dr. Papanicolaou for tests, he had difficulty getting successful results with them.

The Strang Cancer Detection Clinic, which Charlotte Jones referred to, was part of the New York Infirmary for Women and Children and had been established by a very wealthy woman pathologist named Elise L'Esperance, the niece of New York Senator Chauncey Depuis. It was the first clinic to include examination of Pap smears as part of an early uterine cancer detection program in addition to the physicial examination, X-rays, blood and other tests.

Besides being responsible for examining and evaluating Pap smears, my job at the infirmary also was to include cutting, examining, and describing tissue removed from patients during surgery. As soon as I completed my preliminary examinations, these tissues would be then fixed in formalin and cut by technicians into very thin slices, so that they could be mounted on glass slides, stained by special dyes—usually Haematoxylin and eosin—and made ready for microscopic examination. I would examine them under the microscope, but Sophie Spitz would sign the final diagnosis.

Apart from screening Pap smears for cancer cells and examining surgical tissues, I also was responsible for performing autopsies.

I therefore had to be on call at all times. So whenever I went out for the evening and during weekends, I would telephone in to ask whether anyone had died. If so, I had to get to the infirmary to perform the autopsy. Autopsies are best done as soon as possible after death to avoid decomposition of tissues and to allow the deceased's family to proceed quickly with funeral plans. Once I called from a public telephone booth, unaware that a nearby policeman could hear me ask the question, "Did anyone die?" This was routine to me, but when he gave me a very strange look, I realized how peculiar what I asked must have sounded to him.

"Lady, who have you been calling and asking if anybody died?" he asked somewhat sternly. "What's going on?"

"I'm an assistant pathologist on call for autopsies at the New York Infirmary," I told him. "Whenever I'm not at the hospital, I have to call and check if there was a death and if I'm needed for an autopsy." That reason hadn't occurred to him—why should it have?—but on hearing my explanation, with a look on his face that said "now I've heard it all," the policeman let me go.

During my employment at the infirmary I was approached by several Englewood doctors who had established cancer detection programs in their private offices. They collected Pap smears from their patients and, knowing of my growing experience in their examination, they asked if I would examine and evaluate the smears. In order to do this at the infirmary, where I had all of the laboratory facilities I needed for this work, I had to have Dr. Spitz's permission. She refused it, so I revived the tradition of my student years and organized a laboratory in the basement of my house. I worked there in the evenings after Claude was tucked in bed. Soon I built up as flourishing a practice as I could handle. I detected several early uterine cancers, and for this I received many expressions of gratitude from the referring physicians on behalf of their patients. My reputation as a good cancer detective grew and became a source of considerable satisfaction and pride to me.

Working at the infirmary was a mixed blessing. I did get a lot of good experience, and my work doing Pap smears would later prove important to my career. However, the clinic employed women doctors only, and many of these women were what in those days were called "old maids." From my upbringing in Poland, I wasn't used to being confined to an exclusively female environment and, frankly, I felt ill at ease in this atmosphere. They, too, felt uncomfortable with me because I was different. Those who were married, like my boss Sophie Spitz, often refused to have children for fear it would interfere with their careers.

My relationship with my boss was but one example of this. Sophie Spitz was a tall, slim woman with a penetrating look in her black eyes. She arranged her smooth dark hair in a chignon, wore no makeup and no jewelry, and was always impeccably dressed in pastel gabardine suits. She was very temperamental, feared by her subordinates, and difficult to work with. She made me work hard for the little money I earned, never praised me, and for no apparent reason kept me at a distance. She was an excellent pathologist, who was not only in charge of pathology at the New York Infirmary but was also on the staff of Memorial Hospital for Cancer and Allied Diseases. She had published an atlas of tropical diseases and several articles about pigmented malignant tumors called melanomas. However, her knowledge was purely descriptive, based exclusively on studies of the structure of human tissues. She had no interest in or understanding of experimental pathology, and she viewed Dr. Kidd and others who did research on animals with contempt. She respected only those pathologists who did research on human diseases, in particular pathologists who were expert diagnosticians of these diseases.

One day I told Sophie Spitz that Hilary had been elected to membership in the New York Academy of Medicine. "You probably mean the New York Academy of *Sciences*. He's only working with mice," she said sarcastically. I let her know that Hilary was a member of the New York Academy of Medicine as well as of Sciences.

Several months after I began working at the infirmary, Hilary encouraged me to try to improve my distant and somewhat strained relationship with Sophie. He expected that a closer personal contact with her would make my working conditions more pleasant. We invited her and her husband, Arthur Allen, to our house for dinner. We sat having drinks in the family room where Claude, who was now eight years old, was playing with his toys. "What an adorable little boy you have," Arthur said, looking at me. "Won't you change your mind about having children, Sophie?"

"We've discussed it many times, Arthur, haven't we? Let's not go back over it again," she replied curtly.

Once I heard Sophie Spitz gossiping with Isabel Knowlton, her good friend and one of the infirmary's gynecologists. They were admiring the stand of another woman doctor who resisted her husband's plea to start a family. "Having a child isn't incompatible with having a professional life. I have a little boy and, if not for the war, I would have had a second child," I said, unable to restrain myself.

"Well, if a woman wants a child, she should have one," Isabel Knowlton said sarcastically, raising her eyebrows high. Although they seemed to disparage my position on this issue, I suspected they were also jealous that I had a child. Furthermore, my unsolicited entry into their conversation and my remark didn't help to improve my relationship with them, either!

A year later when I went to Isabel Knowlton's office for a routine gynecological examination, she remembered that I wanted a second child. "You have fibrosed ovaries; you'll have a hard time conceiving another child, Irena," she said. I was surprised because I was thirty-two years old and, as far as I knew, ovaries became fibrosed only after menopause. Isabel Knowlton had a mischievous look on her face and I couldn't be sure if what she said was true or whether she may have said it out of spite. But my desire to have a second child must have not been strong enough as yet to seek another opinion at that time.

I thought that Sophie Spitz was narrow-minded and provincial in her attitudes. This was revealed by her reaction to my desire to see my family, who had just managed to leave Poland and go to Sweden. Spitz stated that it wasn't worthwhile to travel to Europe since there would be nothing worth seeing there that I couldn't see in the U.S. She didn't understand how much I might have suffered from having been torn away from my family because of the war, nor how desperately I wanted to be reunited with them. I went anyway.

On my way to Stockholm, I wondered how my family would behave towards me and what it would be like for me to be with them again after eight years of separation. When I arrived, Bronislawa hugged me and, crying, held me tight in her arms. When she released me from her embrace, I looked at her. I could scarcely recognize her. She had been an elegant and well-groomed woman. Now she looked ill at ease, almost sloppy, in cheap, ill-fitting clothes. She also had become fat and was excessively talkative. She spoke about her wartime sufferings in a difficult-to-follow, tiresome torrent of words. It was painful to see how age and the terrors of the war had transformed her. She did not show much curiosity about the state of my marriage with Hilary, about Claude or, in general, our life in America. It was apparent that what she had gone through had made her very fearful and needy. There was no sign of her former nurturance towards me, which I realized I still yearned for although intellectually I understood that now I, not she, had to be the caretaker.

In spite of her altered appearance and behavior, and although I had even less in common with her than I had in the past, I was extremely happy to see her. Gabriel, who had been merely a teenage school boy when I left Poland, had become a good-looking, well-mannered, and knowledgeable young man. He attempted to describe their wartime experiences in a way I could comprehend, without all of the emotion and confusion that characterized Bronislawa's talk. He had already described in his letters how our father had talked about me on his deathbed and how he and Gene, being young men of military age, had hid from the Germans, moving from place to place after our father died.

"Gabriel, are you sure nobody is behind the door? Can't they hear?" Bronislawa restlessly moved across the room. She still feared the Germans long after the war was over.

"We're in Sweden. The war is over. Nobody is listening behind the doors anymore, mother dear," Gabriel told her.

"I want to bring you over to the United States where people feel free from such fears," I added.

Our attempts to reassure her would calm her down for a few moments only. She would then resume her restless wandering and frightened demeanor.

I was so glad to be reunited with Bronislawa and Gabriel. But after spending several days in this emotion-laden atmosphere, I was relieved to fly to London to see my father-in-law, who continued living in England in between his brief annual visits to the United States. By contrast, my time with him was relaxed and enjoyable. It was just what I needed at that point. He cooked tasty meals in his apartment, taught me a few culinary tricks, and showed me how to mend men's socks. He bought me smart suits and a hat, and gave me a gold bar lapel pin studded with diamonds. His kindness and friendship towards me continued to grow. After living in the United States for three years, I still hadn't had enough money to buy nice clothes for myself. The last new hat I had was the one Hilary chose and Bronislawa bought me for a garden party I never attended in Warsaw. Naturally I appreciated what he was doing for me.

I put on my new finery and looked at myself in the mirror. I looked smart. After a visit to a beauty parlor, my hair was cut short, which is the way I preferred it. I had a big smile of contentment on my face. I felt rejuvenated.

Once or twice my father-in-law mentioned his wife with bitterness and irony. "She only wants my money for her relatives. I didn't spend my whole life working as hard as I did to give it away to people who have no right to it." I didn't understand what was behind his words. However, I didn't feel that I should ask him for an explanation.

Shortly after my return to the United States, the plans for bringing my family to America began to be realized. Gabriel stopped in the United States on his way to Canada, remaining with us in Englewood for one month. Then Hilary, Claude, and I drove him to Canada. I was very sad and cried when we had to leave him alone at McGill. It was quite clear that, even though my father was no longer alive, my feelings for my stepfamily were quite strong indeed.

When we returned home from Montreal I found myself often thinking about Bronislawa, who would be the next one to join us in the United States. I recalled how she mothered me from the time I was an infant right up till I was newly married, pregnant, and left Poland during the war. After what I saw of her in Sweden, I knew she would never again mother me, and I had already accepted this reversal of our roles. I still had mixed feelings towards her. I was deeply attached to her, and at the same time she annoyed me. I knew I would always do the best I could for her and give her whatever she might need, although we were never very close and her depression didn't make our comunication any easier. I also knew that I couldn't impose her on Hilary. This would have made him as unhappy as living with his mother had made me. The part of me that resented what he had put me through by thrusting his mother on me all these years wished to give him a taste of his own medicine. But I knew that Hilary wouldn't accept such abuse. We would argue, I would feel unhappy, and he would most likely spend more time away from home with his friends, leaving me alone with Bronislawa. Our marriage was fairly stable now, and I wouldn't risk anything that might disturb our hard-won equilibrium.

After I had returned from Montreal and was back at work one cool, sunny day in October 1948, I was cutting specimens at the surgical bench at the infirmary when Sophie Spitz suddenly announced, "Dr. Papanicolaou is coming to the Strang Clinic today to give a lecture." I immediately sensed the importance of his visit for me personally, no less than for the clinic. By then the daily microscopic examination of Pap smears had become a significant part of my responsibilities. Now, finally, I would have a chance to meet the important pioneer of this new method of diagnosing cancer of the womb.

From the time I first had begun to examine Pap smears, I realized several things. I understood how complicated the preparation of Papanicolaou's stain was. No wonder Bica, my good boss in Brazil, had lost his enthusiasm for it! More importantly, by the time I had examined thousands of Pap smears, I knew that cancer cells differed from normal cells because of their altered structure rather than the difference in the color they were stained with. The structural alterations of cancer cells usually manifest themselves by the enlargement, coarse texture, and irregular outlines of the nucleus—the central portion of the cell. Because of the different chemical composition of the nucleus and the cytoplasm (i.e. the rest of the cell), each have affinity for a different dye. The nucleus usually stains dark blue and stands clearly against the background of the cytoplasm, which may pick up a variety of shades of pink, orange, purple, or pale blue. These differences in color, in addition to the more pronounced structure, are of diagnostic value.

Besides making structural abnormalities of cancer cells more apparent, Papanicolaou's stain offers another advantage. Various types of cancers produce chemical substances that are characteristic of their site of origin. For example, the cytoplasm of the cells of the most common cancer located in the uterine cervix—on the tip of the womb—often produces keratin which stains bright orange with Papanicolaou stain and therefore is readily recognized as belonging to that type and location of involved tumor.

On the day of Dr. Papanicolaou's visit, I followed the others to the conference room, taking one of the few vacant seats at the back of the room. Minutes later a short, stocky man with a high forehead, brown eyes, and scant gray hair entered the conference room in a rather furtive manner, quickly and quietly, taking short steps. In spite of being well dressed in a dark gray business suit, he seemed unsure of himself. But a pleasant smile appeared on his face when he greeted people.

Dr. Papanicolaou was introduced by Elise L'Esperance, the founder of the Strang Cancer Detection Clinic. He spoke in a low voice, which became inaudible at the end of his sentences. He had a foreign accent (he had immigrated to the United States from Greece many years ago), and his lecture was difficult to understand. He spoke about the diagnosis of cancer while he projected colorful pictures of cancer cells on a screen.

When he finished, Dr. L'Esperance asked Sophie Spitz to lead the discussion. "Pap smears provide an excellent tool for cancer detection programs, but the final diagnosis of cancer can be made only by a pathologist on the basis of a biopsy," she stated emphatically.

I was shocked at what I considered to be her rudeness to an invited guest—a man who, without being a pathologist, was responsible for the tests used at the clinic at her hospital. Also, her comparison of the diagnostic value of the Pap smears and biopsies had been unfair. The usefulness of the Pap smears is different than of the biopsies. The collection of the vaginal secretions for the Pap smear test is simple, painless, and inexpensive. It may be done repeatedly without traumatizing the patient, and it permits detection of the presence of cancer too small to be visible to the naked eye. The tissue for the biopsy can be excised only in the presence of a visible growth or, blindly, by multiple small, so-called punch biopsies (and sometimes by a large cone) in order to confirm the presence of cancer detected by Pap smear. These procedures are more traumatic, difficult, and costly.

Dr. Papanicolaou bowed deeply, but didn't take up her challenge. I was surprised that he was so reserved in his response, so modest. His test was now used all over the world. Yet a pathologist was telling him that it wasn't as reliable as a biopsy. He just stood there and listened without a word of protest.

Several days after Papanicolaou's visit to the infirmary, I found out that they needed a pathologist at Booth Memorial Hospital, which was a small hospital nearby. I began wondering what kind of services they needed, perhaps only for the sporadic performance of an autopsy that I could do on my lunch time to make extra money. In trying to find out more about this job, I made the mistake of asking for an interview without telling Sophie Spitz about it. I didn't realize that she was connected with that small hospital in an advisory capacity and that they would seek her advice before giving me any consideration.

She became furious as soon as she found out that I was making inquiries about this position without discussing my plans with her. "You made a fool of yourself looking for a job at Booth Memorial Hospital. They're looking for a well-rounded, experienced pathologist to take care of surgical pathology, autopsies, chemistry, and microbiology. What do you know about blood banks?" she asked me.

As a matter of fact, I had training only in pathological anatomy, which my job at the infirmary required, and she was correct in her assessment of my lack of qualifications for the position at Booth. But she became obsessed by what she viewed, in a way correctly, as my disloyalty. In retrospect, I realized that this was the time when she began to search for an excuse to fire me. But she would have to justify my sudden dismissal; I had worked hard for two years at the infirmary, and no complaints had been lodged against my work.

A few days later, tissues from a tuberculous patient were brought to the surgical pathology laboratory for dissection and examination. I hadn't seen a case of tuberculosis since I left Brazil, but with all my experience handling the organs of deceased tuberculous patients at Miguel Couto Hospital, I felt that I was on familiar territory. Sophie Spitz entered the laboratory just as I finished my examination of these tissues. She took one glance and began to shout that I was spreading infection all over the place by the way I was handling the infectious material. "You must scrub the dissecting table with Lysol immediately. Never again will you be allowed to take care of tissues from patients with tuberculosis. You're fired as of this moment!" she yelled, and flew out of the laboratory without giving me a chance to reply.

Miss Stamm, the chief technician who had worked at the infirmary for twenty years, entered. Seeing tears in my eyes, she approached me with a questioning look. "What happened here? I heard that bitch yelling at you!" she said.

Getting no answer from me, she put her arm around my shoulders. "Listen to me. You aren't the first one this beast has made cry. Let's go out for a cup of coffee. I can tell you a few things about Sophie Spitz," she continued.

The coffee shop next door was nearly empty. Stammie and I installed ourselves at a corner table in the back. "You're dealing with a very perverse and abnormal person, Dr. Koprowska. I wouldn't be surprised at anything she says or does to you," she said, and told me a long and distressing story. I understood then that not much love had been lost between these two women.

The next day, when I came to collect my final check and a few belongings, Sophie Spitz smiled at me, all sweetness. "If you don't like being fired, why don't you go to complain to Dr. L'Esperance," she said.

I thought I had nothing to lose. I went to Memorial Hospital to see Dr. L'Esperance, the former head of the infirmary under whom Sophie Spitz then worked. I didn't realize how malicious Sophie Spitz's suggestion had been. Elise L'Esperance had a special interest in tuberculosis in chickens. Her past studies required the sterile handling of animal tissues. Sophie Spitz had managed to arouse Elise L'Esperance's anger at me by telling her that I had been careless with tuberculous tissues. I tried to explain to Dr. L'Esperance that in Rio de Janeiro I handled tuberculous tissues only in the autopsy room, where no sterile technique was necessary, and all the dissecting tables and knives were scrubbed and disinfected daily by morgue attendants. I was unfamiliar with the different routine used by pathologists at the surgical bench in American hospitals. But Dr. L'Esperance wouldn't listen to my explanations. She told me she endorsed my firing.

Yet what felt like a humiliating experience at the time turned out to be of great future benefit to me. Fortunately, I had remained at the infirmary for two years, long enough to complete the requirements of the American Board of Pathological Anatomy. I was now eligible to take their examination and to advance my career opportunities.

Dr. Pap,
My Mentor

I took a temporary summer job covering for a pathologist at a small private hospital. Although I worried that once this temporary job ended I would have no permanent position, several weeks had passed before I began any serious efforts to look for one. Because of my experience with Pap smears, Hilary suggested that I should try to work with Papanicolaou. But I was afraid that should Papanicolaou call her, Sophie Spitz would give me such poor references that he wouldn't want me to work for him. So I did not get in touch with him right away.

Although my worry about Spitz's comments were not unreasonable, my reaction to Hilary's idea fit a pattern I had developed dealing with him—to initially respond negatively to his suggestions. Possibly I wanted to have the feeling that I was making my own decisions. He had become accustomed to that and knew I rarely would be open to any further discussion when I had such a reaction. I don't know why I responded this way but, in retrospect, I think that, being a less dynamic person than he, I did not want to be pushed into doing things before I was ready for action. Eventually I snapped out of my apathy and followed another of Hilary's suggestions: I went to see Dr. Janet Travell, professor of pharmacology at Cornell University Medical College, whom he knew and with whose research on treatment of burns in animals he was familiar. I then sought the advice of Dr. Kidd, my old mentor and a man I respected and had so enjoyed working with at the Cornell University Medical College.

Dr. Kidd's hair had become white and thinner since I had last seen him three years earlier. But his face was as red and round as in the past, and he had a big smile as he spoke to me. "Since you're now eligible to become a diplomate of the American Board of Pathology, Dr. Koprowska, you should see Dr. Nathan Chandler Foot, the former head of surgical pathology here. He can help you better than I can. For he now spends his retirement working with Dr. Papanicolaou on the floor directly below us in this building. And with your experience with Pap smears and your background in general pathology, he seems like the perfect person to next see and talk with."

Ten minutes later I was walking down the hall with Dr. Foot. He opened the door to Dr. George N. Papanicolaou's office, where the great man sat behind a big desk facing us. "Dr. Papanicolaou, this is Dr. Koprowska, about whom I just called you." Dr. Foot put my curriculum vitae on Papanicolaou's desk.

Dr. Pap pointed to a seat for me. Then he rose from his chair and shook my hand. As he approached me, I became aware of the faint fragrance of verbena about him. Later I found out the source—he used Mary Chess soap.

"I see from your curriculum vitae, Dr. Koprowska, that you're eligible for certification by the American Board of Pathology. I might be able to get a fellowship for you. Not many pathologists are as interested in learning about my method of diagnosing cancer as you are."

I looked at his oval face and thought that he seemed to be a kind and friendly person. His olive-colored skin wrinkled when he smiled. His brown eyes sparkled.

As Dr. Papanicolaou continued, he remained reserved but courteous, giving me the impression that he was a modest man, just as he had during his lecture at the New York Infirmary. I knew right away that if I worked with him, I would be free from the hostility I had found so painful when I worked with Sophie Spitz. But besides my good feelings about Dr. Pap, I had further reason for encouragement. I was very impressed that Chandler Foot, author of a well-known textbook on surgical pathology, had chosen to spend his retirement years working with him.

Now I wished that Dr. Pap would give me a job, but he made no definite commitment during our interview. In fact, it wasn't till a month later that I received a letter from him offering me a fellowship. In the meantime, I was offered a fellowship by Dr. Travell. I was thrilled to receive these two offers and didn't want to give up either one. If I could work in both departments, I believed that I would find the answer to my basic question of whether I would like best to deal with human patients, do animal experimentation, spend my life at the microscope, or select any combination of these activities.

I considered how I ever began building up my experience in pathology. As a third-year medical student, when I applied to become a voluntary assistant in the department of anatomic pathology at Warsaw University, I did so mostly because my close friend Zaira chose pathology. Her mother had been a pathologist in that department and knew all their faculty. I had acted like a copycat, but I also was convinced that knowing pathology would be the best preparation for any specialty I might select in the future. After the beginning of the war, I had always had to accept whatever job I was fortunate enough to be offered. Now, for the first time, I had an opportunity to gain experience in several different aspects of medicine and compare the extent of my own interest in each.

The fellowship in the Department of Pharmacology would give me a chance to participate in Dr. Travell's experiments with electrically induced burns in guinea pigs, which she attempted to treat by ethyl chloride spray. In her private office she had been using this treatment on patients with muscular pains, sprained ankles, and other conditions. Other than my work with Dr. Kidd on tumors of rabbits and mice, I had no experience in the animal experimentation used in research by experimental pathologists as well as pharmacologists. This exposure would renew and expand my contact with medical research. My fellowship in pharmacology also would allow me to participate in their testing of new cardiac drugs on patients, and I had had no contact with patients since my job in Villejuif Lunatic Asylum.

By contrast, the work with Dr. Papanicolaou would involve neither experiments with animals nor contact with patients, but microscopic examination of body fluids and secretions for the purpose of diagnosing cancer—the occupation closest to my actual experience, for which I was best prepared.

Fortunately, I was allowed to take both fellowships, on a part-time basis, for a period of one year (1949). So I began to work with "Bobbie" Travell, as we called her, the same Dr. Travell who would later gain popular fame when she helped President Kennedy with his back troubles. She authored a well-read book called *Office at All Hours* about her experiences in the White House. She was a tall, hard-driven woman with blue eyes and a captivating smile. In contrast to the women on the staff of the New York Infirmary, she had a successful professional career as well as a happy family life. With that in common, not surprisingly, we got along well. I liked her very much and enjoyed working with her, but I had never developed much enthusiasm for producing burns in guinea pigs. And the drug testing trials conducted at Beth Israel Hospital by Dr. Harry Gold from our Department of Pharmacology, in which I was also participating, didn't stimulate my interest either. I discovered that getting patients' histories just to enter this information on questionnaires that were used as part of the drug research, giving these patients general physical examinations, and taking their chest X-rays bored me. None of it held my interest as much as looking through the microscope at cells and tissues, or Dr. Kidd's cancer research experiments in animals.

This was precisely what I needed to find out. I finally realized that my inclination towards microscopic diagnostic work was not merely something that circumstances pushed me into. I still recalled conversations with my father when, over and over, he used to encourage me to study medicine and treat patients, and I would insist that I didn't care about diseases and treating sick people. My lack of enthusiasm for patient care was what had initially delayed my decision to enter medical school until my growing interest in science culminated in a passion for learning more about protozoa—unicellular organisms. It was clear that my preference for laboratory work had early roots and wasn't just the result of outside forces shaping my career. The important thing was that I answered my question. My interest in medicine was laboratory-based diagnosis and experimental cancer research.

My long and important association with Dr. Papanicolaou began in 1949, with my part-time fellowship with him. Dr. Pap was then sixty-five, and I was thirty-two. The examination of Pap smears that I had done at the New York Infirmary had permitted me to learn only how to detect cancer of the womb when looking through the microscope at cells desquamated into genital secretions. Now, in Dr. Pap's lab, I had an opportunity to also look for cancer cells in fluids and secretions from other sites of the body, and thus to detect cancer growing in organs such as the lung, stomach, and bladder.

My work consisted of looking for naturally exfoliated or scraped-off cancer cells in the gastric secretions of patients suspected of having stomach cancer, in urine of patients suspected of having bladder cancer, and in sputum and bronchial secretions aspirated from patients suspected of having lung cancer. It was a brilliant method for identifying cancer, but its success depended upon an improvement in the technique of collecting these body fluids, especially in the case of gastric secretions in which digestive enzymes cause a rapid deterioration of the exfoliated cells.

I sat at a desk and used a microscope in the office I shared with a young doctor named Fred Panico, who was trying to develop inflatable balloons from condoms for the purpose of introducing them into the stomach to collect gastric secretions for the diagnosis of stomach cancer. He would pull nets made from veiling used for women's hats over these balloons before inserting them into the stomach and inflating them there. He expected that cells still unaffected by destructive enzymes would adhere to the nets and be recovered before their disintegration. While doing all this, he would whistle "Some Enchanted Evening." His whistling was great fun and typical of the kind of silly and ironic humor that often breaks out in research and clinical settings, when serious objectives are ingeniously served by sometimes outlandish means and methods.

I became increasingly involved in my work and often would bring scientific papers to read at home. It made me feel more self-sufficient. Up until that time I always wanted more togetherness in my marriage. I often felt lonely and resented it whenever Hilary brought his work home, spent hours playing piano, or decided to have an evening out with colleagues or friends. When I became immersed in my work, I was often glad to have the time to myself, and I needed less attention from Hilary. This improved our marriage.

I spent my days looking through the microscope at a great variety of cells—single cells and clusters of cells. At night I was haunted by images of these cells. The magnificent range of colors that Papanicolaou's stain revealed was often before my eyes, even when I was falling asleep. I was fascinated by the configuration of these cells and wondered how such groups of cells were formed and what interaction might have been taking place between them. Could the relationships between cells within such groups include the exchange of some substance? Could the transfer of this material from one cell to another be instrumental in the transformation of normal cells into cancer cells?

After several months, when I felt confident I could reliably recognize the wide variety of cancer cells found in bodily secretions, I went to Jack Seybolt and told him that I would like to begin screening smears not seen as yet by other people in the laboratory. Jack had worked with Dr. Papanicolaou a year longer than I had, and was his second in command. Up to that point I had been examining only Pap smears, which already had been diagnosed as having cancer cells—or at least screened as suspicious by the technicians. Their job was to place ink dots on the slide next to cells they thought were cancerous. I was the next person to look at these cells so that I could write down what I thought they were. Jack Seybolt then would make a final diagnosis. I wanted to be the first one to find and recognize cancer cells so that I could show them directly to Dr. Pap, who had the final word.

"But you aren't ready yet, Irena. You don't yet have adequate experience. It took other people much longer to learn," he answered me. But he passed on my request to Papanicolaou.

"Give her a chance if she feels that she's ready," Dr. Pap told him, realizing that with my background in pathology, I very likely would learn to find and recognize cancer cells faster than others.

It was then 1950. I received a full-time fellowship with Dr. Pap. During the following two years I became an experienced diagnostician of cancer cells. Increasingly, I was considered to be quite innovative and a real "cancer detective." It was gratifying beyond words, and so challenging. I knew I had made the right choice. And then, upon completion of these two years, I was allowed to issue the official reports of the results of Pap smear tests to clinicians. By then I shared the daily load of examinations of Pap smears equally with Jack Seybolt. We got along well, although we never became close friends. Both of us would always consult with Dr. Papanicolaou whenever we had doubts about our judgment. Dr. Pap remained our mentor and ultimate authority.

But our attitudes toward Papanicolaou were very different. I had been strongly attracted by Dr. Pap's approach to dealing with challenging diagnostic problems. It had an inspirational quality about it rather than rationalization, a quality of creativity that people often associate with the arts but which is very much involved in scientific research. This made me feel a special kinship with him, unlike anyone else I had worked with. Perhaps that's what allowed me to withstand his occasional moodiness and emotional outbursts.

In contrast to myself, Jack Seybolt had no patience with all that and with Papanicolaou's ups and downs. He himself was extremely even-tempered and, in my judgment, rather provincial and dull. He disdained outbursts of emotion. Seybolt was quite critical of Papanicolaou's behavior and personality, considered Papanicolaou to be paranoid, and made derogatory remarks about him behind his back. I thought that calling him paranoid was questionable, even though Pap did worry excessively about people denying him his due, criticizing him, and even stealing his ideas. When he had come to this country Pap went through demeaning experiences, which I'm sure left their imprint. And as far as I knew, in other areas of his life, beyond his work, he showed no evidence of feeling persecuted. It is true he was an emotional man, but some of that was cultural.

Here's an example of the sort of thing that would happen and feed Jack's belief. One day when Dr. Pap and I were working together, alone, he looked at me with tears in his eyes. "You know, Irena, when I was young and unknown I worked with Dr. Stockard, chairman of the Department of Anatomy. He took credit for some of my work on the sex cycle of guinea pigs. And then I developed the smear method for diagnosis of cancer of the womb. Although I was the one who did all the work, Dr. Traut, the head of obstetrics and gynecology at Cornell, insisted on co-authoring my monograph." His voice was full of what I think could best be called self-pity.

Although Dr. Traut had provided Dr. Papanicolaou with the genital smears of his patients, his contribution of research material does not compare with the central intellectual achievement made by Pap and perhaps didn't justify their joint authorship. A recognition of the role of Dr. Traut as a supporter of Dr. Pap's ideas and a supplier of smears from his patients could have been adequately expressed in the form of a note.

As Dr. Pap wiped the tears from his eyes with the sleeve of his jacket, I felt embarrassed by his tears because I admired him very much. He thought that sharing credit with Dr. Traut would diminish the value of his contribution. He did indeed have an excessive fear of having his discoveries stolen from him. Jack Seybolt may have been right that Dr. Pap was actually paranoid, although my feeling was that he was simply too highly sensitive and obsessive about the issue of who would get credit for the work he actually did. But I'm no psychiatrist. I felt bad that he suffered, though I considered his pain to be excessive and unnecessary.

Also, I know that Papanicolaou's feelings about not having received sufficient recognition for his discovery of the Pap smear technique were at least partially justified. He had been repeatedly told by pathologists that cancer could be diagnosed only from biopsies of tissue and not by looking at single cells—tissue being made of huge collections of cells tightly held together. That reminds me again of Sophie Spitz, who exhibited the same attitude in that comment of hers when Papanicolaou spoke to us at the New York Infirmary that October day in 1948. I could still remember her words: "Pap smears provide an excellent tool for cancer detection, but the final diagnosis of cancer can be made only on the basis of a biopsy." How upset he must have been on so public an occasion. But the very fact that he concealed his feelings and acted like a perfect gentleman suggested that he was not necessarily paranoid.

For a long time the medical establishment rejected the Pap test because Dr. Papanicolaou wasn't a certified pathologist and because they were not confident that cancer could be diagnosed without a biopsy. Undoubtedly, his accomplishment was enormous. And to imply anything different was an outrage to which he should not have been subjected. But it usually takes a long time before new discoveries are appreciated, and Dr. Pap bore the brunt of this delay.

"What were you doing alone with Pap in his office so long?" Jack asked me one day. "Did he cry and try to make you feel sorry for him, the old paranoiac?"

"Yes, he cried," I admitted, but I didn't say anymore. I was shocked to hear Jack Seybolt speak so callously. He may have found Pap's behavior unattractive and annoying, but he occupied a leading position in Pap's lab and was benefiting from Pap's knowledge. His reaction seemed to me unduly petty and extremely unkind.

Most old-fashioned pathologists resisted for a long time the requests made by clinicians to evaluate the Pap smears of their patients. But some younger pathologists and some physicians from specialties other than pathology, and even laboratory technicians, were eager to learn this new diagnostic method. As a result, Papanicolaou gave annual training courses at Cornell, which attracted participants from all over the country and from abroad. Their enthusiasm at least partially compensated Papanicolaou for the skepticism of his detractors. Jack Seybolt and I were usually very busy lecturing and giving classroom instruction at the microscope during these courses. I was in constant demand to teach which, of course, made me feel needed and respected.

My contact with Dr. Pap remained frequent, since I would always consult with him about cases that were difficult to diagnose. I would usually go to his office and sit next to him at his microscope to get his opinion and advice. But sometimes it was he who would make a special point of seeking me out to ask my opinion of a slide he had some doubts about. I would use those opportunities to ask him to have a look through my microscope at any slides I was then working with and also happened to have doubts about.

"Dr. Pap, please look at the cells I've marked on the slide," I would often say to get his help in determining if what I was looking at in bronchial secretions were cancer cells or histiocytes, which may resemble cancer cells but are benign. Whenever he couldn't tell the difference right away, he would look at the cells for several minutes, mumbling to himself. I might as well have not existed. But I listened carefully to the occasional words I could catch, and sometimes I could make sense of them. Whenever I could discern what he was saying, I was fascinated. For I loved the intuitive way by which he arrived at his conclusions. There was something almost sacred and ritualistic in this process, and I felt privileged to witness it.

I would always wait patiently for his answer. I never got bored or impatient, although sometimes I would become distracted by the fragrance of his verbena-scented soap. While it wasn't a favorite scent of mine, I'd begun to identify it with him and expected to smell verbena in his presence. I would never dare say anything about this to him. Our relationship never got personal enough for such talk since our close rapport was based on a mutual fascination with the cells we were working with. He always treated me with much respect, as had Dr. Bica in Brazil and Drs. Kidd and Travell at Cornell, but I never shared with any of them the same excitement about our joint observations as I experienced with Papanicolaou.

Mrs. Pap often walked in and out of her husband's office during our consultations. She was a short, plump woman with a pale complexion, faded blue eyes, and gray hair. Her face was expressionless, except when her pleasant smile appeared. She always referred to her husband as "Dr. Pap" and also called him that when she spoke to him in front of others in the lab. Likewise he called her and referred to her as "Mrs. Pap" in conversations with others. They never used their first names while at work. This was the traditional Greek way of addressing each other.

She was in her early sixties and performed the function of a messenger and filing clerk in his department, bringing papers for him to sign or Pap smears from his private consultations for him to examine. Mrs. Pap always had a friendly smile for me, but we never really engaged in much conversation. Our backgrounds, interests, and responsibilities were too different to bring us together often or to have much in common. I thought highly of her, found her pleasant, nonintrusive, not a woman to put on airs because her husband was important.

Once when I consulted Dr. Pap about the smear of a woman suspected of having cancer of the womb, he presented me with an unexpected challenge: "What do you think about these cells, Dr. Koprowska? Are they cancer cells or is it *dyskaryosis?*"

I had never heard this word before. I didn't know what dyskaryosis meant.

"I don't know, Dr. Pap," I answered, admitting that I didn't understand his question, but this whetted my curiosity and I asked him to explain it.

"Well, it's cancer and it isn't cancer at the same time," he replied, leaving me further confused.

I looked up dyskaryosis in the dictionary, but couldn't find it. I asked Dr. Foot, and he didn't know what it was. Seybolt had also heard Dr. Pap use this word but had no idea what it meant. All I could figure out was that it was a Greek term meaning some abnormality of the nucleus of cells. It bothered me that I didn't know what abnormality it was and what its significance was. He didn't explain, I did not understand why, but I was too shy to persevere. I was afraid of angering him. It wasn't until several months later that I found out what he meant.

In 1950, as my fellowship with Papanicolaou continued, I was asked by the admissions committee at Cornell University Medical College to interview their women applicants. This provided me with an interesting challenge. My experience at the New York Infirmary made amply clear that many American women who became physicians felt that they couldn't combine being a doctor with having a family life. Some of them felt "married" to medicine and rejected the idea of having a husband and children. Others stopped practicing medicine to devote themselves completely to raising a family. I knew that it was difficult to be a physician and to have a family as other women did in Poland. One of the reasons Polish women doctors could successfully combine their careers with a happy family life was that they had servants to care for their houses as well as their children; domestic help was affordable for middle class families and readily available. I knew, however, that in the U.S., culture and tradition also played a role. After all, until recently, American women with families who were wealthy enough to have servants still tended not to choose professions; many did charity work instead, and, ironically, it was often in hospitals. At the time, medicine was seen more as men's work or the work of that group of women who didn't lead what was considered to be traditional female lives — having husbands and children. But things were changing, and many women ceased to be satisfied with the prospect of having no career of their own. Even those who wanted to marry and have children began to enter the field of medicine. These women struck me, quite frankly, as softer and more traditionally feminine than many of the women I knew who already were doctors — the ones I had met up with in much of my career in the United States up to that point. But I worried that these young women might be discouraged once they reached the point of marriage and the decision to have children.

Hence during my interviews, I questioned the women applicants about their plans and emphasized the desirability of their continuing to practice medicine after they married and had children. Although I understood it might be difficult, I tried to encourage these young women — future physicians — to find a solution to their problems by relying on their relatives, as many Polish women doctors did, or hiring help even at a financial sacrifice.

However, I went further. I let them know that if they couldn't work this out, and considered desisting from the practice of medicine, they would be wasting a training slot which someone else could use.

"If you plan to quit after you find a husband, you shouldn't occupy a slot which might otherwise be given to a man; he won't give up his career because of marriage," I told the applicants firmly. They did not respond, but I suspect that they were shocked by what they heard from me. I don't know what they thought, but they may not have liked what I said and may have repeated it to the members of the admissions committee, because I was never again asked to interview the applicants.

Meanwhile, I was experiencing major changes in my personal life as well. In 1950 I became an American citizen and immediately brought Bronislawa to live with us in Englewood. This freed Gene to leave Sweden and permitted him to enroll as a student at McGill University, just as Gabriel had done before him.

Gene arrived at McGill University in October 1950, when Bronislawa came to the United States. I expected that the atmosphere of our household , which had always been tense as long as my mother-in-law lived with us—although by then the emotional crises between us had subsided—would become worse with the addition of Bronislawa. Since I'd been working full time, earning money, and advancing my professional career, Hilary's mother had complained about me less. But still I never felt I was the mistress of my house. There were other problems as well. Claude, who had spent so much time with Hilary's mother when he was small, was now ten. He had many friends and was less in need of her care and company. Feeling less needed and having more time to think about her present life, she began to make plans to go back to Europe. She became more preoccupied with herself than with me. Now sixty-seven, she had never learned much English and was totally dependent on us for transportation. Living in an American suburban community, she had fewer opportunities to make friends than she had in Rio de Janeiro, where many Poles like ourselves established their residence during the war. So as some of the old sources of tension in our household disappeared, new ones became apparent with Sofia getting older and more dependent.

The presence of Bronislawa in our house must have made Sofia Semeonovna more uncomfortable. The house was small, but each of them still had a room of her own. Even so, they had very different backgrounds and personalities, had gone through different wartime experiences, and this made their communication and mutual understanding more difficult. They didn't trust or like each other and would never be friends. Each kept to herself, avoiding the other. Hilary did not seem to have any problems with Bronislawa. But he and I often went out in the evening to escape the tense domestic atmosphere their joint presence created.

One of Claude's friends, Walter Hammerle, a son of a baker, lived across the street from us. Claude loved to watch television at his house. Most American middle class women of my generation, the mothers of his classmates, stayed at home and didn't work. Claude was made uncomfortable by my having a career—it made him different from his friends.

"Mummie, why do you have to work? Why don't you stay home and bake cakes like Mrs. Hammerle? Doesn't Daddy earn enough money to support us?" he asked me repeatedly.

"Claude, I've spent years studying medicine and I want to practice my profession," I responded, although I realized that at his age he couldn't really be expected to understand how important my work was to my self-respect and my sense of myself as a person, how much pride I took in it, how I couldn't imagine giving it up.

"Why did my daddy have only one seed to plant in you so that I'm alone and don't have a brother or sister?" was another question he would ask. How was I to explain to him that wartime wasn't a good time for enlarging the family?

"Maybe now that the war is over and our life in America is more settled, we could give you a brother or sister," I once responded.

One time, after listening to Claude's desires for a sibling, I repeated our conversation to Hilary. Remembering Isabel Knowlton's statement that I would have a hard time getting pregnant, and with Hilary's knowledge and apparent approval, I decided to stop using contraceptives.

We spent that summer in Massachusetts, in Manchester-on-the-Sea, with the Bertholds, our friends from Englewood. One day Hilary, Claude, and I went for a ride with our host, Jack Laus, in his lobster boat to see the Marblehead races. But the engine stalled and couldn't be restarted. Our boat crashed on the rocks of Little Misery Island (*most* appropriately named, it seemed to us at that moment). Some hours later, we were rescued by the Coast Guard. A couple of months after our return to Englewood, I discovered that I was pregnant and calculated that the time of conception must have been the night after our sea escapade.

"This summer we almost took your life away, but in the end we gave you a new one," Jack Laus's wife wrote when she learned of my pregnancy.

For our laboratory's Christmas party in 1950, I wore my new maternity clothes for the first time. As soon as I entered, I saw Chandler Foot dressed up as Santa Claus. Many people stared at me, but Dr. Papanicolaou was obviously upset. "I see that you expect a baby. What's going to happen to the course?"

I was very disappointed that he didn't congratulate me before showing concern about work, making me feel that he didn't care about me at all and, instead, cared only about my teaching responsibilities. As I think back about this, I suspect that really it wasn't selfishness that motivated his outburst, so much as the attitude many men of the day had that they could accept a woman working in their profession as long as she didn't present them with obvious inconveniences associated with her biological role as a female.

"I'll be working and teaching until the last day, Dr. Pap," I reassured him. "At worst, I may be unable to give my last lecture."

"But you can't teach in that condition. It's simply not done," he continued in a disapproving tone.

I was shocked by his belief that it would be improper for a pregnant woman to be seen on the podium as a teacher. I insisted that I could teach until my delivery time. But I feared that he might cut short my teaching schedule because of his old-fashioned ideas.

We were crowding around the refreshment table when Karl Hoffamann, a gynecologist who was one of Dr. Pap's research fellows, made a noisy, delayed entrance. He had already had a few drinks.

"Sorry to be late, Dr. Pap," he announced. "I had to see a patient. It was one of those cases in which I didn't know whether she did or didn't have cancer. I wish you could have helped me to resolve it." Karl had begun to shout. "But all I would have heard from you would be that cursed word "dyskaryosis"—it is and it isn't cancer at the same time. It sounds almost like 'La Cucuracha'! Is it a South American dance? Would you mind committing yourself for once in your life and telling us what it means?"

Dr. Pap became red in the face. Angry at Karl's provocation, he even stamped his foot. But at last he spoke.

"Dyskaryosis is a term I use when exfoliated cells derived from the lining of the womb have acquired large irregular, abnormal nuclei, without losing the regular outline of the entire cell. True cancer cells are bizarre and, in addition to the nuclear abnormalities, the entire cell becomes irregular. This change in appearance of the dyskariotic cells to cancer cells is usually accompanied by the invasion of tissues. *Carcinoma in situ* becomes then true cancer."

Finally I understood what he meant. This understanding developed slowly in my mind, but wasn't gained by other pathologists for many years to come. It was a revelation, a new concept, a great discovery. It was more important than to discover an already advanced, often incurable cancer. The detection of dyskaryosis in a Pap smear would give a woman a chance to receive preventive care. This would greatly decrease the likelihood of her ever developing cancer.

That this explanation finally came out now, at a party, was a bit astounding. For years Papanicolaou either didn't know how to verbalize the nature of his discovery or was reluctant to disclose it prematurely. I knew from Charlotte Street, his chief cytotechnologist and long-time associate, he'd always been slow in publishing his findings and liked to review them meticulously to be certain that everything he said could be verified and confirmed. He dreaded error, and he would never discuss his unpublished findings, fearing that they may be stolen. But now, under duress, when challenged by Karl Hoffamann at that Christmas party, Papanicolaou apparently overcame his fears and explained what he meant by that mysterious term, dyskaryosis.[5]

---

5. In differentiating cancer from its precursor (carcinoma in situ) pathologists base their diagnosis on the appearance of the basement membrane separating abnormal surface epithelium from underlying connective tissue stroma. They determine the presence of cancerous invasion if this membrane is broken. These are the criteria of malignancy that pathologists use in making tissue diagnosis. Since no basement membrane is present in Pap smears, where only single cells detached from tissues may be seen, pathologists felt that no distinction between carcinoma in situ and invasive cancer could be made. What Papanicolaou had accomplished by using the term dyskaryosis was to introduce a different basis for differentiating carcinoma in situ from invasive cancer in cervical smears than the one used for tissues. The abnormal cells desquamated from carcinoma in situ have bizarre nuclei, but are not altered as a whole. Whereas in the presence of invasion, cancer cells have not only large, irregular, hyperchromatic nuclei but are totally altered acquiring bizarre shapes.

"Enough of the shop talk!" announced Santa Claus Foot as he handed a cup of eggnog to Dr. Pap, who accepted it with a grateful smile. Once he got over his anger, and maybe even some fear, he was fine.

After the Christmas party, I couldn't stop thinking about dyskaryosis. Increasingly I pondered the importance of what certainly seemed to be a revolutionary concept. Little did Dr. Pap know how strongly pathologists would fight the use of this term. They failed to understand the greatness of Papanicolaou's discovery that cells forming carcinoma in situ not only become more aggressive when they break through the basement membrane, invade, and become cancer, but that they also change their entire shape, that is, become bizarre. Seeing such bizarre cells in Pap smears makes it possible to diagnose cancer.

As soon as I understood the nature of his discovery, I could explain it to others better than Dr. Pap himself could. I was considered an inspired and inspiring teacher by our students. They would seek me out to explain the pattern of dyskaryosis, teach them to recognize it, and distinguish it from cancer cells. I stimulated their enthusiasm for the Papanicolaou method of cancer diagnosis, and this was gratifying. But as I was preaching Papanicolaou's gospel, many pathologists continued to resist the idea that one could diagnose the presence of a carcinoma in situ by finding evidence of dyskaryosis in Pap smears.

One day in 1950, I ran into Sophie Spitz on the street as she was coming out of Memorial Hospital for Cancer and Allied Diseases. She was all smiles when she greeted me. "How are you? What are you doing now?" she asked, as if she were my best friend. When I told her, she said, with considerable outrage, "You don't mean that you are working with Papanicolaou, a man who isn't even a pathologist and who doesn't know as much as you do!"

Memories of her past attitudes and remarks came rushing back, and I found myself upset again. I was indignant at her suggestion that being a pathologist made one superior to a scientist who, though not a pathologist, had made such an important discovery in the field of cancer diagnosis. "There's plenty I can learn from him, even though he's not a pathologist," I said in a cold tone of voice and walked away, leaving her standing there in the street with her mouth open in astonishment at my sudden boldness.

During the period of my association with Dr. Pap, I passed the examinations that were necessary to become a diplomate of the American Board of Pathology. I then had the formal credentials that were required to diagnose cancer. Although a pathologist myself, I firmly believed that in many instances one can make an equally reliable diagnosis of cancer in Pap smears, as in tissues, without the need for a traumatic and costly biopsy. Although in coping with my own problems in life, I was often too passive to speak for myself, I felt the need to speak for my mentor, who often was too shy and reluctant to do it for himself. I preached his gospel whenever I had the opportunity, in the classroom as well as at medical meetings.

Even though I did this because I believed it important, to my deep disappointment and bafflement, Dr. Pap never showed any appreciation of my efforts. Still, my admiration for him continued. I considered it a privilege to help him in the struggle for greater acceptance of his method. I treasured the moments when I sat next to him at the microscope. I still felt a kinship with his approach to science and found his creativity unique, appealing, and very inspiring.

By now I had acquired more professional self-confidence; I knew what I was doing, and I had gained the esteem of others. My status in the field of teaching cancer diagnosis based on cell studies had become established and recognized. But I began to notice that, at times, Dr. Pap behaved as if he resented my professional growth and recognition. As a board-certified pathologist, I had better professional qualifications than he did, and as a teacher I could present his concepts to students more clearly than he could. But I was never aware of flaunting this. It was hard to believe he couldn't have noticed the awe and respect I felt towards him. Sometimes I wondered why I put up with his unkind behavior towards me. But instead of talking to him, I suppressed my anger and remained loyal to him. I feared in talking to him frankly I might risk making things worse rather than better.

Then something happened that I never anticipated. When one of the students asked me a question that I couldn't answer, I offered to ask Dr. Pap. His response startled me. "You should never ask me about my unpublished work in progress, Dr. Koprowska," he said in a stern voice. "I'm surprised at you."

Although I knew he was sensitive about people taking credit for his ideas, I took his reaction as growing evidence that he didn't trust giving me the information because he was jealous of my increased independence and accomplishment. Perhaps he even thought I was asking in order to steal his ideas and take credit for them, especially since I was now gaining a good reputation of my own. It was impossible to know. All I knew was that I felt devastated by the way he had responded to me. Seeing his anger, I swallowed my tears.

Shortly after this episode, I found out something that was further disturbing. Dr. Pap had been working at home on an illustrated monograph about cancer cells, but I did not realize that he was working on it with Doris Holmquist, a graduate student who shared my office now that Fred Panico had left Cornell. My feelings were hurt when I learned about it from Doris, whom he had invited to work with him at his home. I failed to consider that her role in their collaboration was based on her background. She was writing a thesis on abnormal mitoses, and he needed their illustration and description for his monograph.

Doris knew that I had my own project conducted in collaboration with two physicians from the department of internal medicine, Ralph Engle and John Ultmann. We had tried to improve the method of diagnosing cancer of the lymph nodes. It was my first independent study. Envious, perhaps, that I had time to spend on my project, Doris complained that she couldn't work on her doctoral dissertation because Dr. Papanicolaou kept her so busy helping him with his monograph.

"Doris, you should ask him to give you time off for your research. How will you get your Ph.D. otherwise?" I responded. The advice I gave her was sound—it was a recommendation she needed to hear, almost seemed to be asking for, in order for her to be able to move ahead with her own education and career. However, what I said to her backfired on me. In suggesting that she assert her independence a bit, I would soon learn that it was independence that had Pap upset with me. His annoyance with me wasn't simply that he wanted to be secretive about his work. He wanted rather to work with someone who felt less independent than I did. Perhaps he felt an independent and accomplished colleague would expect and deserve some credit that he didn't want to risk sharing.

"Irena, could you ever work for me like a soldier and follow my orders blindly?" he asked me one day as soon as I entered his office.

I hadn't even had a chance to tell him the purpose of my visit when he blurted that out.

Fortunately, despite my devotion and deep admiration for this man and his work, I stood my ground. "No, with all my admiration for you, I wouldn't be able to sacrifice my independence, Dr. Pap," I answered. I was too shy to call him George, although he had encouraged me to do so. A year and a half into our acquaintance, he had begun to call me Irena.

"Now I know that I made the correct decision in choosing Doris Holmquist over you to work with me on my monograph," he said abruptly. "And she had been loyally following my orders until you tried to turn her against me by encouraging her to do independent research." His tone was cold and accusing.

I couldn't believe my ears. It became clear to me that he was working with Doris because, unlike me, he could turn her into a little toy soldier, blindly following his command. He wanted subservience more than loyalty, a helpmate more than a colleague. As a result, he wanted to punish me, and he went out of his way to take Doris into his confidence and exclude me.

The whole situation really got to me. I was stung by Doris's betrayal at having told him I encouraged her to ask for more time for her own work. I had perceived this to be a genuine worry on her part, and I thought my words to her would be held in confidence. And I was crushed by Dr. Pap's obvious rejection of me and his hostility.

Independent Scientist

Despite my unhappiness with Papanicolaou's attitude toward me, our behavior towards each other remained as it had been before he reproached me for my independence. A few weeks after the painful incident with Doris Holmquist, he came to see me, addressing me formally, not using Irena, as he had in the past. "Dr. Koprowska, I may have issued a false positive report for lung cancer. The patient was a house painter and died in this hospital of emphysema," he began. "No lung cancer was found on autopsy. I want you to look at the smear of his bronchial washings and tell me what you think of the cells I marked on it."

He handed me several glass slides, which I immediately put under the microscope. All during this interchange I was feeling a mixture of surprise and flattery. After his recent harsh words to me, I hardly expected Dr. Pap to solicit my opinion, especially in so important a case. So, in spite of his reproaches, he apparently still respected and trusted my judgment.

"Dr. Pap, I don't know if these are cancer cells," I reported an hour later. "But what I do see are cells that look just like what you call dyskaryosis. This patient may have had a carcinoma in situ in his lung, just as women have it in the neck of the womb, often before cancer develops there. I'm not surprised that this man died of emphysema before his carcinoma in situ became a cancer large enough to kill him."

I said this, although at the time our knowledge of the behavior of carcinoma in situ (CIS) of the lung was practically nonexistent. I assumed on the basis of analogy that some CIS of the lung may progress to cancer. The ready accessibility of the uterus permitted pathologists to study the appearance and behavior of many CIS, but this kind of knowledge was not available in the case of lung cancer.

My having found dyskaryosis strengthened Papanicolaou's conviction that his initial report was indeed warranted and could not have been discounted as a false positive. However, the only chance he had of convincing others of this was to get that patient's lung from the autopsy and find there evidence of cancer, however "occult" (small).

"You've worked with Dr. Kidd. Please ask him to release to you the lung from the autopsy of this patient. Then you can look for evidence of a small hidden cancer." He didn't say carcinoma in situ.

Listening to his request, I feared that such an experiment was beyond my competence. How would I know which piece of an organ as large as the lung to excise in order to look for a grossly invisible cancer. The technical problems in detecting such a cancer were formidable. But I was determined to meet this challenge. I also was excited that Dr. Pap was showing such faith in me, trusting me not only with the important task of validating his finding but, in so doing, helping to further validate his method of detecting a real or potential malignancy.

I knew, of course, that besides the scientific value of this experiment, Dr. Pap's ego was involved. He very much minded that his report had been dubbed a false positive. For although a certain percentage of false positives and false negatives are an accepted part of any diagnostic work, they do represent failure to determine the truth. Nobody likes it, but for Papanicolaou it was something he particularly dreaded and took personally.

When I told Dr. Kidd that Papanicolaou had asked me to search for an occult lung cancer in a patient who died of emphysema, even though no cancer was found at the autopsy, he became visibly uncomfortable. My request for a renewed search for cancer carried with it the implication that the autopsy performed by his staff hadn't been thorough enough.

"But the lung has already been examined very carefully and no cancer was found. The patient died of emphysema. Why do you want to repeat this search, Dr. Koprowska?"

"There's no question that this man died of.emphysema, Dr. Kidd," I said, trying to soothe his injured feelings. "But I'll look for a microscopic, perhaps even noninvasive cancer, which would not have been possible to see with the naked eye. Its presence would validate Dr. Pap's microscopic diagnosis. He asked me for my help, and I will have to cut blindly through hundreds of pieces of tissue to look for it, Dr. Kidd."

"As you wish, Dr. Koprowska," he said in a cool tone.

When I left, I carried away with me a large jar containing the lung.

My initial success—obtaining the lung—turned out to be the easiest part of my mission. Now came the hard part, figuring out where I was to look for a microscopic site of cancer in this huge human lung. I had no idea how to begin my search, and I knew of only one person who could help me: Nathan Chandler Foot.

I found Dr. Foot in his office, ready to leave for the day. When he realized what I was trying to accomplish and how desperate I was, he took off his coat and removed the lung from the jar. He put it on a cutting board, picked up a pair of scissors, and cut open all the respiratory tubes in the lung. He looked at their soft, smooth, pink linings, on which there were only a few uneven, red granular areas barely visible to the naked eye. He showed me and palpated these granulations with his finger and asked me to feel them, too. They felt like tiny bumps. I had never seen or felt such bumps before in the course of my training in pathology, but Dr. Foot, as an experienced surgical pathologist who was sufficiently interested in the early diagnosis of cancer to spend his retirement years with Papanicolaou, must have already expected to find them. Then he took a scalpel and cut through some of these granules, removing at their site a few small tissue slices. These he dropped into a jar filled with formalin, which preserves the tissues and is used routinely.

"You may find something there," he said. Then he put his coat back on and departed, leaving me with my specimens.

I took the slices of tissue that Dr. Foot gave me and brought them to the histology technicians, who prepared from them tissue sections suitable for microscopic examination.[6] There were five hundred of

---

6. The technicians first wash the tissue samples in water, then dehydrate them in alcohol and xylene before impregnating them with paraffin. Once this process is complete, the technicians are able to use a microtome (a slicing machine) to cut very thin tissue sections. The tissue sections then can be mounted on the glass slides and stained by hematoxylin-eosin for microscopic examinations.

these tissue sections! In my effort to locate evidence of cancer, I looked at one tissue section after another for the next three days. I was thinking about my challenging project day and night. After examining the first one hundred sections, I became discouraged. I began to doubt that I would ever find any cancer. But in spite of my growing pessimism, I felt I owed it to Dr. Pap to continue looking until I examined every single tissue section. Besides, to stop now would make him quite unhappy, maybe even angry. At this point in our relationship, it would have been very foolish indeed to not go along with his request, to fail to help him in something he wanted so much.

Then, on the fourth day, all of a sudden I saw something that made my heart beat very fast. Here it was, a minute collection of cells with abnormal nuclei in the lining of the bronchial tube, with no cancerous invasion of the tissue underneath it! This was the presumed source of the exfoliation of the cells with abnormal nuclei, that he had found and shown me in the smears of bronchial washings. Now, I was looking at CIS in the tissue from which they had exfoliated into the bronchial secretions. What I found was just what we needed.

Blood rushed to my head, and I felt wet with perspiration. I stared through the microscope for several minutes without moving, glued to the chair. Then I got up very rapidly and ran to Dr. Pap's office, forgetting even to knock at the door. "Come and look at what I have under my microscope!" I exclaimed.

Dr. Pap followed right on my heels. "Carcinoma in situ—I must kiss you!" he said.

Dr. Papanicolaou was elated in a way I had never seen him. He had been vindicated! I had vindicated him! As he kissed me on the cheek, I became aware of a strong scent of verbena from his Mary Chess soap. "This must be published as a case report," he announced. "It'll be the first reported case of carcinoma in situ detected by finding dyskaryosis in a bronchial secretion."

I knew then that my hard work had paid off. He turned back to the microscope to re-examine my treasured findings. After a few minutes, when his excitement subsided, he became more businesslike.

"Who do you think should be the authors of this publication?" he asked me.

"You should be the first author, Dr. Pap," I quickly replied, "because you issued a positive smear report. Dr. Foot should be the second author because, without him, I wouldn't have known where to start looking for the cancer. I found the carcinoma in situ, so I should be included as the third author."

"I don't think that Dr. Foot need be a co-author," Dr. Pap said. "He just helped you to cut a few slices of tissue. He had nothing to do with this case. It was my positive smear report that began it. You found carcinoma in situ in these tissues. You'll get more credit if there's no other pathologist on the report."

I was shocked by Dr. Pap's attitude. Beset by inner turmoil, I didn't know what to do. I didn't want to fight with Dr. Pap, fearing that the price of a fight might jeopardize my relationship with him. Besides, the thought of being the only co-author whetted my own selfish desire for more professional recognition and fame. With such mixed feelings, and under Pap's intense pressure, I agreed to go along with his wish.

And so our report of this case, which was published in *Cancer* in January 1951, appeared without Dr. Foot's name as a co-author. I felt guilty but, interestingly enough, neither Dr. Foot nor Dr. Kidd ever asked me any questions about it. In an attempt to decrease my feelings of guilt, I did manage to include in the text a description of how Dr. Foot found granular areas in the bronchus and cut tissue slices from that site. Fortunately, Dr. Pap didn't overrule that! Reading about Dr. Foot's contribution, despite the absence of his name as co-author, any pathologist would realize how crucial his role had been.

At a couple of professional meetings at which the report of this case was later discussed, in my presence, the case was referred to by the pathologists discussing it as "Foot's case," not "Pap's" or "Pap and Koprowska's." In their opinion it was Foot's case, not only because I had described how he had found abnormal, bumpy sites in the bronchial mucosa and felt that they may have harbored an early cancer, but because Dr. Pap was not a pathologist and I was still unknown to them. The sad irony was that I did deserve recognition for my contribution to this case. I was ashamed that I allowed myself to become indirectly involved in Dr. Pap's competition for recognition with Dr. Foot.

By helping Dr. Pap be vindicated for his "false positive" cytologic report, I had hoped things would become smooth between us again, and maybe he would come to view me as an independent colleague rather than his toy soldier. But this wasn't to be. Something else followed that again demonstrated his jealousy about professional matters and his desire for control. This very disturbing pattern seemed to be building in his relationship with me. I think it was probably fed by my professional growth, and, to my sadness, it would ultimately color and deeply affect my important association with my esteemed mentor, George N. Papanicolaou.

Jim Reagan was a pathologist from Western Reserve University,[7] who had completed our course on Pap smears at Cornell. He went on to gain prominence teaching other pathologists how to diagnose cancer by this method. One day he came back to visit Dr. Pap at Cornell University Medical College. Afterwards, he stopped to say hello to me. While we spoke, he in passing mentioned his current, still unpublished, study of lymph nodes. When I told him that Ralph Engle, John Ultman, and I were doing similar work at Cornell, Jim raised his eyebrows in surprise. "Dr. Pap never mentioned that you were doing this work," he said quietly. He then left to catch his plane back to Cleveland.

I thought that Dr. Pap's silence was odd. I started to worry that this was more evidence of Pap's wanting to keep me from moving ahead. I didn't want to think this, but to ignore it was impossible, and very likely unwise, as I realized it could affect my career adversely.

And my career was very much on my mind. After my joint publication with Dr. Pap of the carcinoma in situ of the bronchus, I had become much more eager to publish my work, and I was hungry to gain recognition. I wanted to offset the harm done to my reputation for failing to include Dr. Foot as co-author of that paper. In this new situation with Jim Reagan, to my chagrin, I saw Pap was again not acting honorably with me, for it would have been to my benefit to have a chance to collaborate with Jim Reagan, or at least to be informed about his research.

What were Pap's motives? Why was he trying to prevent my career growth in a rather sly and cunning manner? I simply couldn't avoid concluding that he was blocking me and refusing to help me further my own research because I was more convenient to him as an associate.

---

7. Now called Case Western Reserve University.

I was in my seventh month of pregnancy and still teaching. Hilary, who had been invited to Brazil on behalf of the World Health Organization, wanted me to accompany him on the trip. Hilary always wanted me to travel with him whenever he was going someplace we had not been to before, or to a place where both of us had fond memories—like Brazil. But with the approaching birth of the baby, I simply felt I couldn't take more time off from my work. Besides, at this point in my pregnancy I wouldn't have enjoyed traveling such a long distance. So I was sorry to let him go alone, but he understood my motivation and went without me, bringing me back a beautiful amethyst brooch.

Since during my previous delivery in France my uterine contractions stopped and I almost lost the baby, my obstetrician scheduled induced labor, fearing that this may happen again this time. I advised Dr. Pap accordingly, saying that I wouldn't be able to give my last lecture.

"You look very well," he said. Couldn't you just postpone it for a few more days until the course is over?" I couldn't believe that he would be so uncaring and insensitive. I had naively thought that over the months he had come to accept my pregnancy, especially since I'd been functioning so well and without letup.

"I'm sorry. I can't." I said smiling, half thinking (or hoping) he was joking and that I was being overly sensitive and misjudging him. But he wasn't. He was serious. He meant it.

At home, nobody except for Hilary knew that I was going to have induced labor, to some extent because I didn't want to cause any concern to Bronislawa, who would be likely to worry about me, but also under the influence of Hilary—always so secretive about personal matters. On the scheduled day, my mother-in-law wasn't feeling well, and I brought her tea in bed before Hilary drove me to the hospital. Bronislawa was still asleep when I left the house. Claude, who had known that I expected to have a baby any day, was used to seeing me leave the house for work in the morning, so he didn't expect me to go elsewhere.

Considering Dr. Pap's suggestion that I could have a microscope placed at a table next to my bed and resume my work right after the delivery, I decided not to give birth to my baby at Cornell. My obstetrician was on the staff of another medical school, and my second son, Christopher, was born at Columbia University Presbyterian Hospital in New York on April 12, 1951, when I was thirty-four years old. My joy knew no end. It was just marvelous to have a baby, the arrival of which I kept postponing for many years because of the war and the lack of necessary stability in my life. This time my pregnancy was not accidental. I really wanted to have a second child, and it felt so good to hold such a delightful little bundle in my arms. He was eleven years younger than Claude, who was ecstatic to find out that he had a baby brother.

Claude came with Hilary to visit me at the hospital carrying a big plant. But since at the time visitors had to be at least fourteen years old, the head nurse who told him this stopped him at the door.

"How do you know that I'm not?" he asked.

"You don't look it," she said.

"You should know better than to judge people by their appearance," he answered; and without further ado he entered my room and deposited in front of me the beautiful plant he brought.

On the fifth day after Christopher was born, I was getting ready to return home from the hospital when my obstetrician walked in.

"I'm sorry, Dr. Koprowska, but your baby has projectile vomiting, most likely due to a strangulated hernia. A pediatric surgeon is on the way to perform an emergency operation."

These unexpected words frightened me. I felt my heart beating very fast, and I became fearful that I would lose my long-awaited second child.

"Your husband's here waiting to take you home. There's nothing you can accomplish by staying at the hospital," he said.

Going back home without my baby was an awful experience. The feeling of emptiness wouldn't leave me for a moment. I felt almost as if I had in fact lost him. The atmosphere at home was very gloomy; it would only come alive with the presence and sounds of a new baby boy. When I told my mother-in-law and Bronislawa what happened, they kept quiet. Then I retreated to my bed. Hilary and I were too upset to talk much about what was going on.

My obstetrician called me in the morning.

"Dr. Koprowska, your little boy was operated on in the middle of the night and tolerated the surgery well. You can see him tomorrow,

Irena with baby Christopher born in April 1951 in backyard of their house in Englewood, New Jersey

although we would like to keep him for another day after that for observation."

Next day, as soon as I arrived at Babies Hospital, I felt so relieved when I saw Christopher sound asleep and obviously well looked-after by the nurses. I spent several hours sitting next to him and just looking at him. Then I kissed him, which made me feel very good, and returned home still empty-handed but much happier. The following day I carried him in my arms to the car and Hilary drove us home, where Claude and both grandmothers awaited our arrival.

I have only a vague recollection of the next several days, except that I was getting used to my second motherhood, so different from the first one, with a husband at my side and no war around us. I insisted on taking care of the baby myself.

Christopher was only one week old when our concert subscription night came up. I didn't feel like going out, but Hilary refused to miss the concert. He invited Gail Theis, his beautiful new technician, to accompany him in my place. They went with our Englewood friends, the Stellars, while I remained at home. I felt miserable that Hilary didn't choose to stay with me, preferring instead to go out to a concert and invite a striking young woman to accompany him.

I also felt very embarrassed that the Stellars would now be aware of Hilary's insensitivity to my feelings. What would they think about it? Would they suspect that Gail was Hilary's girlfriend? And I began to wonder whether she wasn't. I was angry at him, very unhappy, and terribly jealous.

Since Christopher was a good baby and slept very well, I went to bed early. But I couldn't fall asleep. I was disturbed by what Hilary had done. It seemed to me that, so close on the heels of the birth of our second child, and especially after the scare we had had, Hilary's going out at all, much less with another woman, was hard to interpret as anything but a sign that his main focus was on his own pleasure, like the spoiled son I often saw him to be. In spite of my resentment, however, I didn't say anything to him. I didn't want him to know how deeply hurt I felt. So although I suffered, I just kept it to myself.

I took one month off for maternity leave. Upon my return to work I was summoned to the dean's office. I was told that, should I have another baby, I wouldn't get a paid maternity leave, but a leave of absence without pay. Such was Cornell University Medical College's attitude to junior faculty women in 1951.

After Christopher's birth, Hilary insisted that I stop using lengthy and tiresome public transportation and learn to drive. I got a driver's license and bought a car. Quickly, I learned the technique of New York City taxi drivers — swinging right and left to make my way between the cars in dense traffic. Later I became aware that being my passenger was a dangerous and scary experience. *Nobody* liked to drive with me.

Bronislawa, on whom I had been counting to help me take care of the baby, developed gall bladder disease shortly after Christopher's birth. She often was in pain and unable to look after him. As a result, before I returned to work, I hired Eleanor, a sixteen-year-old girl, to help us. Eleanor told me that she knew how to handle babies because she took care of her baby brother who, as I later found out, was her own child, born out of wedlock. She did indeed know how to take care of babies, and took good care of Christopher, but when I asked her to help me with domestic chores I was disappointed. When it came to housework, she was lazy and a poor worker. I had to leave much of our housework undone or do it myself.

One evening, when Christopher was barely three months old, Hilary said, "Come with me to Kenya, Irena. This is going to be a truly interesting trip to a continent that we don't know."

As in the past, Hilary wanted me to share with him the opportunity to discover unknown countries. My jealousy of Gail hadn't completely disappeared, although I tried to justify Hilary's insensitivity towards me by his love of music and unwillingness to waste a subscription ticket. Yet this evidence of his renewed interest in me made me feel better.

I wondered if and to what extent Hilary's apparent fascination with Gail Theis had decreased, how strong it had been to begin with, and if it could just have been male pride to be seen in the company of a beautiful woman. As in all situations when I was jealous because of Hilary's flirting behavior, I never found the answer to my question.

"I wish I could come with you, Hilary, but Christopher is too small a baby to be left without me for several weeks," I replied sadly.

Hilary's trip wasn't only going to be fascinating from a sightseeing point of view. He went to test a new poliomyelitis vaccine that he had developed on chimpanzees. (See the appendix for a summary of Hilary's work on polio.) To accomplish this, he was going to be away for several weeks.

When Christopher was six months old, Gail Theis invited Hilary and me to what was dubbed as a rock and roll party at her parents' house. Hilary told me about this invitation at the last moment. Though the feeling had diminished since the day when Hilary took her out to a concert, leaving me at home with our recently born baby, I was still jealous of Gail's beauty and Hilary's obvious infatuation with her.

I had no idea what a rock and roll party was like or how to dress. Although Hilary usually cared much about my appearance, every now and then, for no particular reason, he neglected to advise me about the proper attire for a given occasion. This was one such occasion. I went in an elegant British-made suit Hilary's father bought me in London. Everybody else was wearing jeans, and I felt very much out of place. There was also a lot of drinking, to which I wasn't accustomed. After three or four whiskeys I threw up, had to lie down, and fell asleep while Hilary danced and had fun with his technicians. He was a popular and sociable person, liked to be with people, and enjoyed parties much more than I ever did. I felt particularly ill at ease with people I hardly knew, and Hilary did nothing to help me. My social discomforts and shyness went back to my isolation in childhood. When I grew up, I had often wished I were different. However, my social reticence apparently bothered Hilary in some way. Although we never discussed it, after this rock and roll party Hilary didn't ask me to accompany him to any other party for a long time to come. This also made me unhappy, but I was too proud to fight it.

I resumed my diagnostic responsibility for Pap smears and lymph node research as soon as I returned to work from my one month maternity leave. With Eleanor looking after Christopher and doing some house-cleaning, and with Hilary's mother still cooking our dinners, I was able to spend long days at the laboratory. Added to that, with my growing ability to recognize single cancer cells and Hilary's established interest in neurotropic viruses (viruses causing diseases of the nervous system) Hilary asked me to join him in an experimental study, although we were working at different institutions. The purpose of our experiments was to discover whether any of those viruses would kill cancer cells. It was part of a new approach in the field of anti-cancer therapy at the time. He began sending me the ascites tumor-bearing mice (that is, mice in which cancer cells grow in abdominal fluids) that he had infected with different viruses, and I would aspirate their abdominal fluids and look for cancer cells.

We were both keenly interested in the outcome of this study, during which Hilary was often away at meetings because he had already become an international figure. So I was the one who mainly dealt with his technicians, supervising them and helping them carry out the details of these experiments. Hilary and I made different, but comparably important, contributions to this research. He conceived the idea of the study, and I judged its results at the microscope. We had no reason to argue. This was one of the few aspects of our life where there was no contention. We collaborated beautifully and rarely argued about science. Our discussions were interesting and never disagreeable. I became very excited when I found out that some viruses did destroy cancer cells. But after Hilary and I published the results of our study, and attempts were made to cure human cancer with these viruses at Memorial Hospital for Cancer and Allied Diseases in New York, we learned—as too often has been the case in cancer treatment research—that the most effective cancer-killing viruses were also lethal to patients. So we failed to find a cure for cancer.

I was just beginning my own experimental research in 1952 with work on mouse ascites tumor and with the study of lymph node imprints. The same year, to help my career move ahead, Hilary arranged for me to present the results of our attempts to use viruses to kill cancer cells at the annual meeting of the Federation of Societies for Experimental Biology and Medicine. Hilary placed himself in the front row, which gave me confidence that he did it not only because he was co-author, but in support of me.

This being my first public presentation of my own research, I still recall how frightened I was when I began to speak. I was afraid I would do a poor job, discredit myself and embarrass Hilary. I thought my legs wouldn't be able to support my weight. But as I proceeded with my talk, I became so involved that I forgot my fears. When I finished, Hilary came up to congratulate me on my "excellent presentation." I knew I had done well and felt happy and proud of myself, but his acknowledgment made me feel even better.

Despite my burgeoning career, I continued my private work at night in my basement laboratory examining Pap smears sent to me by local physicians, a private practice I had started when I worked at the New York Infirmary in order to supplement my income.

Hilary's father came from England to visit us almost every year. Whenever he did, I was always glad to see him, but invariably he quarreled with Sofia Semeonovna about money. I soon came to understand more than I had in England when he had complained to me about her financial demands. Realizing that in the event of his death, his wife would inherit his money and could then do with it as she pleased, he initiated divorce proceedings upon his return to England.

Although from the moment Christopher was born my family life demanded more attention from me, my enthusiasm for my work was not diminished. I still got a thrill preaching Papanicolaou's gospel, and continued to do it with the same enthusiasm as I had before, in spite of his criticism of my independence. But I also was growing more and more excited pursuing my own experimental research. All this was an expected and healthy sign of my growing expertise and commitment to my profession.

In 1951 my younger brother Gabriel, who had then received an American immigration visa, graduated from McGill University with a B.A. and came to spend the summer in Englewood with us. Having Gabriel and Bronislawa with us made me more aware of all the changes that had occurred in my life since my visit to them three years before in Stocksund. I had stepped into the shoes of my late father and became the head of the family.

I was proud of these achievements, just as I was of my own professional success. I had a prestigious fellowship at one of the best medical schools in the country, I loved my work and, above all, my sons were a source of incomparable joy. Things still were tense on the domestic front. The two mothers caused difficulties because of their poor relationship and, in spite of our gratifying scientific collaboration, Hilary and I had only a very uneasy peace. But with my other accomplishments and successes, I was able to withstand these problems. I could set them aside, maybe bury them for the while. They were there and they caused me pain, but they just didn't loom quite as large as before.

In the fall, Gabriel went to Boston to do graduate work in political science at Harvard. He met there and fell in love with Dessie Dêchennes, one of his classmates, and brought her to visit us as his fiancée. Dessie's mother was a New Englander, and her father was a French Canadian. She and Gabriel had very different backgrounds. Bronislawa was distressed by Gabriel's plans to marry, but Hilary and I persuaded her to let Gabriel decide how to live his life.

I was glad that Gabriel had found a companion. I knew she would help him adjust more easily to his new life in the United States. They married in February 1952.

India

In 1952, the same year that Gabriel married, the World Health Organization (WHO) organized an international workshop on rabies. It was to be held in Coonor, a hill town in southern India. Hilary, along with several other members of their Expert Committee on Rabies, taught this course. "This time you *must* come with me, Irena," Hilary said.

I couldn't resist this opportunity. I was happy he wanted me to be with him and also looked with excitement on the chance to travel to a country I had never seen. I was sorry having had to turn down his two previous invitations—his trips to Brazil and to Kenya— so now, without the constraints of advanced pregnancy and a newborn infant, I was thrilled to finally be free to say yes.

This invitation came on the heels of the memorable rock and roll party at Gail's house. I still hadn't forgotten it. But things were changing in my life and in my attitude towards Hilary. I had finally realized that I wasn't going to change him. He didn't behave towards me in the way I wanted him to, but I knew that he cared about me deeply, was very supportive of my career, and was a good father. I was pleased he still valued and enjoyed my company.

It was clear that he wanted to have a somewhat separate life of his own rather than to conform to the more traditional pattern of togetherness more often seen in married couples, and one I had expected. He felt comfortable going about his own business and not always sharing his thoughts with me. Sometimes he would make plans to travel with me, and I would hear about it first from someone else before he told me! His mind was so full of thoughts that he forgot to let me know that he intended to include me in his plans. I realized this after many years of marriage. He preferred talking to me about interesting books he read, and he often urged me to read them. At other times I would find out about what he had read by listening to his conversations with other people.

Often when he would go out alone, I felt lonely, deprived of his companionship. Finally I learned not to reproach him and to use the time I had to myself for writing scientific papers. In all this, I had changed. I found satisfaction in the stability of our relationship, which had grown over the years. I had come almost full circle from where I had been on these matters as a very young wife, when a picture of such a marriage was not at all what I had in mind. But I felt that I had changed with my own personal development and my expanded role in the family, and my successful professional life. And, besides, I discovered that as I reproached him less about things that made me unhappy, the kinder and more thoughtful he became towards me.

I was entering a new phase of my life, one that was better suited to conserving energy for my work and preserving a marriage to a man I cared about deeply. My attitude was that this was a wonderful chance to see an unknown and mysterious continent together with Hilary, and to feel wanted by him. So before going to India, all that remained for me to do was to deal with a few obstacles that had cropped up on the home front.

Christopher's pediatrician felt that, at the age of one, he was still too small to be without his mother for several weeks. And Bronislawa didn't like being left in charge of his care. But I was now a far more experienced mother and did not share the pediatrician's exaggerated concern about leaving a child for a few weeks without me. I saw Bronislawa's complaints as evidence of her general unhappiness, for which I had sympathy but over which I simply had no control. She would only be alone with Christopher at night, and Eleanor was doing the everyday chores involved in the care of a baby of Christopher's age. So, assured that no one would be unduly put out and that Christopher would be cared for just fine, I decided to go to India.

Claude was spending his summer vacation at l'Ecole Nouvelle de Châtaigneraie in Switzerland where we expected him to learn French. But as we found out later he roomed there with Fazl, a boy from

India, and they spoke English all the time. Sofia Semeonovna kept very much to herself, avoiding Bronislawa, and not participating in the care of Christopher. She made it clear to us that she had already fulfilled her grandmotherly obligations taking care of Claude and that it was Bronislawa's turn to look after our younger son.

India was the first Asian country we had ever visited. When we arrived in Bombay, we checked in at the Taj Mahal — an old-fashioned Indian hotel, which we found strange and uncomfortable. With no air conditioning we had a hard time falling asleep during the hot and humid nights. The big ceiling fans they had, instead of cooling, just moved stale air around. The top parts of the doors were cut out for ventilation, but with no cool air their main effect was to let in the noise of other hotel guests and servants moving about the hallways. All night long we heard the patter of barefooted people walking in the hall and their whispers in a language that we didn't understand. These sounds, and the fact that there were no locks on the doors, gave us no sense of peace or privacy.

On the first morning we were there, when I sat on the toilet in our bathroom, a man walked in without knocking at the door and offered me a cup of tea. At first, I was astounded and embarrassed, but from his demeanor I quickly sensed that this was his duty, and I wasn't supposed to mind or pay any attention to his presence, nor he to what I was doing.

The next evening we had dinner at the house of a local Lederle representative, who drove us back to our hotel. Through the windows of the car, we could see many people sleeping on the sidewalks. Before the street lights went off at midnight, we caught a glimpse of a man leaning against the lamp post; he had been reading. When the lights went out, he closed his book, stretched out, and went to sleep on the sidewalk.

Everywhere in the street there were red stains from the betel nuts, which Indians chew and then spit. I first thought that they were spitting blood. I was quite overwhelmed by the extreme poverty I saw virtually everywhere I went, and I wondered if any attempts to improve the lot of the enormous population of India could possibly have any chance to succeed. The longer we were there, the more compassion we felt for the enormity of human suffering to which we had so suddenly been exposed.

The World Health Organization, which thus far had been primarily concerned with the control of infectious diseases, mainly in the undeveloped countries of the world, had begun to consider programs to control cancer because new epidemiological data indicated that certain types of cancer, such as cancer of the womb, had been quite common in India. Because of this, while Hilary was busy with the preparation for the workshop on rabies, Dr. Khanolkar, an outstanding tumor pathologist and director of the Tata Memorial Cancer Institute in Bombay, asked me to give a lecture there on the early detection of cancer by Papanicolaou's method. After my presentation, which had been well received by an audience who asked me many questions, Dr. Khanolkar invited me to submit a paper based on my lecture to *The Indian Journal of Medical Sciences*, of which he was the chief editor.

From Bombay we flew to Coonor, the small town in southern India where the workshop on rabies was to be held. Upon our arrival in the hotel room, Hilary left me to unpack and change for dinner while he went to meet with members of the workshop organizing committee. I had been looking forward to freshening up and relaxing when I heard a swishing sound of wings and saw a bat fly into the room through an open window. I froze in fear and placed myself flat against the wall waiting for the creature to fly out of the window. But an hour later, there I was, still standing motionless while the bat was furiously flying above my head, hitting the walls around me with its wings. When Hilary returned, he chased it out and we had to rush to be on time for dinner.

The specter of poverty that first hit us in Bombay followed us throughout India. "A local woman has just thrown herself with her starving children into a well," Hilary reported on our way to dinner. Thinking about the despair of a mother killing herself and her children because she had no food for them was so depressing that it made me feel guilty, looking forward to eating our meal. It was hard to deal with these feelings.

Dr. Pierre Lepine, from the Pasteur Institute in Paris who, like us, was in India on his way to the workshop on rabies, would, whenever he was with us for a meal, watch over our diet. He wanted to make sure that we wouldn't get sick eating raw salads and fruits, or any milk products. When chocolate profiteroles topped with whipped cream were served for dessert, Pierre Lepine pushed his plate away with disgust. "I told you not to serve us any cream," he reminded the waiter, who took Lepine's plate back to the kitchen.

But the waiter left the door open, and through it we could see him licking the cream from the cake. When he finished, he brought the very same profiteroles back and placed them in front of Pierre. "Here's your dessert without cream," he said.

In Coonor, the children were dying of Kwashiorkor, which is a form of liver cirrhosis that results from starvation, and different from liver cirrhosis associated with alcoholism and with certain viral infections in well-fed populations. When my professional identity became known at the local medical association in Coonor, I was invited to lecture on the early diagnosis of cancer by single cells. As I saw these children sick with Kwashiorkor, I couldn't help but wonder how many of them would live long enough to develop cancer.

At the conclusion of the workshop on rabies, we were invited by the governor of the province to a lavish garden party. The next day Hilary and I went off on a sight-seeing adventure. Near Coonor was an area where the rich tropical vegetation had been preserved. This virgin territory, called Mudumalai, was a tropical forest with wildlife sanctuaries and provisions for visitors to take guided elephant trips through its terrain. There were no roads, and the elephants carved their way through the jungle by using their trunks to pull out trees, one at a time. The sounds of the birds were heard everywhere. Our guides saw to it that we moved in the right direction, as we managed to emerge back into civilization, although we were almost eaten up alive by the insects. It was an amazing experience.

After returning to Coonor, we visited the huts of the Toda people—a nearby hunter's community of which only several hundred people still remained. This primitive tribe killed most of their newborn girls so that males would predominate. When the men were away hunting, the women stayed in the huts polishing cooking pots and oiling their hair. Because they were less numerous than men, each had to live conjugally not only with her husband, but also with his brothers.

I recall our visit to Bengalor where we met the physicist, Sir C.V. Raman, who in 1930 became a Nobel Prize laureate for discovering what has come to be called the "Raman effect." This effect is elicited by splitting light rays passing through crystals. His research was done in an institute established for Sir Raman by a friendly Maharajah and equipped with semiprecious stones for his studies. Carrying a big bunch of keys, Sir Raman took us in the middle of the night to visit his totally deserted institute. He and Hilary enjoyed talking to each other while I admired the display of gems.

The next morning we were to leave Bengalor, and the famous man offered to see us off. "Would you like to know the secret of how I got the Nobel Prize?" he asked Hilary at the airport. Then without waiting for an answer, he continued, "I found out that a scientist from eastern Europe was about to publish a discovery similar to my own. I then telegraphed my paper to the British scientific magazine, *Nature,* so that it would be received and thus hopefully printed first." I was surprised that he not only shared this amazing bit of information with us, but that he shouted the story in Hilary's ear so loudly that everybody could hear.

We were amazed by his shrewdness. Years later I actually traced the publication of his discovery which he had telegraphed to *Nature* and a long paper later published by his competitor, another European scientist, in a different scientific journal. I could not help imagining that with his habit of working at night at his own institute, Sir Raman might have spent a good part of a night waiting for the opening of the telegraph office to be the first one to cable his discovery.

After leaving Bengalor we flew to Iran, where we were lavishly entertained in Tehran at the home of a wealthy Iranian, Mr. Khosrowshaki, whose son had worked with Hilary at Lederle Laboratories in Pearl River, New York, and arranged this visit for us. There was a long road from the main entrance gate to the mansion itself. That road, though outdoors, was covered with Persian rugs. After reaching the mansion we were received outdoors first on the front terrace where snacks were offered. Then we were invited indoors to a thirteen-course banquet, which for me was torture to consume, since I managed to develop a gastrointestinal upset towards the end of our visit in India.

Old Mr. Khosrowshaki sat at the head of the table flanked by his seven sons. Neither his wife nor any of the daughters-in-law were present. Following Moslem tradition, the old man wouldn't let the women of his family be seen by male visitors. The wife of the American cultural attaché was the only woman aside from me who attended this banquet. She and I were received with courtesy as the wives of invited guests. The absence of the other women made me feel very odd and uncomfortable. I felt disloyal to them, sitting there with their husbands in their absence. I asked several times if I might go to the women's quarters to meet our hostess and to thank her for this magnificent feast. Each time I was told that she would join us later, which she never did.

According to Iranian custom, we were expected to leave immediately after dinner so as not to appear that we were still hungry. As soon as our thirteenth plate was empty, we departed, carrying with us two small Persian carpets, a farewell gift from our host.

Stops at the market and the Pasteur Institute, the director of which was French and a member of the W.H.O. Expert Committee on Rabies, completed our visit to Tehran. The visit at the Pasteur Institute was interesting because it gave us an insight into the extent to which Iranians depended upon the French to run things efficiently. They feared what would happen to the facility when they took it under their own direction. Seeing the market had been a fascinating experience in a different way because of their displays of turquoise stones, famous Persian rugs, and Russian samovars.

Our trip to India and Iran was really the first time we had spent several weeks together sharing new experiences. Removed from our own daily life at home and at work, we had then a sample of a normal life that other married people have. No wonder I liked it so much and also that I realized that upon our return it wouldn't continue in the same way.

On the way back from Iran we stopped at Rome, and my feeling of leading a separate life from Hilary returned briefly when, straight from the airport, inexhaustible Hilary went alone to see a magnificent performance of "Aida" with real elephants on the stage. I refused to attend, exhausted because of the diarrhea that already had bothered me in Iran.

When we returned, we again had to face the usual mundane difficulties of our everyday life. Fortunately, we found Christopher in satisfactory condition, and Bronislawa complaining as usual but about nothing really important. We had arranged Claude's return from Switzerland to coincide with our own homecoming. Soon thereafter, new problems at home became apparent. My mother-in-law was no longer able to control Claude. For example, she couldn't stop his wild bicycle racing next to the busy highway that ran right in front of our house in Englewood. We decided that, for his safety as much as for the sake of a good education, we ought to send him away to Lawrenceville, a Princeton prep school.

Until the recent arrival of his baby brother, Claude was the center of attention at our house, and we had not prepared him for living away with a group of other boys. Once at Lawrenceville, he missed home and telephoned every day to talk to us. Since he had to talk from a public room and couldn't complain about his life at school as much as he wanted without being heard, he found a useful solution to this problem. "Please, speak only Polish to me," he pleaded with us. His native tongue, rejected firmly ever since his arrival in the United States so he could be like other boys, returned to him promptly, and he has retained it ever since. His insistence on speaking Polish may also have expressed his wish to identify with us and to return home. We of course visited him at Lawrenceville almost every weekend. Claude's housemaster became a marvelous surrogate parent for him, and he taught Claude a lot about getting along with people, which he hadn't had much opportunity to learn in our household. In spite of missing home and resenting being away, Claude ended up enjoying Lawrenceville.

But I never knew how Claude felt during parental visits at school. He was amongst a minority of students whose parents had never divorced and had only one parent visiting them on respective "Father's" and "Mother's" days. A large number of boys had their step-parents in addition to their biological parents visiting them. Sometimes I wondered if he did not feel deprived.

Once Claude was settled and I was back at work, I wrote the article based on my lecture in Bombay as Dr. Khanolkar had requested. This paper was about how cancer of the womb, lung, stomach, urinary bladder, and other sites of the human body can be diagnosed from cells in body fluids and secretions. When I showed this paper to Dr. Papanicolaou, he read it and said, "It's a good contribution."

His praise pleased me, but given what I had seen emerging in his attitude towards my developing career, this instance of approval didn't really surprise me. In the paper I was presenting mainly what I had learned from him, and not the results of my independent research. With both sadness and resentment I doubted that he would have praised me if the paper had reflected the original research I was involved in. Even though my new and independent work was based on the methods developed by Pap, it was moving beyond what he had done. Thus, my original work could easily have and really should have been a source of pride for Dr. Pap. But it seemed that when he couldn't direct it, he felt undermined. And what lay ahead proved this weakness of his even more.

Not long thereafter, a new organization of physicians and technicians interested in the propagation of the Pap smear method was established. It was called the Inter-Society Cytology Council, and its first session was held in Philadelphia in November 1952. Every one of us who worked with Dr. Papanicolaou attended. I neither knew ahead of time who had organized the meeting, nor had I seen the program. This was typical of my ignorance about the professional politics associated with my work and career—I never even thought to make any inquires about such matters. I thus had no idea that there would be several presentations of papers from our laboratory, all of them by people working under Dr. Papanicolaou's direction, and since Dr. Pap was one of the organizers, there was little doubt that their invitations to speak were initiated by him. I, however, would learn that I had not been included.

When I arrived at the conference and finally saw the program, I became furious. I realized that he had excluded me from presenting the results of the research I was doing in his lab. There just was no way around it. I should have been given an opportunity to present the results of my independent research at this important professional forum. Not inviting me to participate was another instance of his inappropriate jealousy and intolerance of any research I did that wasn't completely under his aegis and direction.

I swallowed my tears as I sat in a big convention hall listening to the presentations of Jack Seybolt, Doris Holmquist, and others from our laboratory. It was more than I could take. My indignation built. I couldn't stand the tension. Somehow I had to make known the work I had been doing, despite Dr. Pap's considerable efforts to prevent me from doing so.

The moment the chairman of the session asked if anybody in the audience wished to speak, I raised my hand. I was given the floor. I took this opportunity to speak about my experiments. I described how I was preparing Pap smears using the abdominal fluid of mice to study the effect on cancer cells of the viruses with which these mice were infected. I was proud and aware that my research, unlike the other work presented at this meeting, was not limited to studies concerned with cells seen in human secretions but that it instead dealt with experimental studies in animals.

At first the audience was surprised, but after I finished people began to ask questions and make comments. Unfortunately, though, there wasn't much time for discussion. But the lack of discussion time didn't matter. I had gotten across two things: the ideas that were at the core of my work, and the fact that I existed and was doing something important which was related to Pap's work but moving beyond it. By the time I finished speaking, my anger was replaced by a feeling of relief. I had succeeded in making my studies known to other people, and in so doing I felt I had begun to establish my very existence as a scientist.

Following this meeting, I gave two formal papers at the annual meetings of the New York Academy of Sciences and the Federation of the Societies of Experimental Biology and Medicine. Hilary had joined these two societies some years before, but I had not. Therefore, I asked him to introduce my papers. Their presentation turned out to be a very important moment in my career. Following this event, I became recognized as an independent cancer researcher.

While this was just what I wanted and what I believed my work now deserved, it added more fuel to the fire of Dr. Pap's resistance to my further experimental work. My work paid homage to Dr. Pap by substantially increasing the usefulness of his methodology. However, after that 1952 meeting of the Inter-Society Cytology Council, my admiration of Papanicolaou as my mentor was severely diminished.

Still, I continued to carry out the responsibilities I had for Dr. Papanicolaou's cytology laboratory, just as I had before, with the same care and loyalty. But I also pursued my chosen path of research, my joint project with Hilary on the effect of viruses on cancer. After completing this project, I began to investigate the gradual development of chemically produced cancer of the womb in mice. I had induced cancer of the womb in mice with chemicals and examined their vaginal Pap smears in order to discover when cancer cells acquired their characteristic appearance and behavior. I was hoping that this would facilitate an earlier recognition, and possibly the prevention of cancer of the womb in women.

In 1952 I began to examine the Pap smears of mice each week, as they developed cancer and ultimately died of cancer of the womb. In contrast to my collaborative studies with Hilary, this research was being done with Dr. Pap's greater approval, and even support for it from his grant. Still, he had his reservations about it and one day asked me, "Why do you have to work with mice? It's a pity, because we know so much more about guinea pigs."

I was surprised and annoyed by his remark because his reason for the use of "we" was that *he* knew more about guinea pigs than about mice because years earlier he had studied the sexual cycle of these animals, studies that took place before he had become interested in cancer. So again, in his imperious way, he now wanted me to use guinea pigs simply because he had used them.

"Dr. Pap, I can't work with guinea pigs because they rarely develop cancer. But it's very easy to induce cancer in mice," I responded.

After this, he showed no further interest in the progress of my research. He could see I wouldn't bend to his wishes to keep me foolishly under his strict control. He actually had begun to realize that my independent work wasn't based on any gratuitous effort to rebel or separate from him, but out of the same spirit of scientific curiosity and inquiry that motivated his work. I had removed any illusion that I would only do work under his direction. I had a hard time shaking my bitter disappointment that he, the man I so admired, my mentor, wasn't proud of my professional growth and independent achievements in cancer research, that he did nothing to advance my career, and even appeared envious of my success. So now I rarely sought him out to discuss the progress of my research. I realized there was simply no point.

Despite this sad turn in my relationship with Dr. Pap, my independent research as well as the general respect for the work I had done in close conjunction with him were being greeted with more and more acknowledgment and respect in the wider scientific community.

I had been invited to join several prestigious national and international scientific societies. I no longer needed a sponsor to submit my papers for presentation at meetings.

As my professional recognition grew, life at home was going through important changes. Bronislawa's presence in the household, the impressive development of Hilary's and my professional lives, the easing of our marital tensions (which made Hilary far less accessible to Sofia Semeonovna and to her control), and Claude's departure to prep school all had a diminishing impact on the importance of Sofia's role in our home. I was able to realize that, without her help, I probably would not have been able to become as successful as I had. But with her diminished role, Sofia began to reformulate her relationship to us. She no longer had reason to live with us. She now felt her presence to be unnecessary. What was left of her grandmotherly duties could and should be handled by Bronislawa. Her only remaining function in the household was being the family cook. One day, when Hilary started to complain about the monotony of our dinner menus, that was too much for her to take.

"If you don't like the way I run the house, you can do it yourself from now on. Here's your household money. I'm through," she called down a few moments later and she dropped her purse from the top of the staircase onto the floor of the hall. Holding the purse strings keeps people in a position of power, which Sofia Semeonovna relinquished by her symbolic gesture.

Sofia Departs

Throwing her purse down the stairs was my mother-in-law's way of relinquishing her remaining family responsibility, that of the much depended-upon family chef. At first I took her leaving the cooking chores to me as a punishment for Hilary's recent criticism of her meals. And it was a penalty, since I neither knew how nor had the time to cook. I did not then understand the full meaning of her gesture. Therefore, Sofia Semeonovna's sudden announcement of her departure several weeks later took me by surprise.

I had been totally unaware that she had been thinking for a year or more about going back to Europe. In fact, she already had begun preparations for her travel. I am certain that she had discussed her plans with Hilary because she needed his help to organize and pay for her travel. I resented being left unaware of all this.

Although I was concerned about my unexpected new cooking responsibilities, I was glad that I finally would become the mistress of my own home—which I never really was as long as Sofia was in the house. It wasn't only because of my ambition to assume a leadership position in our household that I was relieved to see my mother-in-law leave. It was mainly because of the suffering to which Sofia Semeonovna had subjected me and my long-standing resentment of her dominance over Hilary. I couldn't help but wonder if she might not have left had I behaved more warmly toward her and been less bothered by her presence over the years. However, my prediction of a grim future for her was quite unwarranted.

Hilary's mother went to France and settled in Nice, where many of her old acquaintances lived and where she enjoyed the company of other Polish and Russian emigrants like herself. She didn't seem to worry about how she would support herself. She knew that Hilary would help her as long as she lived, and she was right.

In spite of my complex feelings at the time of Sofia Semeonovna's departure, I had to address the immediate problem of who would prepare the family meals. I couldn't turn to Bronislawa, whose preparation of bland meals would have no appeal to Hilary, so I hired a housekeeper who cooked for us. One day this woman put me to shame. She said that if I had the intelligence to become a doctor, I should be able to learn what any uneducated woman knows — how to cook. I never forgot the rationality of her words, and I began to prepare family meals on and off.

My father-in-law, who continued visiting us at least every other year, knew from Hilary's letters that Sofia had left us, and he perceived that a new challenge lay ahead of me. While still in Europe, he hired a Swiss housekeeper for us and paid her way to the United States. "She is an excellent cook and loves children," he told me. "She will keep your house clean, and you will be able to carry on your own work with more ease. This is too much for you, Irena. You need this help if you are going to have the energy and freedom to pursue your career as before."

I listened to him, uncertain how his arrangements would work out for us. But I was then in a very difficult situation. Eleanor wasn't taking care of the house and only minded Christopher. Bronislawa, who wasn't much used to doing housework herself, developed inflammation of the gall bladder. The woman I had hired to cook for us wasn't very satisfactory and gave us notice. Fortunately, when twenty-eight-year-old Hedy Erni arrived, I realized within the first few days what a help she would be to me. And happily, Christopher took to her immediately. So I stopped trying to acquire cooking skills after putting in a full day's work, and I parted company with Eleanor without shedding tears.

One day Christopher started limping and was diagnosed as having a mild case of Legg-Perthés disease. This rare condition results from a poor blood supply to the small vessels of a hip joint. We went from one physician to another at leading New York institutions, and they all recommended various forms of immobilization.

We acquired a television to help keep him still, and Hedy was very resourceful at keeping Christopher entertained in bed. But in spite of her efforts, this vivacious child became sad and apathetic. Dealing with this change was very distressing. I took him for consultation to the New York Hospital for Special Surgery where I had the traumatic experience of seeing many handicapped children in carriages or walking with the help of various orthopedic devices. I had visions of Chris becoming like one of them. But after returning with Christopher from our visit at the Hospital for Special Surgery where they still insisted on his immobilization, Hilary and I decided to seek advice elsewhere.

I flew with Christopher to Boston to see Dr. Greene, a pediatrician who objected to the immobilization of children with this condition. He looked at Christopher and told him to walk.

"There's nothing wrong with him. Don't restrain this child," he told me. From that day on Christopher stopped limping, and I was relieved of an anxiety that I had lived with for a year. In retrospect Hilary and I felt rather critical of the New York and Philadelphia physicians' approach to Christopher's treatment. We could never understand why they insisted that keeping him active which was bound to provide a better blood supply to his affected hip joint was not more likely to promote healing of a small lesion he had there than immobilizing him.

We would always bring Claude home for the weekends during his grandfather's visits. Surprised at seeing television at home, he reproached us for having bought it for Christopher. Claude reminded us that he never had a TV and he had to go to a friend's house across the street to watch it. He did not realize that we had bought one for Christopher because during his period of lameness we believed that Christopher needed to be kept in bed at all cost. We ourselves had no habit of watching TV and there was no compelling reason why we should have purchased one for Claude.

My father-in-law felt that Claude needed more discipline than he was getting in our household and would assign various chores to him. He would tell Claude to cut the grass in the summer and shovel the snow from our driveway in winter. Claude, who didn't want to do it but feared his grandfather's anger, always managed to gather neighborhood kids and convince them to do his work for him. Like Tom

Sawyer, he merely supervised their performance. I don't know what arguments he used to make them work, but they did. His grandfather was annoyed that Claude didn't perform these chores himself and yet he had to be impressed by Claude's managerial skills.

Since my father's death I had been the head of my blood family— Bronislawa, Gabriel, Gene, and myself—so I watched with interest the progress of the education of my half-brothers. After receiving his Bachelor of Arts degree from McGill University in Montreal, Gabriel obtained a Master's degree in political science at Harvard in 1953, the same year that Claude entered Lawrenceville School and my mother-in-law moved to Nice. Being a bookworm by nature, Gabriel took additional courses in library science and eventually became a librarian, first at Harvard University and then at the University of Massachusetts.

Bronislawa still lived with us. During her gall bladder operation in 1953 at New York Hospital, the attending physician arranged for me to be present during her surgery. "Gene, where are you now? I love you so much," I heard her moaning, as she was falling asleep during the anesthesia. Listening to these words was painful to me. Here I was, taking care of Bronislawa in every way: financially, medically, and emotionally. But my efforts weren't enough for her. She still missed Gene, who could neither help her nor be with her now. I felt guilty for feeling such resentment because I realized, of course, that Gene would have been more a comfort to her than I was.

Bronislawa recuperated slowly after surgery.

Other important events occurred in 1953. Gene presented himself for his Master's degree at McGill. After an hour of grueling questions, the examiners told him that his performance was so outstanding that they accepted it for a Ph.D. rather than for a Master's degree. When Gene was in Montreal writing his doctoral thesis, Bronislawa finally recovered from her surgery. Missing her sons, she went to Boston to stay with Gabriel and Dessie. There she was a lot closer to Montreal, which meant she also could see Gene more often.

In the midst of all these family events, there also were indications of an increasing recognition of my own scientific efforts. Unlike the first meeting of the Inter-Society Cytology Council (when my formal participation had been blocked but where, through my strong determination, I found a way to participate instead of just attending the conference), at this second year's meeting in 1953, I was asked by the organizing committee to contribute a paper. Dr. Pap wasn't able to attend this particular meeting because he had the flu, but in spite of his physical absence, I made his spiritual presence felt in a rather funny way, which I can't resist describing.

The membership of this scientific organization had increased, as had the familiarity of the members with a variety of cells exfoliated from the lining of human cavities. Listening to the formal presentation of Dr. S. from Cleveland, who projected on the screen the picture of atypical but not cancerous cells he had seen in sputum and observed in respiratory secretions of several alcoholics, I became annoyed. He had not conducted any control studies and had attributed presence of these cells to drinking alcohol, as if this could be the only thing capable of causing enough irritation to result in the appearance of such atypical cells. His presentation had upset me over and beyond a justifiable criticism of his conclusions.

"Is there any discussion of Dr. S.'s paper?" the session chairman asked the audience.

"I would like to make a comment," I said, picking up the nearest microphone. "The cells just shown by Dr. S. have often been seen in Dr. Pap's laboratory in the sputum smears of patients with inflammatory conditions associated with infections and exposure to irritants. We used to call them Pap cells because they were first observed in the sputum smears of Dr. Pap himself at a time when he had a Chronic Bronchitis. Certainly exposure to alcohol, among other causes, could also lead to the formation of such atypical cells."

My point had been made. I needed to say no more. But scientific truth, it turns out, was not all that was now motivating me, no matter how correct and appropriate it was to have made the point I did. I realized that my colleagues with a good sense of humor could not fail to perceive how emotionally involved I had become in defending Dr. Pap against any suspicion that he might have been an alcoholic, which nobody thought he was. I could feel everybody's eyes on me as I became red in the face. I overheard remarks loaded with irony and innuendo, suggesting that I was engaged in the defense of my idol. And I realized that some of my colleagues were highly amused by my performance.

"You wouldn't let anything nasty ever be said about Dr. Pap, would you, Irena?" Jack Frost, my colleague from Johns Hopkins, asked me, smiling, during the intermission.

This moment gave me a sudden insight into my filial devotion to Dr. Pap. Despite all his attempts to thwart my progress as an independent investigator, and despite all my resentment about his lack of support, I still felt protective of him. I now realized that Papanicolaou didn't impede my work out of malice. He acted more like a domineering parent who tries to keep his child close to him as long as possible. Although he wasn't my parent, he knew and I knew that he was a very influential force in my intellectual life, a very special mentor. It was complicated. I was his spiritual child, but like all children I had grown up. The connection was still one of reverence and deep respect, but with my coming of age I had to become his adult child, his colleague.

When Dr. Pap's retirement approached in 1953, I was convinced that I would make as good a director of his laboratory as anyone. Yet I did not declare my interest in the job because I was equally certain that I would not be offered the opportunity. I didn't want to fight a lost cause and I also hated to play the role of victim of sexism. Although I did believe that gender was part of the issue, I felt that more was involved in the choice of Papanicolaou's successor at Cornell.

Jack Seybolt was eventually chosen to succeed Pap as director of the laboratory, which by then had been renamed the Papanicolaou Cytology Laboratory. Jack was a real Milquetoast, but he was a male, an American, and a Cornell graduate. Seniority was also a factor in his choice. For all these reasons, I always knew that he would be chosen.

I was more qualified in terms of my scientific contributions than he and I knew that quite a number of my colleagues shared that opinion. The administration likely would not have supported my choice since I was a woman, an immigrant, and not a Cornell graduate. Dr. Pap himself had been discriminated against in the past because he was an immigrant—more reason why he wouldn't likely go against "the boys" at Cornell. He never said anything to me about the choice of Jack as his successor, and of course I never asked. However, I often wondered what he would have done had he realized that for years Jack Seybolt told anyone who would listen that the old man suffered from paranoia.

The decision had a considerable impact on my future at Cornell. After five years with Dr. Pap at Cornell, I was to be promoted from research fellow to research associate. But those were not tenure-track positions. Thus, without being named director of the lab, my chances for getting tenure were closed. So was any opportunity for future advancement at Cornell. Once I became aware of this situation, I began to think about exploring other opportunities.

In the summer of 1953 I went to the First International Cytology Congress with Hilary and Claude. We stopped in Nice to visit Hilary's mother and we brought her with us to Vienna. There was plenty of sightseeing to keep the three of them occupied while I attended selected scientific sessions.

Several weeks after the Congress in Vienna, I again went with Hilary to Europe, this time to Switzerland. We had dinner in Basel at the Kunsthaus Restaurant with his friend, the late Dr. Niels Jerne, an immunologist who was a Nobel Prize laureate. When we arrived Jerne, having already consumed most of two bottles of wine by himself, was in an ebullient mood. He and Hilary almost immediately became involved in a scientific discussion about the cellular mechanisms of body defenses and other immunological problems. Feeling excluded from their conversation since the subject was their area of great expertise, I let my thoughts drift. I recalled how I used to be haunted by pictures of the cells I saw when I began working in Dr. Papanicolaou's laboratory. During the day I could see them through the microscope, but at night their picture remained in front of my eyes. Some of these cells were discrete and isolated; other cells appeared in groups.

Groups of atypical but nonmalignant cells often form tight clusters in the presence of inflammatory conditions. One usually can observe cells wrapped around each other in these clusters of cells, detached from the sites of inflammation. Similar clusters of cells wrapped around each other but with abnormal large, darkly staining, irregular nuclei may be cancer cells, and these at times may be difficult to distinguish from clusters of nonmalignant cells associated with inflammation. Seeing the tightness of both kinds of clusters, I began to wonder whether any exchange of contents occurs between cells within these clusters and whether such an exchange may lead to the transformation of cells derived from sites of inflammation into cancer cells.

Suddenly, I became aware that Hilary and Jerne were talking about the activation of the body's defense mechanisms by cluster-forming cells. Listening to what they said, I felt a sudden need to ask Jerne the question that just came to my mind. "Could the cells lining the body cavities, which once detached often form clusters, induce changes in each other leading to their transformation into cancer cells? If so, they would be using mechanisms similar to those the cells of the immune system use in the fight against infections."

To Jerne, the great immunologist, deep in conversation with Hilary, my interruption was most annoying. "You're a very foolish woman, Mrs. Koprowski!" he said, paying no further attention to me.

I was crushed. Jerne obviously was not interested in being side-tracked from his talk with Hilary. I felt bad at the time that Hilary, in not defending me to Jerne, seemingly had been trying to show off in front of his much admired but rude friend and that he too resented my interruption of their conversation. But when we returned from Switzerland, Hilary described this incident to our sons, stressing the rudeness of his drunken friend. As often in our life, Hilary's attitude changed depending on whom he was talking with at the time.

With Sofia no longer living with us, and my growing comfort of being able to run the household with Hedy's expert help and superb cooking, I thought 1954 would be a more uneventful year for us. But an unexpected accident occurred that contradicted those expectations.

During my father-in-law's visit that year, he, Hilary, and I planned to meet for dinner in New York. My father-in-law appeared late. "Let's start eating, Irena. Hilary will be joining us later," he said.

My father-in-law didn't seem to have much appetite. It wasn't until after I had my dessert that he gently broke the news to me.

There was a minor problem in the house and Hilary may not be able to join us at all tonight," he said. "There's been a small fire."

In spite of the extreme delicacy with which my father-in-law prepared me for the bad news, I felt that my heart had stopped beating.

Apparently he, Christopher, and Hedy had been home when they began to smell smoke and discovered the fire. By the time Hilary returned home from work the fire engines were extinguishing it. Hilary's father agreed to meet me alone for dinner. He decided to delay breaking the news to me until after dinner to give me at least a chance to eat and rest a little after work before being told about it.

Actually, most of the damage to the house itself was from the water used to extinguish the fire. Our clothes and other items stored in closets and drawers became so impregnated by the odor of smoke that we couldn't use them anymore. But the house had not been destroyed and we could live there. According to the firemen, the fire most likely had been started by an unextinguished cigarette butt inadvertently thrown into a wastebasket. My father-in-law suggested that Christopher, who was then three years old, must have been playing with matches and that he was responsible for the fire. But Hedy Erni, who didn't smoke, and who was at home with him and Christopher when the fire was discovered, was very much annoyed by my father-in-law's suggestion and denied such a possibility. In the end, we were never able to find out what had happened.

The house was still smelling of smoke when Earl Ubell, a reporter from the *New York Herald Tribune,* called. He came to the house that very evening to interview Hilary about the live oral Polio vaccine, which he knew Hilary had developed. As we sat at the kitchen table, Hilary described the development of the vaccine, the credit for which had been increasingly connected with the names of Salk and Sabin.

Seeing Earl's intense interest in this story, we were looking forward to forthcoming press releases. But when not a word about it appeared in the newspapers, Hilary called him to find out what had happened to their interview. We deduced from his noncommittal reply that his story was not approved for publication. This was our first experience in the U.S. with what looked to us like press control.

After Ubell's visit I was finally able to address some of my professional problems.

When Dr. Papanicolaou retired later that year, he remained at Cornell, maintaining his office there, still supported by the previously awarded grants that had not expired as yet. He also received money from private consultations on Pap smears. But now, having my chances for career advancement blocked at Cornell, I had to plan my professional future. The issue was where to turn and whom to consult.

Fortunately, the person that I would have most wanted to turn to, Dr. Pap, was still available to help me. And, over the past months, some very noticeable improvement had taken place in my relationship with Dr. Pap.

With his retirement, possibly because he was still physically there in the same building but not in an administrative position to exercise any real power over me, things became easier still. My feeling of spiritual kinship with him returned. He still had a research grant from the National Cancer Institute and he continued to see to it that the cost of my research and salary were covered by it, just as they were before. As he became warmer towards me, I thus began to feel that he was genuinely concerned about my fate, and I knew I would be able to rely on him for recommendations and advice on how to move ahead with my career.

Leo Koss, a colleague of mine and prominent cytopathologist at the Memorial Hospital for Cancer and Allied Diseases, told me about an opening for an assistant professor of pathology at the State University of New York Downstate Medical College in Brooklyn.

The chairman of the department was Pat Fitzgerald, a fine researcher. He had received excellent training — from the Memorial Hospital for Cancer and Allied Diseases (connected to Sloan-Kettering Institute), where Sophie Spitz, my former boss from the New York Infirmary, was on the staff. Pat now was looking to fill a vacancy in his department at Downstate with a pathologist who was experienced in the use of Pap smears, so that he could provide this service for a large division of pulmonary diseases at King's County Hospital. In this part of their medical center, there was considerable interest in the application of the Pap smear technique to the early diagnosis of lung cancer. Since this was an area in which I had already published original research, I was virtually a perfect candidate for the position.

If I recall correctly, I went ahead and applied for this position. But when the job was offered to me, I didn't want to decide whether to accept it without the advantage of Dr. Pap's advice. I found him in his office at Cornell, where he came every day to carry on his work, very much as he had before he retired as director. When I told him about the position at Downstate his reaction was very positive, more so in fact than I ever anticipated. "Becoming a faculty member at

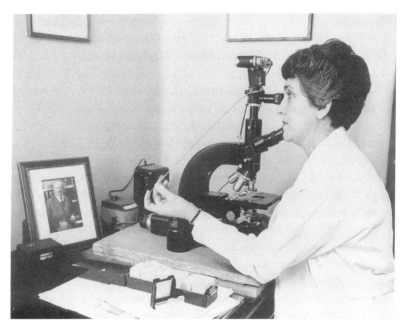

Irena at the microscope with a photograph of Dr. Papanicolaou in front of her (1954)

Downstate is a good career opportunity for you, Irena, and you and I will be able to have joint lung cancer research projects if you'll be there," he said.

Although I was glad he felt good about the position itself, I was especially surprised and happy on account of his unexpected state-ment about our collaboration. This was the first time that he had ever expressed interest in a scientific collaboration with me as a colleague. That was a prospect I found extremely appealing and was something I had wanted for a long time. Thus, I accepted the job with absolutely no hesitation at all—a decision I never regretted. And Pat Fitzgerald was one of the reasons for that. As it would turn out, Pat Fitzgerald was by far the easiest and most accommodating person I worked with in my entire career.

With my move to Downstate, Dr. Pap encouraged me to apply directly to the National Cancer Institute for support of my project, and this is the way I obtained my first research grant. On the day I left Cornell, I received several farewell gifts. These included a photograph of Dr. Pap on which he inscribed, "To Dr. Irena Koprowska. With affection and esteem, George N. Papanicolaou."

I was touched. Without thinking, I responded quite spontaneously, by saying, "Thank you, George." And with that I called him by his first name for the first time. What a wonderful way to end my association at Cornell, where it was George Papanicolaou who had been such a force in my life, so central to the entire direction of my career. And at last I now felt we were true friends and colleagues.

"I'll keep your photograph next to my microscope," I told him, "and whenever I have any doubts about whether I'm looking at cancer cells, I'll ask myself, What would Dr. Pap say?" I meant it. I still needed the illusion that he wasn't far from me and that, whenever I was in doubt, I could always direct my questions to him.

"Much good it would do to you," he said smiling, obviously pleased by this expression of my reverential feeling about him.

When I began working at State University of New York Downstate Medical College in Brooklyn, Pat Fitzgerald gave me space not only for establishing a Pap smear laboratory, but also for my experiments with the mice. The accommodations were modest but had a somewhat amusing history. I had an office in a former elevator shaft, and I kept my mice in what used to be a men's room. But I was happy. I hired two research assistants, and we resumed further studies on the development of cancer in mice.

Soon after I moved to the State University of New York, both Dr. Pap and I were invited to participate in a nationwide lung cancer study supported by the American Cancer Society and Veterans Administration. This was the collaborative study to which he had alluded when I consulted him about the job at Downstate. The participants of this study included four directors of the cytology centers studying sputum for the detection of lung cancer, and six of the Veterans Administration Hospitals. Dr. Pap and I each directed one of the centers. All the participants of this project worked as colleagues and were very much interested in learning how useful screening of the sputum Pap smears would be in the early detection of lung cancer.

The results of this study made apparent that very small cancers detected by the microscopic examination of sputum smears couldn't have been detected by a mere X-ray of the lungs. Thus, a further validation of Papanicolaou's method had been achieved by this study.

Now that I had left Cornell, Dr. Pap and I saw each other at least twice a year and often spoke on the phone in connection with our participation in this lung cancer project. Our meetings were increasingly warm and friendly. He now accepted me as his grown-up spiritual child, one he could treat with respect as a colleague and not one he had to dominate and control. And it was abundantly clear that he was genuinely happy to help me in any way he could.

Along with these changes in my professional life, there were important developments on the home front as well. In 1954 Gene obtained his Ph.D. from McGill University, and he was offered and accepted a position as assistant professor of economics at the University of New Brunswick in Canada. Before moving there, he came to visit us in Englewood, and when he left for Canada he took Bronislawa, who had returned from Boston and was back in Englewood, to live with him in Canada. She lived with him happily for many years to come.

Painful Adjustments and Slow Understandings

During Claude's summer vacation after his first year at Lawrenceville, we hired a biology professor from Brown University to spend time with him on a daily basis and accompany him to museums, the zoo, parks, and other places of interest or educational value to a growing boy. This teacher helped Claude establish fish tanks in our house and was responsible for the development of his life-long interest in marine biology.

In 1956, when Claude was sixteen and we were spending our summer vacation in Bar Harbor, Maine, Claude had a job in the Bar Harbor Research Laboratory. While there, he was taught how to remove ovaries from mice for their famous animal experiments on hormonal activities, but although he became skillful in the performance of these surgical procedures, he wasn't planning on becoming a physician. His years at Lawrenceville had been very productive. Not only did he do very well in his school work, he had lots of left over energy. Thus, when we were in Bar Harbor, he found his way to the summer theater company and acted in several plays in their summer repertoire.

For the first time that we know of, he met and became attracted to a girl. When we found out that she was from Cranberry Island—a community known for inbreeding and hereditary feeble-mindedness—we became concerned about her genetic background. Although we had no evidence that this particular girl was feeble-minded, and the likelihood that Claude at sixteen would end up marrying this young girl was really quite a far-fetched notion, somehow we felt sufficiently threatened that we decided not to return to Maine.

Irena with Hilary at their first house in Englewood, New Jersey (1954)

With our two growing sons, the house in which we lived on Rockwood Place in Englewood was no longer large enough for our needs. Claude was now bringing his Lawrenceville friends home for weekends, Hilary needed a room to work, and we needed a larger bedroom than the one we had. In 1956 we sold our house and acquired a larger, beautiful, and better constructed house with an oak-paneled study and a fireplace in every room. But we had little opportunity to enjoy our new home because, due to unexpected events, we had to move to Philadelphia only a year and a half later.

At Lederle, Hilary had been allowed freedom to pursue his interests in basic medical research although he became aware that with recent changes in their policies, a decrease in support for basic research was to be expected. But by then Hilary had made considerable progress, acclaimed worldwide, on the development of the first safe and successful polio vaccine made from an attenuated live virus. (See appendix.) However, as with most institutions, petty jealousies and personality problems made things very difficult for him. It also had become clear that, despite the considerable success Hilary was having with the safety and effectiveness of his polio vaccine, his working at a private, for-profit, nonacademic institution was an impediment to the national recognition of his accomplishment.

All these factors contributed to Hilary's realization that remaining at Lederle was not a very good idea. Although Hilary hadn't reached the point where he was aggressively pursuing another position, in 1957 he was offered the directorship of the Wistar Institute of Anatomy and Biology in Philadelphia. The opportunity to revitalize an old and prestigious institute, affiliated with but independent from the University of Pennsylvania (where Hilary also was offered a professorship), provided him with an appealing challenge. His acceptance of this offer would mean selling our new house, a change of jobs for me, and a new school for Christopher. Claude was in his last year at Lawrenceville and had already been accepted to Princeton University, so the move would affect him the least.

The prospect of all these changes frightened me. For the two years since I had left Cornell in 1954, I had been assistant professor of pathology at Downstate and director of the Cytology Laboratory at King's County Hospital. I was engaged in an exciting collaborative lung cancer project with Dr. Pap, supported by the American Cancer Society and Veteran's Administration. I also was pursuing my own experimental research in the development and early diagnosis of uterine cancer in mice. I was happy, liked the people I was working with, and was anxious to continue where I was. The laboratory was one I myself had set up, gathering all the necessary tools for my work. I was settled, respected, and felt comfortable in the Department of Pathology, where I also taught medical students. I had absolutely no desire to leave my job, but I would never seriously consider remaining in Englewood and have Hilary commute from there to Philadelphia.

When Hilary's negotiations with the Wistar Institute approached their final stage, he encouraged me to inquire about my own opportunities in Philadelphia, which thus far I hadn't even thought of. I was so unhappy about the prospect that I just buried my head in the sand. Up until this point I waited until Hilary made up his mind that he would accept the Wistar directorship and then I explored my options. By then I was forty years old and a very marketable professional person. After a few inquiries, I was asked to come for interviews at the Hahnemann Medical College (now called Hahnemann University) and at the Women's Medical College of Pennsylvania (now called

Medical College of Pennsylvania). I was able to schedule both interviews for the same day. As it happened, each medical school where I went for an interview offered me an associate professorship with a better salary than I had in New York.

I selected Hahnemann, where I also was offered the directorship of the cytology laboratory. Besides that, the dean, Charlie Cameron, was the former medical director of the American Cancer Society. Since I was working in the field of cancer research, I felt that could be important for me. In addition, Cameron was a special person — besides being a glamorous and influential Philadelphian suburbanite, an excellent speaker, and a good writer, he was a great admirer and friend of Dr. Pap.

Needless to say, Dr. Pap was delighted with my choice. "I know that Dr. Cameron wants to develop a first class cytology laboratory," Dr. Pap said. "Because of that he'll support your efforts, and it will be a good place for you to carry on your research."

During my interview at Hahnemann, Charlie Cameron had mentioned that the Department of Pathology was without a chairman and that Joe Imbriglia, the acting chairman, wasn't a strong candidate for the permanent chairmanship. Charlie then asked me if I would be interested in the position. It was a flattering offer. However, I didn't jump at this opportunity. "Frankly, no, Dr. Cameron," I said, perhaps too rapidly. "I want to develop a good cytology laboratory where research, teaching, and diagnostic work would be conducted at a very high level of excellence. The chairmanship of pathology would require too many conflicting responsibilities."

Considering my past hardships working under a boss like Sophie Spitz, it would have been wiser on my part to have given his offer at least some consideration. Even though I didn't care for a primarily administrative position, I was able to cope reasonably well with administrative problems. I also was concerned about responsibilities for teaching and for the supervision of the performance of autopsies, surgical pathology, and clinical pathology. In some of these areas, especially clinical pathology, I hardly had adequate experience since I had devoted so many years to developing expertise in cytopathology. I feared conflicting commitments and short-changing my standards of excellence in cytopathology. It would have been more practical to have accepted the offer of chairmanship and become my own boss, but in retrospect I don't regret that I didn't sacrifice my integrity.

Dr. Cameron didn't press me to show interest in the chairmanship of pathology, but I subsequently found out that they had difficulty attracting an outside chairman. In spite of reservations on the part of the search committee, before long Joe Imbriglia became the chairman.

Confident that I had a good job in Philadelphia, Hilary accepted the directorship of the Wistar Institute and moved to live and work there in April or May 1957, coming home for weekends. We decided to move as a family to Philadelphia in the summer of 1957. By then I would have completed my academic responsibilities at Downstate, Christopher would be out of school, and we could all have a nice summer vacation.

Hilary began to work hard and enthusiastically at Wistar. He also began looking for a house for us. I continued my job in Brooklyn until the end of the 1956–57 academic year to bring my experiments to completion so that I could publish my work. Pat Fitzgerald accepted my resignation with dignified regrets and was most generous to allow me to transfer my research equipment, bought from the grant the National Cancer Institute gave me, to Hahnemann. Three of my associates decided to come with me to Philadelphia, including Father Bogacz, a Polish priest with a Ph.D. in biology from the Pasteur Institute in Paris, who was my research associate, my chief cytotechnologist, and a research technician.

In the meantime, I went to Philadelphia several weekends looking for a house with Hilary, but nothing I saw was suitable. Then, after two months of a frustrating search, Hilary found a lovely and well-constructed Tudor house in Wynnewood, a small suburban area on so-called Main Line, very close to Philadelphia. That summer we moved to Philadelphia, and then we took our sons for a long vacation to Europe.

Our return home in September was very traumatic. Within a week we received a telephone call that Hilary's father had died of a heart attack in Manchester, England. Hilary and I took the first available plane to England. It was very painful to see the body of Hilary's father and to attend his funeral, which had been organized by a nephew who worked with him at his Manchester office with the help of Paul's close friends. His memory was very dear to me as I mourned him with Hilary. We were sorry that we had not visited Paul while in Europe that summer, but we had expected him in the United States in the fall to see our new house. We remained in England several days to take care of his estate and to terminate the lease on his Manchester apartment.

His father left Hilary all his money. Hilary knew how important his father had been to me, how caring he was of me, how generous, and how much I loved him. To compensate me in some way for the loss of his father, he bought me a mink coat before we left London. It was my first one, and wearing it made me feel very elegant. His doing this moved me and made me feel even closer to him as his wife, almost as if in losing his father he needed more connection with me. It made me feel very special and loved.

When we moved to Philadelphia, we bought a puppy so as to have a watch dog and a companion for Christopher, who missed his Englewood friends. We called our boxer Bronco, and he became an important member of our family. Aside from selecting a school for Christopher, we had to organize our new household, which depended heavily upon finding adequate help. We placed an ad in a Swiss paper and found a German housekeeper who was a reasonably good worker but who never became a very intimate member of our household. Finding adequate sources of food shopping and other necessities became a tiresome chore, which used up a lot of my time.

Hilary was very busy reorganizing the Wistar Institute and traveling in search of promising young scientists to attract there. He was happy doing it. But with all the drudgery I had on my hands, I had to await satisfaction from my own professional work until the renovation of the space for the cytology laboratory at Hahnemann was complete. This took several months because my laboratory was going to be built in a top-floor apartment vacated by the former Hahnemann caretaker. In the meantime, I was given a very small place to keep my mice. My research associates remained idle, impatiently awaiting the day when we would be able to resume our work.

I found the move itself to be quite strenuous and draining, far more than previous ones had been, including when we came to this country from Brazil. Once in Philadelphia, I had a difficult time settling in, getting used to my new surroundings, becoming comfortable enough to be able to get on with my life. In part the difference could have been that when I arrived in the United States from Brazil I was a good bit younger—twenty-seven years of age. But since forty is hardly old, I'm not sure age was the major factor. I really think it had to do with my resisting the move psychologically, because this change came at a time in my career when I was well established and happy.

As soon as better accommodations for our animals became available at Hahnemann, my research technician transported the rest of our animals and equipment by truck from Brooklyn to Philadelphia. Now we had to get organized for new experiments.

In the midst of all these new stresses, I discovered that I needed to wear glasses. Although this is something that often happens at forty, I viewed it—perhaps because of all the unwelcome changes and overall stress—as evidence of some personal decline. So forty, which can often be a glorious time in a woman's life, with family and career established, became a difficult age for me. The need for glasses somehow sparked in me a fear of becoming less attractive. Being the wife of Wistar's director, I happened to be the only working woman among the wives of their staff scientists. I valued my career but did not wish to sacrifice my femininity. I wanted to look attractive and hide the signs of my aging.

I began to have trouble concentrating and making decisions. I often didn't know what I wanted and felt the urge to cry. I became anxious and depressed. It was awful. But Hilary became concerned and spoke about my anxiety and depression to a colleague with psychiatric experience, who advised me to take Miltown, an antidepressant much used in those days. I felt less anxious using Miltown, but I became apathetic and, fearing that this might interfere with the alertness needed for my research, I stopped taking it. But with the return of my symptoms, I knew I had to do something.

I then saw a woman psychiatrist in New York. She made me aware of the stressful nature of my adjustment to new situations I encountered in Philadelphia. What made it especially hard was the feeling that Hilary, who enjoyed every bit of his new life, somehow did not give me a chance to share enough of it and participate in his efforts and entertainment. But now I reached the point where there was just too much discrepancy between his joy of life and my constant frustrations; I felt that we had been drifting apart. The concern about this must have been the real reason for the anxiety and depression I felt after our moving to Philadelphia. I was unhappy, but I did not believe that continuation of the sessions with my New York psychiatrist over and beyond the first one was going to help me. In any event, it wasn't worth the time, effort, and money to keep seeing her. Having arrived at this conclusion, I decided to deal with all these new and complex demands on my life through my own efforts and adjust the best I could.

My regret at having reached forty and feeling unattractive was alleviated by a flattering incident. When Hilary was away, Dr. L., a famous French cancer researcher, came to our house rather unexpectedly. In an attempt to make him feel at home and to show him my pleasure in welcoming his visit, I invited him to sit down next to me on the sofa where, to my surprise, he grabbed me in his arms and attempted to kiss me passionately. While I was pushing him away, thinking that as yet I hadn't become so unattractive, Hilary was turning the key in the front door. Dr. L. freed me from his embrace and rushed to the door to greet Hilary. Within a matter of minutes they were discussing science. Later, I found out that Dr. L. had an illegitimate son who was conceived during a more successful encounter with the wife of another scientist.

In spite of my difficulties in adjusting to our new life in Philadelphia, I managed to establish a friendship with another woman. One of the first people I met when we moved to Wynnewood was Sasia Nowicki, a Polish woman who was a professor of architecture at the University of Pennsylvania. She was the widow of the very famous architect who designed the United Nations building and shortly afterwards perished in a plane crash. She had two sons, the same ages as Claude and Christopher. The similarity of our national backgrounds and our efforts to combine demanding academic positions with family responsibilities soon led to the development of our friendship. We could talk to each other about our problems and often could give each other good advice how to cope with them.

Sasia lived only fifteen minutes away from us by car, and I used to see her quite often. She became one of the few women friends I had in my adult life. Stefa F., whom I took with me on a brief vacation when we lived in Brazil and who taught me how to make exceptionally tasty scrambled eggs, was another. Most of the women I met were either the wives of my husband's colleagues, with whom I had nothing in common because they were mainly focused on domestic concerns, or women scientists who had no interest in family matters and who, like Sophie Spitz, were often cold, hard-driven women from whom I felt alienated. Stefa F. and Sasia were different. With neither of them did I have the kind of intellectual kinship I had with Dr. Pap, but these women were very educated and sophisticated, and with them I had a common frame of reference. They understood what it is to have a passionate involvement in a career and still have deep concern with and commitment to family and personal issues. Being able to talk to them provided me with considerable relief. Sometimes we would just speak about ordinary problems and matters. Sometimes we spoke about some of our more profound inner feelings and turmoil.

I did wish that I had a woman friend with whom I could also share my feelings and interests in science, much like I could with George Papanicolaou—who was the one person in the world of science who had the same intuitive approach to scientific discovery that was so vital to me. It would be wonderful to have that with a woman friend in whom I could also confide the deep personal things I spoke of with Sasia and Stefa F. But I suppose it is probably quite rare to find such a combination, and I'm thankful I found those two women, both intelligent and loyal friends and confidantes, real helpmates in some rather troubled moments of my life. Without them I don't know what I would have done.

I had barely gotten used to our life in Wynnewood when Hilary decided to give a big dinner party at our house for the members of the Wistar Institute. We invited a few scientists, some of whom had followed him from Lederle, and some, who were new, mostly young and promising European researchers, whom he had persuaded to join him. In all, we had about fifty people, including the wives. I wasn't used to giving big parties, but I realized that as the wife of the institute's director I would often be expected to entertain.

Before dinner I saw two slightly tipsy wives of Wistar scientists holding cocktail glasses in their hands and talking rather loudly in the living room. "Isn't it terrible when the wife of the director tries to compete with her husband?" I overheard one of them say, as she spilled a good part of her martini on our rug. I felt a pang hearing this, wondering whether this was how these women, none of whom had a profession or a job, felt about me. Like so many middle class American women of the 1950's, they took care of their houses and children, proud that they were under no economic pressure to work and unaware that they were failing to achieve their own human potential. The opinions and behavior of these women helped me understand why I had so few women friends.

Poland Revisited

"We're going to Poland!" Hilary announced with great excitement one day as he came home for dinner. No prospect could have sounded less appealing to me. It was 1958, and Poland was governed by a totalitarian communist regime.

"They've been sending scientists to the U.S., and not all of them have been communists. Remember Przesmycki from the Polish State Institute of Hygiene?" Hilary continued enthusiastically. I recalled a distinguished-looking man with poor hearing. "He was the one who made arrangements to feed children in Poland with my polio vaccine when it is delivered. Now, in gratitude for this, the Polish government has invited us to visit Poland as their guests."

"But won't it be dangerous to accept this invitation, Hilary? Once we are there, couldn't they prevent you from leaving and make you stay and work for the Polish government?"

"Don't be silly, Irena. We're American citizens now and we're in no danger of being forcibly retained in Poland. We'll go this summer and take our sons with us." As he spoke to me, he walked about the kitchen. But despite his enthusiasm and air of confidence, he had sensed my hesitancy.

"Don't you want to go?"

I was rather anxious, but I could also feel myself beginning to get excited. So after a moment's silence, I responded to Hilary and said, "I guess I do." The prospect of seeing Warsaw again after nineteen years had started to thrill me.

The trip then became one of the foremost things on our minds, and we became occupied with making all the necessary plans. On a warm July morning in 1958, Hilary and I and our two sons landed at the Warsaw airport. It was a dramatic and emotional moment for me. When I left Poland in 1939, I was a spoiled young woman, barely out of medical school, unhappy to be leaving my father and family, pregnant, going off with my new husband and his family. I had plenty of reason to feel insecure and uncertain about the future. I realized that so much had happened since then. I had weathered some frightening wartime experiences, lived in several countries, become an American citizen, was now an associate professor of pathology, the wife of a famous scientist, and mother of two sons. It hadn't been easy, but my uncertainty and insecurity of those former years had certainly vanished.

But that wasn't all I was feeling. My thoughts were darting all over—the places I wanted to visit, the people I wanted to see, a huge rush of so many memories I had stored from the past. All four of us were guests of honor of the communist government. Our visit was widely publicized. We were met at the airport by representatives of the Polish State Institute of Hygiene, by Hilary's cousin Joanna, and several friends and former classmates, all carrying flowers.

We checked in at the Grand Hotel. This once elegant hotel had become a decaying building with shrapnel holes that had been filled in and patched awkwardly. The lobby was furnished with ugly, cheap furniture and was drab. Even though we were accompanied by government representatives, we experienced a long wait and indifferent service at the reception desk. Our rooms were adequate, but modest.

We had time to freshen up after our travel, but no time for any rest, for our schedule was full of continuous activities. Both Hilary and I had been invited to give lectures at the Polish State Institute of Hygiene. That was the first item on our itinerary and was scheduled for that same day. On our way out of the hotel, as we passed through the lobby, we were surrounded by old friends, colleagues, and strangers seeking to catch our attention. But we had no time to talk to them. We had to give our lectures—Hilary first, then I.

Hilary spoke about his live poliomyelitis vaccine. He described its discovery. That story had made Hilary a national hero. Thus, the audience was fascinated to see him in person and listen to his account of the development of his vaccine. When he ended, they applauded for a long time.

Giving a lecture after that was bound to be anticlimactic, no matter what the subject. Nothing I could speak of would have the emotional impact that the prospect of conquering polio in Poland had. When I chose my topic, I felt I had two options: either talk about the early diagnosis of uterine cancer by the Pap smear, or discuss my animal experiments with early development of uterine cancer. I didn't expect that I'd arouse much interest with the latter, so I chose to talk about the early diagnosis of uterine cancer by Pap smears. But my mind wasn't focused on what I was about to discuss. I was distracted. I was reacting strongly to being back in Poland after so many years and to the enormous changes that had taken place in my circumstances. As I walked down the aisle towards the podium to deliver my lecture, I remembered coming to that very same lecture hall as a student to listen to the immunology lectures of Professor Hirshfeld. I felt so proud to find myself now the lecturer, a sign of how far I'd come in my profession, which had started here so long ago. And although I was pleased to be giving a lecture, pleased to have accomplished what I had, I also was worried about how I looked, worried that I looked old at forty-one, hoping that my carefully chosen and delicate facial makeup was successfully hiding any signs of aging. I was very self-conscious. I walked slowly and noticed that the audience followed my footsteps very closely. When I recognized the faces of old friends I had never expected to see again, I was deeply moved, as was my audience. Some of them had tears in their eyes. I stopped several times to hug and kiss those who were closest to the aisle, whom I could easily reach. Zaira, my friend from our childhood days through medical school, was smiling through her tears as we embraced.

When I got to the podium and delivered my lecture in Polish, my audience listened with interest, but of course I couldn't tell at the time what mainly interested them. Polish physicians already were familiar with cancer detection through Pap smears. I mentioned the detection of cancer at other sites of the body by the study of cells in body fluids. After my lecture, no pathologists expressed any interest in my work, but I heard many comments about the purity of my language.

I might have done better talking about my experimental cancer research in mice or I could have saved myself the disappointment by declining to give a lecture. I might have offered instead an informal discussion with scientists to give them an opportunity to ask more general questions about science in America. But because my return to Poland was so emotionally overwhelming, I did not realize what was likely to happen.

After the lecture and during much of our time in Poland, I found myself saddened as I heard old friends speak of their hardships: poverty, lack of food, medicines, clothes. "Working hard gets you nowhere unless you have a Communist party membership card," we often heard people say. We were repeatedly confronted with a gloomy picture of the realities of life in Poland. People didn't trust each other and saw no future for themselves or for their country. Listening to them, my mind would return to the conditions in Poland right before the war, and I wondered about the relationship between what happened then and the present. I couldn't forget the shameful scenes at the Warsaw University Medical School when a group of anti-Semitic students succeeded in their demand that separate seats be assigned to Jews. In fact, some of my former classmates told me they regretted their past attitudes. So we obviously couldn't blame the Germans and Russians for all of Poland's failures. It was hard not to wonder, had there been a stronger resistance, if post-war Poland would have been a better place.

In spite of our memories of the shameful mistakes of the past, we joyfully celebrated the reunion with all our colleagues. Several visits had a special emotional meaning for me. I went and saw the tomb of my mother, and I was grateful that it was still standing and in good condition, because I was thinking about my father and that this would have made him happy were he still alive. Sadly, my search for his grave yielded nothing. I then visited Wikcia, our former nanny. She burst into tears as she hugged and kissed me at the door of her modest apartment, and then fed me a potato soup she had cooked for her bedridden husband. Next I visited Mme. Rogóyska, my beloved French tutor.

I tried to delve into my past as I visited Vera L. and Szpilka, my classmates from the gymnasium. But we had only a short time together—it was frustrating, but there just wasn't enough opportunity to talk about all that I wanted to.

I also met with Witek Kula, the young man who used to kiss my teeth. He had become a well-known historian. We danced together at a party, but we didn't talk much. The whole time I was dancing with Witek, he had a smile on his face. He was clearly happy to have me in his arms once again. He invited Hilary and me to visit him in his apartment before we left Warsaw. We went, and while Hilary was engrossed in a conversation with his wife, Witek handed me my old leather-bound diary. He had kept it for a quarter of a century. It was preserved in perfect condition, and still bound by its pink silk ribbon. I found very touching his meticulous care of my girlish musings, and although I considered that this might have been the result of his historian's instinct for the preservation of archives, I preferred to think it was a vestige of his former love for me. However, being with him again made me realize I had no regrets that I didn't bring my pillows and go off and marry him as he had asked me to long ago when I was nineteen.

I would have been happy to see Janek G., the idol of my teens, who was practicing surgery in Lodz, but unfortunately I had neither time nor facility of transportation to go and visit him in this industrial town about twenty-five miles from Warsaw. With all the other emotions I experienced in Poland, this did not turn out to be the major disappointment I had expected it to be.

The partially annihilated apartment house where my family had lived on Hoza Street had been rebuilt, but I don't know when and by whom. I forgot when and how it ceased to be our family's property. I remember that Bronislawa, Gene, and Gabriel sold the second, more valuable house on the Hoza Street property to LOT, the Polish Air Line, when they needed money in order to leave Poland. The building in which the school of my girlhood, the Gymnasium of Popielewska Roszkowska, was located was not damaged by the wartime bombing. But there was no trace left of the nearby pastry shop on Bagatela Street with its elegant outdoor café, where we used to go for tea and cakes. The empty lot where it once stood became a sad reminder that so much that was important from my past was irretrievably lost.

My father's property on Solec Street, where I was born forty-one years before, didn't exist anymore. Nor was there any trace of the flour mill and our old residence, all of which formed an integral part of my childhood recollections. The church across the street still stood, and in place of the mill and our residence there now was an open space with tree-lined roads leading from the street in front of the church to the Vistula River.

As I walked through the streets of Warsaw, I became excited whenever I spotted familiar sights—ones that were unscathed by the war, or even those that bore some scars but still retained their basic look and structure. I also was delighted by Warsaw's renovated old town. It was very beautiful. Its renovation had been accomplished by architects who used the eighteenth-century paintings of Canaletto to guide them in the reconstruction. But sticking out like a sore thumb in the center city was a much newer edifice, the hideous, monumental Soviet-style Palace of Culture.

Our family sightseeing included a visit to Cracow, the ancient capital of Poland that is approximately 100 miles south of Warsaw, to show our sons the national treasures: Wavel—The Royal Castle, and the thirteenth-century wooden altar sculpted by Witt Stwosz in Marjacki Church.

Thanks to Dr. Baranski, an associate professor of pediatrics at the University of Warsaw, whose wife had spent one year working with Hilary under provision of a Polish American scientific exchange, we were able to visit my in-law's former country place in Celestynow. When the post-war communist regime was established, they built a hideous brick building on the site of our former beautiful strawberry beds and turned the family house into an orphanage. The old house, however, was still there, thankfully. It was empty and abandoned. In our desire to create some continuity and connection with our family tradition, Hilary and I took photographs of Claude and Christopher on the steps of that little house where Hilary and his cousin, Leon Gerber, had their pictures taken twenty years before.

While we were there with Dr. Baranski, he told us a joke about Professor Michalowicz, who taught us pediatrics in medical school and who disappeared during the war. After the war, when other people were returning from the front, prison camps, and hiding places, there was still no trace of Michalowicz. He was therefore presumed dead. Some of his friends who mourned his loss were involved with spiritualism, a movement that had gained some popularity in Poland among certain intellectuals after the war. They arranged a kind of seance for him, during which his ghost was summoned from the "other world". When several weeks later Professor Michalowicz actually turned up and was spotted in the streets of Warsaw, it came as a shock to all those who assumed he was dead, but his spiritualist friends believed that it was his ghost that had been seen!

Told that his ghost had already been seen at a spiritualistic session, the Professor quipped, "Apparently impostors also exist in the other world."

Claude and Christopher each had rather different reactions to Poland. Claude, who spoke Polish, felt at home in Warsaw and ventured into the streets on his own. But Christopher was bored and unhappy. Some of this had to do with their difference in age at the time of our visit. Claude, being eighteen, was able to get around on his own and appreciated being in a city so full of history and new things to see. But seven-year-old Christopher didn't share those interests. Fortunately for everyone, Claude agreed to take him to Nice to visit their grandmother, Sofia Semeonovna, and we allowed them to go. Then Hilary and I remained alone in Warsaw for several more days.

There were lots of people who still wanted to see us. Some were curious about our life in America; some wanted our help in obtaining medicine, journals, and even clothes, which they couldn't get in Poland. Listening to their stories, we were overwhelmed with compassion. But soon we became emotionally exhausted and were ready to leave. We realized that despite our deep affection for Poland, we would not want to live there now. Life there was very difficult, and different from what it had been when we lived there before the war. We, too, had become different, and the people we knew also had changed. Except for memories, we didn't have much in common with our old friends.

So, as glad as we were for that chance to visit, it was with deep sighs of relief that we departed, leaving behind the remnants of our lost past. From Poland we flew to London where our sons awaited us, and together we all returned to Philadelphia.

When we came back home, we became aware that Claude was having problems with school. He was in a pre-med program at Princeton because he felt that we expected this from him. He was doing well in biology and organic chemistry, but he didn't like chemistry which required more memorizing than thinking. Also, he was having difficulties with physics and didn't care for the professor who taught it. Although we had been somewhat aware of his discontent, we didn't realize how serious it was and, thus, were hardly prepared to find him unexpectedly home and hear that he wanted to drop out and enlist in the Marines!

Claude was apologetic, feeling that in not doing well in this pre-med program he both disappointed us and was wasting our money. We had never put any pressure on Claude to select the pre-med program, although we had pointed out the merits of being a physician. Now faced with the danger of our son dropping out of college altogether to become a Marine, we became ready to help him with the selection of other college-based educational opportunities.

"Claude, we really don't care if you become a physician. We would like you to acquire a good education, be able to make your living, and above all be happy," Hilary said in a soft tone of voice. I was relieved to realize that Hilary and I felt the same way about the need to be more flexible in helping Claude to speak up and make a wise choice of his future career.

"Given a choice, what would you really like to do in life, Claude?" I asked him.

Claude hesitated. "I wasn't going to say because I don't expect you to agree, but since you asked, I must tell you that I've been painting."

He had brought home some canvases, which he planned to store in the attic. Now he decided to show them to us.

Hilary had a thoughtful expression on his face as we examined Claude's paintings. I was amazed at how little we knew about our own son's desires, dreams, and activities. I blamed myself and felt guilty about not spending more time talking to him.

Fortunately, John P. Fox, our old friend from the Rockefeller Foundation, arrived to visit his son at Haverford College and unexpectedly came to see us during that weekend. After listening to our problem, he advised us to consult a Professor Wade at Princeton about what to do. We did, and he fully supported Claude's decision to drop out of Princeton. Fortunately, he proposed other options to him besides the Marines.

"Let him go to Italy and enroll at the University of Florence, where he can study the history of art and learn Italian," Wade said. He told us that after one year in Italy, Claude would be able to re-enter Princeton University and enroll in a special program in European civilization. Claude then would graduate with a B.A. degree just a year later than if he had remained at Princeton and hadn't gone off to Italy.

We were in favor of this plan, which fortunately Claude found appealing. He went off to Italy to study art. He spent six months at the University of Florence and saw the great paintings of the world. He then went to Rome, where he studied how to restore old paintings. When he returned to Princeton he had a solid knowledge of art history and could now speak Italian in addition to English, Polish, and French.

Dr. Pap's Death

Within one year of moving to Philadelphia, I established at Hahnemann a Pap smear laboratory for early cancer detection and resumed my studies of how cancer of the womb developed in mice. My research was conducted under provision of the grant from the National Cancer Institute and I was allowed to transfer it from the State University of New York Downstate Medical College in Brooklyn to Philadelphia. I also was able to continue collaboration with Dr. Pap on the American Cancer Society Veteran Administration's Lung Cancer Study, which by now had entered its stage of completion. In spite of all these positive activities, my work was not entirely free of annoyances. Unfortunately, Joe Imbriglia, the man whom I had indirectly helped to become chairman of pathology, competed with me for financial support that I expected and needed for the support of the cytology laboratory.

Thanks to Charlie Cameron's intervention, I began receiving consultations from the private offices of the chairman and the senior faculty of the Obstetrics and Gynecology Department. I used this income to support the cost of performing Pap smear tests in the lab. However, since I was new on the staff, some physicians understandably continued sending their private patients' Pap smears to Joe Imbriglia. It was my hope, though, that eventually all the Pap smears done at the hospital or in the private offices of staff physicians would be sent to our lab.

Joe had other ideas. He continued to compete with me for the Pap smears from staff physicians' offices. He processed and examined them for his own private gain in another part of the Department of Pathology separate from the cytology laboratory.

In retrospect, I have to admit that I did not fight him as strongly as perhaps I should have. My primary interest should have been building up the volume and resources of the Pap smear service laboratory. But, fighting your department chairman is very difficult, and I was very understanding of Joe's financial needs. He was a self-made man who had a large family to support and probably needed this income to supplement his salary. He also was working at another hospital. I could understand his position, although I resented it.

At that time, I also had many other interests and activities and did not want to lose my time and energy on fights with Joe Imbriglia. In addition to the Pap smear work and the studies on lung cancer detection by sputum and bronchial washings, I was primarily interested in my experimental work. One day my associate, Father Bogacz, installed a filter in the window of our laboratory to collect city dust. He and our research technicians made an extract of this dirt and applied it to the wombs of mice twice weekly over a long period of time. They painted the wombs of another group of mice with tobacco tar, and used a third group of animals as untreated controls. We ended up producing cancer of the womb in several mice in both the tobacco-treated and the air pollutant-treated groups. The mice who received neither tobacco nor city dust did not develop cancer.

Using experimental animals, we were trying to prove that tobacco tar, as well as air pollutants, produced cancer of the lung. But the application of these substances to the lining of the respiratory tubes was very difficult and couldn't be done on the long-term basis necessary to induce cancer. Fortunately, the lining of the respiratory tubes consists of a membrane that is similar to the membrane that lines the womb, to which it is easy to apply substances that you wish to test. In addition, because the development of cancer of the womb may be readily detected by Pap smears, we thus also had a method for detecting whether the substance produced cancer. So, in selecting the womb to learn about the development of cancer in the lung, we had both a scientific rationale for using that site (the womb instead of the lung) and a developed and respected test for determining the existence or absence of cancer there. After presenting the results of this study at the annual meeting of the American Society of Cytology, I was interviewed by Earl Ubell of the *New York Herald Tribune*. This was 1959. Thus, long before tobacco was accepted as a major cause of cancer, I had made that discovery in my laboratory in Philadelphia. But I was never given credit for proving that tobacco tar, as well as air pollutants, produce cancer. Science, like virtually every other aspect of life, is not immune from prejudice and politics. Although it is difficult to say for sure, I have some ideas why my discovery wasn't acknowledged. "It's the wrong end of the body to apply tobacco to," someone joked. Who would want to use our method of studying the cancer-producing effects of tobacco and air pollutants after it had been ridiculed in that manner?

Another factor in my failure to receive credit for my discoveries was that I didn't have sufficient ambition, aggressiveness, and perseverance to bring my achievements more forcibly to the attention of the scientific community. As a result, my fame remained limited to a relatively small circle of cancer researchers and experts in early cancer detection.

In 1959, two years after I began to work at Hahnemann, Dr. Cameron asked me to organize a cytology symposium as a way of dedicating and marking the official opening of my laboratory. He suggested that we invite Dr. Pap. Although I was quite pleased at the prospect of having a symposium to dedicate the cytology lab I had developed from scratch since coming to Hahnemann, I must confess I felt resentful that Dr. Cameron suggested Dr. Pap rather than me to be the main speaker. I suppose I still felt some lingering resentment towards George. But mostly I think I saw this occasion as one that could really launch me at Hahnemann, and beyond, as a prominent and respected figure in the field of cancer detection. With Pap as the speaker, I knew that I would be overshadowed, and the potential for my career would be seriously compromised.

Naturally, I hardly felt I could say this to Charles Cameron. I also realized that having Pap there would be a feather in Hahnemann's cap, which made the possibility of his going along with my suppressed ambitions quite remote. So I kept my feelings to myself, but the resentment didn't fade.

On the day of the symposium I asked the head of the public relations committee to meet Dr. Pap at 30th Street Station and accompany him to Hahnemann. To this day I've always wondered if my not meeting him at the station was because of my feelings of resentment. As I "argue" it out with myself, another part of me says,

"Irena, you're being foolish. How could you have left Hahnemann when you were running this conference? Your presence was needed and you saw to it that he wasn't left to fend for himself, which would have been rather inconsiderate." Fortunately, Dr. Pap didn't seem to be affronted one bit. He was pleased to have been invited and to see what I had accomplished. In fact, the symposium itself, attended by eighty people, went quite well, as did the dinner at my house for the speakers and my family. We had good food, wine, a relaxed atmosphere, and interesting conversation. Then Dr. Cameron took Dr. Pap back to 30th Street Station, and he returned to New York.

When word of Hahnemann's symposium spread among the members of the American Society of Cytology, several of my colleagues from that organization made a point of letting me know they had heard that the symposium was a great success. This response made me realize that, even with Dr. Pap being the main speaker, the symposium had some direct benefit for me, and I had gained increased prestige in the eyes of my professional colleagues.

Working as hard as I did to carry out my experiments and maintain all the work associated with my career, I needed and almost always had good domestic help to take care of my home and family. When I didn't I simply left many tasks undone and devoted myself to searching for a housekeeper again. At one point, when I simply couldn't find anyone, my old and good friend from Brazil, Stefa, with whom I had continued to maintain contact, sent me an excellent Portuguese housekeeper, Maria da Conceição Pereira.

In 1960 there were some personal developments in our family. Gabriel and Dessie adopted a baby girl, Maria Alina. Gene, who went with Bronislawa at the end of his sabbatical to Haiti, decided to remain in Port-au-Prince, even though the group Gene had gone there with, the American Economic Mission, returned to the United States. Gene stayed on as a consultant to the Haitian government. In spite of the terrorism characteristic of Duvalier's regime, Gene's job was a challenge to him as an economist. He succeeded in helping the Haitians to develop several programs intended to improve their financial situation and for export of agricultural products.

That year Hilary decided to spend Christmas with his mother in Nice. He suggested that I take Claude and Christopher to Haiti to see Gene and Bronislawa. The Ton-Ton Macout, who exercised so much control over the citizens in Haiti, were not yet considered a threat to American visitors. So we went.

Gene met us at the airport and took us to Petionville, where he and Bronislawa lived in a beautiful house with a swimming pool in the hills outside Port-au-Prince. They had five inefficient people working at their house, which was some help. The next day we left Christopher under Bronislawa's care, and Gene took Claude and me to see a voodoo ceremony and participate in the local observance of Christmas.

We entered a small house where a black man in a red robe sat in front of a Christmas tree. Being agnostic, I didn't come to celebrate Christmas, but I participated in the ritual so I could experience it firsthand and so as not to stick out. I joined a line of women that moved slowly, allowing us, one by one, to face the man in the red robe, who would then pat each of us on the belly and pronounce some words of blessing. Then, several men in red uniforms marched through the house. After that ritual was over, we all went to another room for refreshments of cookies and coca-cola. The man who sat in front of the Christmas tree joined us, but instead of drinking cola he sipped from a bottle containing a colorless fluid that had some kind of weed in it.

Gene then took Claude and me to the hills. There we saw women moving to the beating of drums in a ritualistic frenzy. I felt deeply impressed by both of these exotic ceremonies, the character of which was so new and strange to me that I began to wonder how Gene felt living in a country where they are common. Long after our return home, the memory of these rituals returned and became part of my daydreaming.

I found Haiti to be a beautiful country and, notwithstanding the appalling poverty and Duvalier's dictatorial regime, we enjoyed our Christmas vacation. After Christmas, Hilary returned home. The interest provided by my Christmas in Haiti and the pleasure of seeing Gene and Bronislawa rewarded me for the disappointment of spending the holiday period without Hilary. Both of us returned to our work immediately, trying to catch up with the accumulated backload. Claude resumed his studies at Princeton; Christopher went back to the Haverford School. The rest of the year through the end of the following summer proceeded relatively uneventfully.

Then, on August 24, 1961, the surgeon general of the United States Public Health Service made an announcement endorsing Albert Sabin's, not Hilary's, polio vaccine. This meant that it would be Sabin's vaccine that would be used for a massive inoculation campaign in the United States. Given the priority of its discovery and the widespread testing that Hilary's vaccine had received both for safety and effectiveness, it was clear that the monopoly established by Basil O'Connor, head of the March of Dimes, was the main reason for the reluctance of the surgeon general to endorse a vaccine produced outside their control. The decision was made on political and not medical-scientific grounds.

"How could you do it to Koprowski? Hilary was the first to develop the vaccine," Karl Habel, a good friend of Hilary's from the National Institutes of Health, asked Dr. Smadell, a member of the committee that made the recommendation to license the Sabin vaccine.

"We had to choose one. Sabin is an old boy from the Rockefeller Institute, and he was supported by the National Foundation for Infantile Paralysis. His name is also easier to pronounce than Koprowski," Smadell explained.

The failure to gain recognition for his pioneering work in the conquest of polio was a big blow to Hilary. He became angry and bitter, but more inclined to discuss with me his disappointments and the events leading to them. It was ironic. In the early 1950's, Hilary had received a great deal of publicity in the daily press, which credited his vaccine with stopping the polio epidemic wherever it was given. He was honored by the widespread use of his vaccine in our native land of Poland. But now, his only reward was for the successful use of his oral polio vaccine with the children of the Belgian Congo. For that he was awarded a medal from the King of Belgium.

But Hilary wasn't destroyed. While he minded missing out on the recognition for his hard work, he now had the peace and time to further his other scientific work.

My laboratory at Hahnemann also continued to develop. I now had generous federal support, some of which I used to establish a school of cytotechnology, the students' stipends being provided by a grant from the National Institutes of Health. I organized a program to train these cytotechnology students to screen Pap smears for the detection of cancer cells.[8]

After Dr. Bogacz accepted a professorship of biology at LaSalle University, a Portuguese woman doctor, Maria Fernandes, came to work with me. She helped me grow, in culture, cancer cells from tumors of the womb in mice. The purpose of these experiments was to find out and compare how cancer cells look and behave inside and outside of the animal body. Maria Fernandes spoke very little English, which helped me retain my command of the Portuguese language.

The American Society of Cytology was interested in the propagation of the Pap smear method for the diagnosis of cancer of the womb. Unfortunately, the interest of this Society in my research, which was initially aroused by the novelty of my approach, didn't last long. But my enthusiasm continued, and I enjoyed carrying out my research and making whatever progress I was able to make.

That same year, 1961, Dr. Pap left Cornell after being there for so many years and fulfilled his lifelong ambition by becoming director of his own cancer research institute, which he established in Miami. By now he was an old man, and these new responsibilities were too much for him. I visited him in his new institute and at his home in Miami Beach. As we sat at the microscope in his spacious and comfortably furnished home office, I spoke to him about my research while he listened with interest. After a while he started mumbling to himself, a sign he was thinking out loud, just as he did when I brought him smears for consultation at Cornell so long ago. "You're doing so much . . . I made a mistake," I heard him say.

I didn't dare interrupt his train of thought to ask what he meant by that, what mistake he had made. He may have regretted his failure

---

8. Once they completed the program, which was full time and lasted one year, these cytotechnologists were qualified to work in other hospitals and perform examinations of Pap smears. Our program taught them how to examine the smear, recognize abnormal cells—which could possibly be cancer cells—and mark them for the pathologist. This allowed the pathologist to focus in on those cells and thus spend time deciding whether cells marked by the cytotechnologist were or were not cancer cells (i.e., making diagnosis of the Pap smear rather than also having to do the initial screening). It is essential for a successful cancer detection program based on the use of Pap smears to have extremely well trained technologists, and my program was dedicated to accomplishing that.

to help me become his successor at Cornell or to achieve a more powerful position in the American Society of Cytology. But I no longer felt the old resentments. Now I was intensely happy because, whatever it was that he meant, he made me feel that I was close to him — closer than ever before.

In January 1962 I had dinner again with Dr. and Mrs. Pap at their Miami Beach home. After dinner he and I sat side by side at the microscope. He was seventy-eight, and I was forty-five. I took a good look at him. He still hadn't aged physically or mentally. But he had altered emotionally for the good, having become a happier man now that his lifelong dream had been fulfilled. I also realized that our relationship had changed. I no longer viewed him as an apprentice would a master. He was my friend and colleague.

The pleasure of this visit was spoiled only by my noticing a strange sensation of the coldness of his hands as I was taking my leave. This reminded me of the feeling of my father's face, which had also felt cold when he saw me off for the last time at the Warsaw train station in 1939. I had a premonition that I might not see Dr. Pap alive again. A few weeks after my visit, I sent Mrs. Pap some roses as an expression of gratitude for her hospitality. She received them on the morning of her husband's death, and didn't understand how I knew he'd died.

"Irena, how did you know that Dr. Papanicolaou died that night?" asked Charlie Cameron, who happened to be their weekend house-guest on the night that Dr. Pap died.

I didn't know, of course. But it was uncanny. The news hit me hard. I was shocked and felt a deep sense of loss.

It was raining as I left Philadelphia for the funeral in New York. I felt very lonely. The church was filled with his colleagues, students, associates, and admirers. I sought out Mrs. Pap. She was composed in her grief and didn't cry.

But when I approached the open coffin I didn't recognize Dr. Pap's familiar olive complexion; his face was purplish-blue, testifying to his cardiac death. I looked in despair at the face of the man who meant so much to me. Never again would I be able to sit and talk to him at the microscope. I would miss him. Feeling as if I were losing a father for the third time, I couldn't control myself and burst into loud sobbing.

Death of Sofia Semeonovna

By 1962, my academic career was well established. I already had published forty scientific articles in reputable national and international journals. I was a member of a good number of professional organizations, a Fellow of both the American Society of Cytology and the International Academy of Cytology, a consultant to the World Health Organization, and I had met all the academic requirements for promotion to full professorship.

One day Hilary suggested that I should request the promotion. But Joe Imbriglia stood in my way. He had another candidate in mind and claimed that the departmental budget didn't contain funds to pay the salaries of two additional full professors. "Promotion means more money, Irena. On the basis of his seniority, I have already proposed the promotion of Karl Koiwai. He has a large family to support," Joe told me.

"Why hasn't Karl been promoted before, Joe?" I asked.

"Because unlike you, he didn't make his name known through publications." Joe's words sounded like an accusation, as if he were critical of my achievements. Joe obviously knew that Karl's seniority and family financial obligations were insufficient reasons for his promotion to full professorship. I wondered whether this must have been the reason he had not suggested that Karl be promoted in the past. But now with me having made such advances, getting much recognition and so many publications, he felt that this was the time to propose Karl's professorship before he would be virtually forced into promoting me instead.

"Do you think that I should be punished for my publications?" I asked.

"Irena, I'm sorry, but I have no money for your promotion."

"But you have it for Karl," I thought. I had neither the nerve nor thought it wise to say so aloud. Instead, I responded: "I don't care about the money, Joe. I can forego my raise. But I want to be promoted to full professor, if you agree that I deserve it."

Since Joe himself had few publications, I wondered on what basis he had been appointed a full professor at Hahnemann. I felt bitter. I knew from what Charlie Cameron had told me when I was interviewed for the job that Joe hadn't been well thought of as a candidate for chairman, which is why Charlie had asked me to consider the post. Yet now that he had been appointed, he was my boss, in a position to decide whether I would be promoted despite the fact that I had accomplished more professionally than either he or Karl. If I had expressed my interest in the pathology chairmanship when given the opportunity, Joe would never have achieved his present position of power over me.

I felt angry and even a bit humiliated by my dependence on Joe. Nevertheless, I was glad I had spoken up and voiced my demand. Much to my surprise, I was promoted and Karl was not. I can only speculate that the promotion committee refused to nominate Karl to full professorship and that Joe saw no further reason to object to my promotion, since it wasn't going to cost him money. With my promotion, a one thousand dollar merit increase was added to my salary. While I resented this negligible salary increase, instead of full professorial pay, I was proud and happy to become full professor. I didn't know then that I had become the first woman physician ever to have attained the rank of full professor at Hahnemann. I was told that many years later, when I was invited by the Women Faculty Committee to give a lecture at Hahnemann.

I suspect I would have handled this differently had it happened after the rise of the women's liberation movement. Although I never liked making an issue of gender discrimination, I am well aware that it was a factor. I was a married woman, and this made it easy to view me as not needing a salary—I had a husband to support me. Equal pay for equal work was not part of the consciousness of the time, nor was it considered wrong to propose promotion of someone with less qualifications because he was a man and I a woman. Today, this behavior would be considered an affront, a matter of frank sex dis-crimination. But things were quite different then.

In 1962 I was invited by the World Health Organization to go to Iran to evaluate the Tehran Cancer Institute as a future cytology teaching center for the Middle East. There, I met several Iranian pathologists who had trained in the United States and now were likely to be leading figures in this future regional cytology training center. In addition to observing their facilities, I became concerned about their inadequate financial compensation, which wasn't enough for the doctors to make a living. Therefore, it wasn't surprising that they were unable to maintain the standards of excellence necessary to become first-class teachers because each had to have several jobs to support themselves and their families. I presented this situation very realistically in my report and made a recommendation that faculty of the future training centers should be better compensated.

Being in a Moslem country then was very different from my first exposure to Iran, when Hilary and I had traveled there from India ten years earlier, in 1952. On the first visit, when we had gone to dinner at the mansion of Mr. Khosrowshaki, I had been made very uncomfortable and distressed by the subjugation of women by their husbands in that household. But on this visit I was now impressed to see many liberated women. I wasn't sure the extent to which their liberation occurred during those last ten years, or whether on my second visit I had to deal with more educated professional women than I had on my previous visit. Some of the women I met now in the hospital at which I came to lecture and to acquaint myself with the population of the patients had been trained in making Pap smear tests at Johns Hopkins University Hospital in Baltimore.

After my lecture at the Tehran Cancer Institute on the early detection of cancer at various sites of the body, I donated my teaching aids to them and prepared my evaluation of their facilities for the report I was to submit to the W.H.O. regional office.

I then left Tehran and headed for Alexandria, Egypt, where their regional office was located. In my report I described existent facilities and discussed the shortcomings. I made it clear that I was most concerned about inadequate compensation of Iranian pathologists trained in the U.S. who were destined to become training center faculty. But I saw the advantages of having American-trained faculty to be in charge of regional instruction in early cancer detection.

I had brought with me from the United States a letter of introduction from Dr. Harold Stewart of the National Cancer Institute, which was addressed to Dr. Gazaryeli, the leading pathologist in Alexandria. Besides being a leading American pathologist, Dr. Stewart was a well traveled man who felt that I should take advantage of being in Egypt to see its most famous historical sites. Dr. Gazaryeli invited me to his house for dinner. During the weekend his son Mohammed, also a pathologist, accompanied me on a visit to the Valley of Kings in Upper Egypt. This turned out to be an exciting adventure, besides being a marvelous sight-seeing experience.

It happened that Kruschev was on a visit to Egypt just as Dr. Gazaryeli was attempting to get train tickets for us from Alexandria to Cairo. When it turned out to be difficult, he told them that I was a member of Kruschev's party and that he merely accompanied me on this trip. When we arrived at Cairo and got off the train, we stepped on the red carpet prepared to welcome Kruschev! Visiting the Valley of Kings became one of the most thrilling experiences of my life, especially when Dr. Gazaryeli helped me to the forbidden descent inside the tomb of Tutenkhamen and, once there, assisted me in taking photographs of his splendid blue and gold sarcophagus.

With my career and reputation burgeoning, I had many invitations to give talks at national and international meetings. This included a request by the World Health Organization to prepare a document on the early diagnosis of cancer by Papanicolaou's method for the report of their Expert Committee on Cancer, which was published in 1963. The National Academy of Sciences invited me to discuss with them my role in the preparation of this document and praised me for it. My subsequent work as a consultant for the W.H.O. had me traveling to Switzerland and all over Latin America, and many years later to India. In Rio de Janeiro I even represented them at the International Cytology Congress held there in the early 1960's.

After traveling by myself, I usually felt good about the work I had done. But I was always glad to be back home with my family.

In June of 1962, Claude graduated from Princeton and decided to enroll at Johns Hopkins School of Advanced International Studies in Washington, D.C. He frankly admitted that he wasn't at all sure what he would end up doing. "At the moment I have a diplomatic career in mind," he said. But when he saw my surprise at this vast change from what he had selected to study at Princeton, he added, "I don't think that I could make a living teaching art."

His education was expensive, but at least he was getting a good one. And from what I could tell, even though I had been a bit skeptical about his reasons for choosing his new field rather than art, he seemed to enjoy his studies. In addition to school, as was typical of Claude, he had a busy social life and fell in love with a classmate, Judy Reilly.

Hilary enjoyed Claude's friends, and now I noticed he acted more as his companion than his father. This was in sharp contrast with me — for I was more conscious of the generation gap between myself and Claude's friends than Hilary was, and I often felt ill at ease when we were present at the social gatherings Claude had during our visits to his Washington apartment.

In the summer of the following year, 1963, Hilary suggested that he, Christopher, and I go to the International Fair in Brussels. Hilary would go to Europe first in order to attend a scientific meeting. Then Christopher and I were to fly to Paris a few days later, spend a couple of days there, and then go to Brussels where Hilary would meet us at the airport.

Before he left for Europe, Hilary approached me with an unexpected suggestion: "Why don't you treat yourself to an appointment with Alexandre, Irena? He is a very famous hairstylist in Paris. The most elegant women of the world are his customers." Saying this, he handed me a magazine with a picture of and a long article about this well-known hairdresser. Hilary was always interested in people, in fashion, and in any kind of new development. So I did not consider his unexpected suggestion strange. He wanted me to take advantage of an opportunty to have my hair styled by a master. He then surprised me with another idea of a rather different nature: "I will ask Françoise Haguenau (a scientist who was a friend of Hilary's) to get tickets for a striptease show I know Christopher would enjoy seeing. He's twelve and entitled to see one." I did not think that seeing a striptease show was a necessary educational experience for a twelve-year-old boy, but I would not argue about it. Frankly, I was more amused than annoyed by Hilary's suggestion.

So while Hilary was making necessary arrangements with Françoise Haguenau, I wrote a letter to Alexandre asking him for an appointment. A few weeks later I flew to Paris with Christopher. We were met at the air terminal by Françoise Haguenau, and she drove us to the Hotel Royal Monceau in her small Renault.

By three o'clock in the afternoon, Chris and I were seated at the Tour Eiffel restaurant. In spite of the many gourmet dishes on their menu, Christopher insisted on ordering a hamburger with French fries and a lemonade. I didn't hear a word of French around us. It was pretty obvious that this place was patronized strictly by tourists. Our two table companions, women teachers from the southern United States, spoke loudly in English and, like Chris, they ordered American food. It struck me as odd that grownups would take the time and spend the money to travel to France and not want to treat themselves to one of the world's best cuisines.

Well fed but exhausted, we returned to the hotel for a nap. The show at Casino de Paris began at nine o'clock in the evening. At first, several groups of scantily dressed women entered the stage and danced. Then a single, more fully clothed actress proceeded to take off her clothes, one garment at a time, to the accompaniment of loud music, until she was completely naked. Immediately someone covered her with a huge shawl.

I was not embarrassed to have Christopher see this show, since in our family everybody was used to seeing each other nude when swimming off the boat on our vacations in the Caribbean. But an elderly Canadian couple, sitting in front of us, turned around repeatedly and looked at me with highly raised eyebrows, as if to say, "Do you think this is a proper show to take your young son to see?" I thought that the attitude of these people showed their narrow-mindedness and that the show itself was a harmless performance. I recalled that, when I was Christopher's age and in Paris with my parents, they also took me to a show at Casino de Paris. There was a lot of dancing and some undressing, too, but I remember comments made by my aunt who lived in Paris at that time that my parents could take me to Casino de Paris but not to Folies Bergères, where the shows were more suggestive and not intended to be seen by youngsters. Christopher might have heard from his peers about Folies Bergères striptease shows, and this explains why after we left the theater he admitted to me his disappointment.

The next day, after a long walk around Paris, we found ourselves in front of a movie theater showing an Alfred Hitchcock film. My feet hurt from our tour and I was looking forward to sitting down. But in Paris children weren't allowed to see crime-related movies, even in the company of adults. I wondered about the French judgment concerning what was appropriate entertainment for youngsters: a striptease show, or a Hitchcock movie. I seriously doubted whether they could prevent juvenile crime by not letting their children watch an Alfred Hitchcock film.

After two days of sightseeing I went with Christopher in the morning to my eight o'clock appointment with Alexandre at his elegant beauty salon on rue St. Honoré. Unprepared for a long wait, I hadn't thought to bring any books either for me or for Christopher to read. I flipped restlessly through the pages of the fashion magazines that were there for their patrons. As time passed and the wait became longer and longer, it was very tiresome and annoying. I tried to make it more tolerable by convincing myself that women have to suffer to be beautiful. In the meantime, Christopher spent most of the time rolling back and forth on an elegant round couch in the center of the waiting room, periodically asking, "How much longer do we have to be here, Mommy?" Unfortunately, I knew as little as he did about this. At noon, quite miraculously, a lunch plate appeared in front of Christopher. He became quite happy for a while, but after another hour he began getting difficult. I too felt annoyed and worn out by waiting. Asking at the desk about how much longer I would need to wait resulted in assurances that the wait would not be much longer. But in spite of feeling guilty about letting Christopher be bored and restless to satisfy my selfish wish to have famous Alexandre cut my hair and not to disappoint Hilary, I would not dream of leaving. I had faith that Alexandre would come eventually, and it is in my nature to go through with all the necessary efforts to achieve a goal I have set up for myself. In spite of not having had any lunch, I refused to leave, so strong was my determination to wait, no matter how long.

It was not until five in the afternoon that the world famous hairdresser finally appeared and I had a chance to get a good look at him. Alexandre was a medium-sized man with dark hair, black eyes, and a charming smile; he looked tired and obviously was embarrassed that he had scheduled my appointment on the day of a big fashion show, where his services had been indispensable.

Then Alexandre began cutting my hair. I watched him and I listened as he told me that he was very careful to preserve the direction of the natural growth of my hair. Then he shaped it until it looked smart and flattering. Finally, when he was finished, he gave me the hand mirror so that I could see the back and sides. I looked like a different woman. I was more than satisfied; I was thrilled. At that moment, the wait ceased to matter to me, although I'm sure Christopher wouldn't have agreed.

In order to maintain this hair style after I was back home and without his further involvement, he gave me a sketch (which I still have) that illustrated for the benefit of my Philadelphia hairdresser how to carry out the details of his hairstyling technique. I also asked him about what kind of hair dye he would recommend for me. "Please don't ever dye your hair, Madame. It's beautiful as it is. When your gray hair becomes completely white, it will be even more beautiful. But once you start dying it, it will look mousy. Please listen to my advice. Goodbye, Madame," he said. And I did listen to his advice. I never dyed my gray hair, nor even used a rinse.

The next day Christopher and I flew to Brussels, where Hilary met us at the airport. "What did you do to your hair? You look stunning, Irena!" Hilary exclaimed when he saw me. Hearing that made the interminable day-long wait for Alexandre really worthwhile.

A year after our return from this European vacation, Claude obtained a Master's Degree from Johns Hopkins. It was 1964. He had by then abandoned the idea of becoming a diplomat. He returned to Philadelphia and applied to study international law at the University of Pennsylvania. But he ended up going to Penn's Annenberg School of Communication. With Claude back in Philadelphia, we remodeled our Wynnewood house to include a studio apartment for him. It was cheaper than to rent him one downtown.

After graduating, Claude was offered a position as a crime reporter at *The Washington Post*. He was given his own column and byline, which is every beginning reporter's dream. This development seemed to make him quite happy. He proudly displayed the photograph of me with a long knife bending over a dead body in a Rio de Janeiro city morgue. It seemed a perfect picture for the office of a crime reporter, implying criminal background on his maternal side, and I must say, as his mother, it pleased and amused me that he had it hanging there.

The following year, 1965, I began to have difficulties obtaining support for the experiments on the development and early detection of cancer of the womb that I was carrying out on mice. The priorities of the National Institutes of Health, which award cancer research grants, had changed. Applications concerned with genetics and/or molecular biology now had a better chance of being funded than did experimental cancer research based on studies of changes in the appearance of the cells during the development of cancer. I was at a disadvantage because I had made the mistake of not keeping up with new developments in genetics and molecular biology. I felt that the amount of time and effort I'd have had to spend to acquire a good knowledge of these expanding fields of medical research would slow down the progress of my experiments. In making this decision, I underestimated the trend to support molecular biology and genetics. The other types of research proposals likely to be supported were oriented toward treatment of cancer, rather than its causes and early detection. In spite of the abundance of money provided for chemotherapy, I failed to receive the support I needed. My grant to study cancer cells in cultures wasn't renewed.

After Dr. Maria Fernandes had left to go first to Washington and then to Brazil with her husband at a time that coincided with my grant coming to its termination, I had no more funds to hire a successor. I had to wait an entire year for the approval of my next application for a new research grant.

During that year I switched my major efforts from experimental work to the teaching of cytology to medical students. I developed a set of color transparencies that illustrated the appearance of normal cells and cancer cells in smears prepared from human secretions from those organs of the body where cancer and other diseases frequently develop: the uterus, lung, colon, and urinary bladder. Claude knew about the extensive collection of pictures of cancer cells I used for teaching medical students. He convinced the 3M Company to provide me with their newest equipment, and he suggested that I use it to develop a sophisticated audiovisual course on the Pap smear method of early cancer diagnosis. With the enthusiastic help of one of Hahnemann's sophomores, Clare Novotny, I did just that, and thus I pioneered a new approach to teaching cytology. This course was well received by Hahnemann's medical students and became part of their pathology curriculum.

Things were changing in Wynnewood. Our boxer, Bronco, was getting old. Fearing that we would be left without a family pet, I mated him and we got one of his offspring, whom we named Fuller. When Bronco died the following year, Fuller was already a member of our household and took possession of Bronco's armchair. He turned out to be a good pet, was particularly devoted to me, and remained with us for the rest of his life.

That same year, Hilary went to Nice for the celebration of his mother's eighty-third birthday. He invited to this birthday party several remaining members of her own family who lived in France, but he did not ask me to accompany him on this occasion. A few months later, we received a telephone call from her physician in Nice. My French being more fluent than his, Hilary wanted me to carry on this conversation. "Tell Dr. Koprowski to come immediately if he wants to see his mother alive. She had a stroke and is dying," the doctor was advising.

"Please go instead of me, Irena," Hilary pleaded with me.

I was surprised by his request. I felt the strength of his wish and the complexity of his feelings. I realized that his mother wouldn't know who was with her. Admittedly, being emotionally less involved and speaking French well, I would be in a better position than Hilary to take care of any necessary arrangements. His incredibly deep attachment to his mother overwhelmed him, and he needed more time to prepare for her loss. He simply couldn't endure the sight of his mother dying, and he needed me to spare him that suffering.

The next day I flew to France. When I arrived in Nice, Sofia Semeonovna was still in a coma. Her physician said that she might not survive the night. Her steel blue eyes were closed most of the time. When they opened a little, I thought that I detected in her eyes some sign of recognition of my voice. From what I saw, despite how ill she was, I didn't think she was about to die immediately.

I spent the night in a hotel room, and the next morning I returned to the hospital. My mother-in-law's doctor asked me if I wanted him to terminate her by euthanasia because she would never be more than a vegetable. As it was, they were not taking any extraordinary measures to keep her alive by breathing machines or by any other means. "No, I have no right to make this kind of decision. Neither have I the heart to ask my husband to do this. Please keep her alive as long as you can," I replied.

I then called Hilary, and I also spoke to Leon Gerber, his cousin, who now practiced medicine in Paris. They felt that there was no point in keeping my mother-in-law at the hospital in Nice, yet Hilary feared that she wouldn't survive a flight to the United States. Leon suggested I arrange for her to be transported by ambulance from Nice to his apartment in Paris. Leon's wife, Claude, was a nurse and would take excellent care of his aunt, for both she and Leon were very fond of Sofia. Once that was settled, I flew back home.

A few months later we visited Hilary's mother in Paris. She was still in a coma. We noticed that she continued making involuntary motions with her right hand. We gave her a pencil, which she was able to hold and use to make markings on the paper. But we couldn't distinguish any words or meaning in them. Realizing that the excellent care she received at Leon's house was the best that we could do for her and easiest on ourselves, we left her there and returned home. There did not seem any point in trying to visit her again.

Good news awaited me in Philadelphia. In 1966, the year after the renewal of my grant had been refused, I at last was awarded a new research grant from the National Cancer Institute. I hired Dr. Park, a capable Korean pathologist, to assist me in the resumption of experiments involving the use of chemicals to produce cancer of the womb in mice and to study their Pap smears throughout the development of their cancer. As in the past, I used mice for this study because the development of cancer of the womb in these animals is very similar to the natural evolution of cancer at this site in women. But now, in addition to watching the early appearance of malignant cells in Pap smears collected from these mice, we also grew and studied these cells in cultures. We wanted to compare the appearance and behavior of the cells throughout the evolution of cancer in these animals as they appeared in Pap smears and after they have been grown outside of the animal's body. Would they remain the same or change?

If we found that the appearance and behavior of the cells derived from an early cancer remained the same after being grown in cultures outside the animal body as they were upon removal from animals, it would be easier to experiment trying various means to interfere and even reverse the development of cancer. Once we were confident that something worked on the cells grown outside of the animal's body, we could try it on the cells growing in the animal as well. Ultimately it could be then tried on people.

So we removed from the wombs of these mice tiny pieces of tissue containing cells from very early cancer. This type of research is referred to as *in vitro* research and, as I've already indicated, can provide valuable information and is a lot easier than working with cancer cells growing inside of the bodies of animals *(in vivo)*.

These experiments were very tedious to perform, but they were productive and useful, for we discovered that the appearance of cancer cells grown *in vitro* was similar to how they look *in vivo*. Thus by studying this process in mice I was able to learn much that would very likely be applicable to the development and hopefully the arrest of cancer growing in humans. But we were still a long way from reversing the appearance and behavior of the cancer cells to a normal state—and only such reversal could be useful in attempts to eliminate cancer in human beings. I devoted almost all of my time to this research, delegating much of my responsibilities for diagnostic work and teaching to the highly qualified associates I had at the time.

In 1967, eight months after she had her stroke in Nice, Hilary's mother died in Leon's apartment. She was eighty-four years old. Hilary flew to Paris when his mother was cremated. By the time she died, he had known for many months that she was gone. This sad event may have been easier for him to witness than the actual process of her dying. Sofia Semeonovna's ashes were placed in an urn at Père Lachaise Cemetery in Paris. Now, whenever Hilary goes to Paris, he puts fresh flowers in front of her urn and, whenever I accompany him, we bring flowers and meditate there for a few moments.

Unanticipated Problems

After Hilary's mother's death, I did my best to help Hilary cope with his loss. I became a more caring wife, doing for him things that I remembered she had done. I also became more interested in his problems, which he now mentioned to me more often. I paid more attention to his clothes and cooked him dishes he liked, as his mother had done. In fact, although I was very committed to my research, I waited on him hand and foot. I could see that this made him happy, and I got great pleasure from this, too, for it made me feel more valuable to Hilary, whose approval and attention were so central to my happiness. With my devotion, I helped him bring out the strength of his character that had been so long suppressed by his mother's domination. Now it became apparent that he was a strong man rather than a weakling.

In 1967, Conceição got married and left. Suddenly I had to do everything myself — clean the house, shop for food, cook, launder, and take care of the dog. I gave up any hope of finding another housekeeper and looked for someone just to clean the house and do the laundry.

That same year, when my domestic help situation was still quite tenuous, I was contacted by Kaja Bielecka. She was the daughter of Vera L., who had been my friend and classmate when I was a young girl in Poland, attending the Popielewska-Roszkowska Gymnasium. Vera and I had spent many Sunday afternoons gossiping in the hayloft on my parents' property at Solec Street. During Hilary's and my 1958 visit to Poland I had visited her and she told me that she had a daughter, Kaja. Heksa, another classmate of mine who'd been living in London for years, was good friends with Vera and maintained contact with her. She wrote me that Kaja, who was then in her late teens, had recently gone to London as an au pair. She was unhappy with her job and wanted to come to America. Hilary thought that we should know more about Kaja before deciding whether to bring her to live with us. It happened that Hilary was to travel to Europe and had to change planes in London at Heathrow Airport. So he could meet and interview Kaja there. After his return from Europe, Hilary told me that during their talk he found out that Kaja had some love affairs behind her and that she seemed to like older men. This information created in me very mixed feelings, but I was so desperate for domestic help and so wished to accommodate the daughter of my old school friend that I disregarded my concern about her behavior in our household.

Kaja was a slim, dark-haired twenty-year-old girl with flashing black eyes. At first, she was euphoric about having her own room and home-cooked food. She offered to do all the housework in return for her room and board, and I accepted this offer at face value. But once I started assigning her work, she became very resentful. She began to behave in an odd manner and to avoid all contact with me.

One evening I had a hospital meeting. When I returned home, Hilary told me that Kaja had been looking very sad. So he felt sorry for her and took her to the movies in the hope it would cheer her up. I didn't say anything, but I resented that Hilary was more sensitive to Kaja's moods than to my feelings. I asked myself immediately why, in an attempt to cheer up Kaja, he took her to see a film that I might have enjoyed seeing with him.

Thus, Kaja's entry in our life initiated a recurrence of occasional difficulties in my relationship with Hilary. I said nothing to Hilary or Kaja about this incident because her presence in our house made us also realize her problems. Kaja aspired to a better future than being an au pair. But she wasn't clear as to what she wanted to become and was not inclined to discuss it with me. One evening I tried to have a talk with her about her plans.

"I'm sorry, but I have a headache and I'm going upstairs to lie down," she said.

Since Hilary was working in the den at his desk, I went upstairs to take care of paying the bills. Half an hour later, I heard voices and came downstairs. I saw Hilary and Kaja with brandy glasses in their hands sitting close to each other on the sofa. Kaja's head was slightly bent over the back of the sofa, and she had a dreamy look on her face. This sight infuriated me.

"Brandy is no good for a headache, Kaja. Please return to your room and leave me alone with my husband," I said angrily. After Kaja left the den, Hilary simply got up from the sofa and moved to his desk to resume his work. I followed him. "I can't understand you, Hilary," I said. "You told me this evening that you had to work, and I gave you a chance to do it. Yet you had time to have a drink with Kaja."

"If you had ever had a daughter, you would have made her miserable, Irena. You are completely lacking in any understanding of young girls."

Hilary's critical remark increased my anger at his and Kaja's behavior. He acted innocent and treated me as the guilty party, when quite the opposite was the case.

Of course, I had been concerned all along about bringing Kaja to live with us, but I had been trying to sweep my worries under the rug. Now they hit me with full force. I became alarmed and wondered if she was trying to seduce my husband by making him concerned about her.

Still, his remark got to me. Could he have been right? Was it true that if I had had a daughter, I would have made her miserable? Might my lack of empathy have kept me from seeing that it was quite legitimate for him to have interrupted his work out of pity for Kaja? I returned upstairs to my room feeling miserable. I was fifty and approaching menopause, and all I needed was a pretty young girl of twenty in my house who preferred older men.

From then on, Kaja became even more antagonistic toward me while continuing to seek Hilary's attention and sympathy. She also tried to endear herself to Christopher, but she antagonized him by making critical remarks and complaining about me to him. Christopher, who was very interested in psychology, looked at Kaja in a different light than I did. "She's a sociopath," Christopher remarked.

While I was having these problems with Kaja, Claude, then twenty-eight, was flourishing at *The Washington Post*. He came home frequently for weekends, bringing friends. One weekend he arrived with a married couple, their two dogs, and a young girl he had recently met at a party. Elizabeth Cole Gustafson, a Smith College student, was nine years his junior.

Sunday morning, while everybody else still slept and as I began to prepare breakfast, Elizabeth came down to the kitchen. She told me that she was born in Washington, D.C., of Swedish parents. It impressed me that she had wanted to be a clinical psychologist since she was nine years old. I was amazed that she knew so well what she wanted to become. I was thinking about how often Claude had changed his mind about his future.

A few days later Claude called to thank me for an enjoyable weekend. "What did you think of Liz?" he asked.

"I liked her a lot. I think it's about time that you became interested in a nice girl like her," I told him.

A week later Claude called again. "Mom, I proposed to Elizabeth. She accepted, and we would like you and Dad to come to Washington for our engagement party." I was happy because I had a strong feeling that Claude and Elizabeth would complement each other well.

A diamond ring that we had found in Hilary's father's safe deposit box in England made a nice engagement ring for Liz. From then on things moved rapidly, and soon we were planning a 1968 wedding. Liz wanted a big church wedding in Washington. Claude became annoyed because he and I had a small ceremony in mind. I took him aside. "If you care enough about Liz to marry her, why won't you fulfill her dream?" I suggested.

That settled the issue, and all of us accepted the idea of a big church wedding. Hilary invited members of the Wistar Institute and chartered a bus from Philadelphia. Stanislaw Kryszek and Jan Majeranowski, our classmates from medical school who were now practicing medicine in the United States, also attended. Following Polish tradition, they had a few drinks with Hilary and Claude just before the wedding.

"What's the difference between a Polish wedding and a wake?" Jan M. asked.

"There's one less person to drink at the wake," Kryszek promptly replied.

I knew Liz was the girl I wanted my son to marry, and yet I felt a sudden sadness at the thought that I was giving my son away to another woman. I would lose first place in his heart. My eyes became moist for a brief moment. But then I smiled—this was the way it should be.

We took Kaja with us to Claude's wedding. During the reception, unknown to us at the time, she told several people how unhappy and badly treated she was in our household. Shortly after our return to Wynnewood, Kaja told Hilary that she was going to New York. She left our house the next morning without saying good-bye to me.

"No good deed remains unpunished," Hilary said, trying to humor me. He realized my predicament, but it was cold comfort.

In 1968, the same year Claude married Liz, Christopher graduated from Haverford School and entered Princeton University. He came home on weekends, using Claude's former studio apartment.

I was now entitled to a sabbatical leave at Hahnemann, but unexpectedly my research grant from the National Cancer Institute wasn't renewed. I had hoped that Hilary and I could take our leaves at the same time. Hilary had made arrangements to go to Munich for his research leave to study the behavior of ducks with Konrad Lorenz. Also, I had just hired an associate, Dr. Chang, to carry on a substantial load of hospital diagnostic tests based on Pap smears and thus give me more time for experimental work, graduate education, and cytotechnology training. These programs also lost their support and now I was required to devote my time to teaching a general pathology course to medical students which I didn't like. Anyway, there was no longer enough money in the department for an additional pathologist. After having hired Dr. Chang, instead of letting him go so soon, and having lost interest in my job, I decided to look for another opportunity for myself.

Dealing with Bosses

No sooner did my interest in other opportunities become known when I received a telephone call from Renato Baserga, the new chairman of pathology at Temple University. A few days later I was sitting in Baserga's office at the medical school, and we were discussing my coming to Temple.

Baserga offered me the position of director of cytology at Temple University Hospital, as well as a professorship of pathology at the medical school. I would report to Diane Crocker, the new chief of hospital pathology. He promised as well that I would become tenured in one year. My salary would be about thirty percent more than what I was getting at Hahnemann.

I went with Baserga from the medical school across the street to the hospital to meet Diane Crocker. I saw a slim woman in her mid-forties with immaculately groomed, smooth dark hair in a simple elegant navy suit. She smiled as she stretched her hand toward me. "I'm glad to meet you, and I'm very happy that you agreed to come," she said cordially.

In striking contrast to the well-equipped facilities at Hahnemann that I was about to abandon, only a very small area was allotted to the Temple cytology laboratory. But everything else was more promising. My salary would be higher than at Hahnemann, and I would be able to bring my cytotechnologists with me. I knew of no better options in Philadelphia, and I didn't want to consider relocating geographically. I discussed it with Hilary, and we both felt that I should accept Temple's offer.

I expected that coming to a more research-oriented department at Temple would increase my chances of getting a new grant. What I didn't realize, however, was that Baserga, my new department chairman, valued me primarily as an expert in diagnosing cancer cells of hospital patients, a profit-making procedure. He wasn't about to facilitate my research activities. This contributed to some of my future disappointments.

When I began work at Temple in August 1970, Hilary was in Munich. Our separation was very difficult for me. I had no companionship and nobody with whom to discuss my new job. Several aspects of my situation at Temple were immediately distressing. I was disappointed that no office had been assigned to me prior to my arrival at Temple University Hospital. Parking was a problem too, although I had been assured of a parking space during my interview with Baserga.

But the worst aspect of my job was dealing with Diane Crocker. She was younger than I was, had no recognized accomplishments in research, and was mainly interested in data processing. Although at Temple she was chief of hospital pathology, she had never before occupied a position of authority. "Isn't it wonderful to be in a position of power. One can do anything one wants to." She surprised me with this statement only a few days after my arrival.

During the first few weeks of my employment, she often made flattering remarks about any new outfits I wore. At departmental conferences, Diane Crocker was constantly in sight. She sat next to Renato, smiling sweetly at him and as it seemed to me deliberately engaged him in conversation, preventing me or other members of the department from talking to him.

Baserga was glad that Diane Crocker relieved him of dealing with the hospital administration, clinicians, the residents training program, departmental conferences, and pathology services. In return, he allowed her to exercise power over the members of the pathology department. I became her favorite victim.

Although her knowledge of cytology was negligible, she made the decision that she personally would cover the cytology service during my absences. Whenever I was away, she harassed E. Lou Bridges, my chief cytotechnologist, making derogatory remarks about my cytologic reports. She also looked into her desk drawers to examine their contents.

Soon she dealt me a much more severe blow. I had brought with me the 3M equipment, with which Claude had helped me to create an audiovisual teaching course at Hahnemann. No other school had this type of teaching aid, and I was very proud of it. When I mentioned this course to Diane Crocker, she said that she would have the departmental teaching committee, which she chaired, review it. Several weeks later she told me that the Department of Illustrations at Temple used a different kind of audiovisual equipment, which was not compatible with mine. Her decision was that my course couldn't be included in the Temple pathology curriculum. It was placed instead for optional use at the medical school library.

At the time, I was receiving requests for this course from members of the American Society of Cytology, the International Academy of Cytology's Committee on Education, and the World Health Organization. My materials were used to teach medical students at Johns Hopkins and abroad in Iran and in Australia. But according to the judgment of Diane Crocker, its use at Temple was not suitable.

At Temple my role as a teacher became negligible. I gave a lecture to medical students only once a year. I was assigned to teach students in laboratory modules, which had usually been the responsibility of junior faculty, pathology residents, and pathologists from affiliated hospitals, but not of Temple medical school senior faculty.

I still had no domestic help. Being unable to find satisfactory live-in help, I hired a totally inexperienced woman and began to train her myself. I had to teach her even how to peel vegetables, use the vacuum cleaner, and launder. Fortunately, Inez was willing to learn and had a pleasant disposition. She still knew very little when Hilary returned for a visit from Munich.

"You're crazy, Irena. This woman will never do!" he declared after being home for half a day. But the effort I invested in training Inez started paying dividends. Our relationship became one of an apprentice and master, free from the usual labor-management resentments. I was rewarded for my patience. Soon I gained not only a maid, but a dedicated member of our household.

During Hilary's brief visits to Philadelphia, we didn't have much opportunity to relax and enjoy being together. When I went to Europe for our promised vacation in Portugal, Hilary arranged for me only an overnight stop in Munich, making no effort to acquaint me with his new environment, about which I had been curious. Hilary said, "We've only one week for our vacation. Let's go to Portugal as soon as possible."

Hilary always wore many different hats, and he changed them depending upon whom he happened to be with at the time, creating different images of himself to people who knew him but who differed in their perceptions of what he was like. Perhaps I didn't fit in with the image he created for himself in Munich, and this was why he didn't want me to stay there any longer than was necessary. The bonds of our marriage, which had become stronger after Sofia's death, seemed to be weakened by his absense.

I returned from our vacation in Portugal to face new problems at work. I had come to Temple on a tenure-track position, with the promise that I would be granted tenure in one year. But Diane Crocker succeeded in having the discussion of my tenure postponed for one more year. By the time I realized that she was an abnormally mean person, I was ashamed that I had tolerated her behavior so long. I was ashamed to admit it to anybody other than my family. I became obsessed with Diane Crocker's hostility towards me, and when Hilary returned from Munich I could hardly talk to him about anything else. I was miserable.

One day Claude came to visit us with Liz. By then he had left *The Washington Post* and had a job as an editor of *Research Reports* in Bethesda. "I made a big mistake. I should have gone to medical school," he announced. Then he added, "I can still do it."

He was twenty-nine years old. This time neither Hilary nor I offered to pay his tuition. "I'll get a job and support us both," Elizabeth proposed. Claude submitted applications to eighteen different medical schools, all of which rejected him. Then, three days before the beginning of the academic year, he was called by the office of the State University of New York, Downstate Medical College in Brooklyn, and offered a slot which had become vacant. An applicant who had become pregnant relinquished that spot.

During his first year of medical school, Claude lived alone in Brooklyn. Elizabeth, who by then had entered graduate school, had still to complete her internship in clinical psychology at St. Elizabeth's Hospital in Washington, D.C. They saw each other every other week at our home in Wynnewood, half-way between their house in Arlington, Virginia, where Liz still lived, and Brooklyn.

In the meantime, I persevered in writing applications to the United States Public Health Service for grants to support my research. This time I wanted to grow, outside of the human body, the cells obtained from the wombs of women who had carcinoma in situ—i.e., from a cancer precursor that hasn't as yet begun to invade the tissues. In the past I had grown in culture cells from mice with chemically induced cancer. But this time I wanted to use human cells so that the results of my study would be more applicable to the understanding of the evolution of cancer of the womb in women. These efforts paid off in 1972, when I was awarded a three-year research grant from the National Cancer Institute. Suddenly my situation at Temple improved. I was now entitled to space for a research laboratory at the medical school. At once I was freed from many departmental duties, including performing autopsies and the preparation of conferences. My teaching load was decreased. All this removed me from the dominance of Diane Crocker.

Finally I received tenure. Feeling more secure, I began spending more of my time hiring personnel, purchasing equipment and supplies, organizing my research laboratory and planning experiments. Failing to find an experimental pathologist of Dr. Park's competence, I hired an available Ph.D. biochemist to use biopsies to grow cultures of the epithelial cells lining the womb. When he failed to establish long-term cultures of epithelial cells, I decided to study instead fibroblasts, which are cells that grow underneath epithelial cells and provide support and nourishment for the lining cells. Fibroblasts grow easily in cultures.

Having established cultures of fibroblasts from the necks of the womb of women with and without early cancer, I compared their respective properties. I discovered that, unlike normal fibroblasts, the fibroblasts underlying a carcinoma in situ resemble cancer cells. The fibroblasts that support and nourish epithelial cells from early cancer of the womb agglutinate (make clumps of) a wheat germ protein known as Concanavalin A, which is a characteristic reaction of cancer cells. Normal cells don't agglutinate Concanavalin A. This was an important discovery because, contrary to the existent concept that cancer of the womb develops only from the lining of epithelial cells, we had demonstrated that other cells also participate in this process of cancerization. When I published with Dr. Chandhuri, my new associate, the results of our study in *Cancer Research,* our paper attracted attention from the national and international scientific community, and we received many requests for reprints. In fact, our paper was listed among the cancer research papers of special importance for 1972.

My Sabbatical

After Christopher graduated from Princeton, he became a student at the Temple University School of Medicine. Christopher lived at home during his first two years of medical school and we were often alone when Hilary was away attending meetings abroad. It helped us to become much closer than we had been since his childhood. "I'm your Pipsiadelko Pomponik" (Little Pompon-Peeps), he would say. He enjoyed repeating this babyish name, which was all he could say in his ancestral tongue.

When he became aware of occasional domestic tensions, he began to criticize my attitude toward his father. "Mom, don't drive Dad away from home," he told me one day. I was shocked, because I didn't realize that I was doing this.

"Mom, you're very inflexible. Please give in sometimes, and you'll see that things will get better. Dad is a very complex human being. But he's a kind man and quite easy to manipulate."

"I never meant to drive your father away from home," I told him. "It is true that sometimes I say unpleasant things to him when he goes out alone and is insensitive to my feelings."

"This isn't the way to deal with him. Don't ever reproach him, Mom, when he leaves you alone. Ask him instead with tearful eyes, 'What have I done to deserve being abandoned?' Tell him how much you missed him when he comes back. This will make him feel guilty. He's basically a good person. The next time he'll be more considerate of your feelings."

Of all people, my younger son was the only person who ever spoke to me about my relationship with Hilary, and it was he who taught me how to deal with his father. In some ways Christopher resembled his father, and because of this he understood him better than anybody else. I learned from this "baby of my heart," as I used to call Christopher, how to deal more effectively with my husband.

I decided to follow Christopher's advice and be more flexible, giving in on matters that were less important to me than to Hilary. I planned my strategy as I would plan a scientific experiment. I took a pad of yellow paper and a pen, and I put a longitudinal line separating the left and right sides of the page. I put a heading on the left side column, "Hilary Wants," and wrote "I Want" on the right side. Then I identified and listed our separate wants.

These desires were apparent from our past arguments. For example, Hilary complained about my objections to his bringing home guests for dinners, the monotony of meals, and my lack of interest in my hairstyle and fashionable clothes. I was concerned about the extent of his demands upon my valuable time and efforts. I complained about his failure to give me adequate notice before bringing home unexpected dinner guests. I really had no time to create gourmet meals because he would often call me at the last minute. As for my loss of interest in my appearance, he took me out with him rarely and, when he did, it was usually on short notice. I had no time to dress properly, so I had stopped caring how I looked. I wanted more of his companionship and more sharing in his cultural and social life.

Just as I decided on my strategy, Hilary came home late for dinner and immediately started making demands. "Go to the garden and pick some fresh basil, Irena. Don't let it go to waste. I'll make green pesto for the pasta," he said as soon as he walked in that night.

I had made other plans for our dinner, and I was greatly tempted to tell him that it was late and that if he wanted pesto, he should have let me know ahead of time. Our cleaning woman could have picked the basil during the day. But I recalled Christopher's advice. "I'll be happy to, Hilary," I said instead. "Would you also do something to please me? There's a movie I want to see. Can we go, when you have a free evening?" I added smiling.

"I'll be free tomorrow night. Let's have an early dinner and go out," Hilary said, looking at me with surprise and also smiling.

I was encouraged by the initial success of this new system. It worked then, and it continued to work. After a while my relationship with Hilary became much happier. We both had to give up something. But fortunately, different things were important to each one of us. I started going more often to beauty salons, bought new dresses, and became interested in trying new dishes. He began to bring guests for drinks at home and then take all of us out to eat. He also got subscriptions to the Metropolitan Opera for the two of us.

In 1972 Hanka, the daughter of Joanna, one of Hilary's cousins, spent a month with us on her way from Poland to Toronto where she would be employed as an au pair. I liked this pink-cheeked eighteen-year-old girl with her blond hair and endearing smile. In her very tight dungarees, flaring at the bottom in the manner of a fish tail, she reminded me of a mermaid. Hilary, who had come from a close-knit family on his mother's side, considered it his responsibility to look after his cousin's daughter. So we maintained contact with her while she was living in Canada.

In 1973 Hilary began suffering from leg pain as a result of a dislocated lumbar disc. He tried all kinds of treatments to avoid surgery. He needed attention, and I needed more help at home to provide it. Hilary had a solution. When Hanka's employment as an au pair girl in Canada was approaching its end, she confided to Hilary that she didn't want to return to Poland, and sought his advice about coming to the United States. Hilary showed me her letter as I was lifting the heavy sandbags necessary for traction for his leg.

"Let's be realistic, Irena," he began. "If Hanka doesn't return to Poland, she'll need money and someone to guide her future. She expects our help, which we can provide more effectively if she were to stay with us. She may also become useful. She can cook. We can bring Hanka to this country on a working permit as a cook because she graduated from a culinary institute in Poland. That would be the fastest way she could come to the United States as an immigrant."

I had my doubts about assuming quasi-parental responsibilities for Hanka, concerned about additional expenses and lack of privacy. But I needed more help badly and ended up agreeing.

Hanka came to live with us in 1973. She was then nineteen years old. Gradually she assumed the responsibility for cooking, food shopping, and planning menus in our household. Hanka was a good cook, and she became a big help to me. We gave her only a modest amount of money, but paid all her expenses. I noticed Hanka's occasional moodiness and that Hilary was very sensitive to these moods and her aspirations.

When Claude's wife, Elizabeth, announced her pregnancy, I stopped thinking about Hanka. I was worried about this additional financial responsibility, which I realized would be ours since Claude was a third-year medical student and wouldn't be able to support his family for several more years. But when Elizabeth gave birth to a son whom they named Hilary II on January 21, 1974, Hilary and I were equally thrilled. "I don't mind being a grandfather, but I don't like being married to a grandmother," Hilary liked to joke whenever anybody asked him how he liked being a grandfather.

Hilary's leg pain persisted in spite of traction and other forms of treatment, including chiropractic. Finally he agreed to subject himself to surgery for a dislocated disc. In November of 1974 Claude accompanied him to Tennessee for his operation because I had to present a paper at the annual meeting of the American Society of Cytology on that day. But as soon as I read my paper, I flew to Memphis to be with Hilary. "So your cytology meeting was more important to you than your husband," Hilary reproached me, knowing that he made me feel guilty and enjoying it.

Several months after Hilary's operation, Baserga relinquished his chair. "Irena, now that Renato stepped down from the chairmanship of pathology, the search committee wants to know whether you're interested in this opening. We think that you would be an excellent chairman," Walter Levy, one of the associate professors, pleaded with me.

I was surprised. It had never entered my mind to become a department chairman. The chairmanship of the department had never appealed to me, and I was also convinced that I stood no chance of getting it at Temple. The department had two other full professors more powerful than I, and both with more seniority. Either Wallace Clark or Emmanuel Farber certainly was more likely to be appointed, and I wanted to avoid the humiliation of the defeat. I behaved as I did years before at Cornell when I never indicated my interest in becoming Papanicolaou's successor. "I'm flattered that you consider me worthy of the chairmanship, Walter," I answered. "But I don't think that I would be given serious consideration."

I returned home that evening, and while I waited for Hilary to tell him about my conversation with Walter Levy, Christopher, now twenty-three, came home. "Chris, how would you feel if I entered the competition for the chairmanship of pathology at Temple?" I asked him.

"Mom, you're absolutely crazy! You already have enough problems as head of the cytology section, and you have to struggle for your grants. Just imagine spreading yourself still thinner. You'd have even less time to spend at home than you do now. Dad would complain. He might even want to divorce you," my son concluded jokingly.

Christopher was wrong about his father's reaction to the prospect of my chairmanship of the department. Hilary thought that I should have sought it. But I had already made up my mind not to.

A few months later Wallace Clark became the chairman of our department. He came to see me four weeks later during the preparation of the departmental budget. We sat in my small office, and he closed the door from the adjoining laboratory, where technicians were looking through the microscope screening Pap smears for cancer cells. "Irena, I'm concerned about your salary. It's very low," he said.

I was surprised. I had come to Temple in 1970 at a salary that was 33 percent higher than my pay at Hahnemann. I thought I had made a good deal.

"Irena, your salary is very low," Wallace repeated. "It's below the minimum for a full professor. It can't remain this low. I have to give you a significant raise to bring it within the range of your rank." I listened without understanding his point.

"Why wasn't I given a salary within the range of my academic rank when I came here three years ago?" I finally asked. "And why are you so willing to upgrade it now, Wally?" He became visibly embarrassed.

"Dr. Tassoni, your predecessor, the former cytology director, had only the rank of an associate professor. When he left, his salary, paid from the hospital budget, became available and was given to you, although it was below your full professorial rank. Since then the National Institutes of Health have become interested in the salaries of academic women. Grants are being withheld from institutions in which discrimination against women is discovered. We simply can't underpay you any more. The dean of the medical school offered his discretionary funds to upgrade your salary. Concerning other budgetary matters, I can't approve your request to support the technicians' continuing education program or pay for their travel to the annual meeting of the American Society of Cytology. Sorry about that, Irena." He didn't wait for me to reply, but opened the door and walked out of my office.

I remained seated, flushed with anger and feeling thoroughly confused. So this is what they did to me at Temple. Knowing how low my Hahnemann salary had been, they felt that the pay they offered me was a sufficient improvement so they wouldn't have to offer me the salary of a full professor. They wanted to correct this situation only out of fear that this might cause trouble for the institution. But to make up the difference, they were unwilling to provide me with adequate support for the cytology laboratory. They didn't seem to appreciate my efforts to make my laboratory one of the leading teaching centers in the country.

I was happy that my salary had been raised from $33,000 to $45,000, the lowest limit for a full professor. For the first time in my life I would have a decent salary. At the same time I was furious that I had been deprived of an income which had been due to me for several years. I knew that many women were suing academic institutions because of this type of discrimination. I would have a strong case if I were to sue to demand my back pay, but the legal procedures this would have entailed were sure to be long-lasting and aggravating.

In 1975, my fifth year at Temple, I at last earned the right to a sabbatical. Hilary's back surgery had been successful, and he felt fit after his convalescence. Hanka, who was still living with us, had taken over the bulk of my domestic responsibilities at home. Our housekeeper Inez, who by then had been with us for five years, kept the house clean and took care of the laundry and the dog. I knew that my current three-year research grant wasn't going to be renewed. I needed to learn new technology to improve my chances for a future grant.

One day I reminded Hilary that, five years earlier, I had foregone my sabbatical in order to get a new job at Temple. Now, in 1975, I had earned another sabbatical and would like to use it profitably. I asked him if he could take a second study leave so that we could go some place together.

"I can't take a second study leave now because of the construction of a new wing at the Wistar Institute," Hilary said in a firm tone of voice. "But you should go alone and go as soon as possible, Irena. The boys are away from home, I'm well, and the house is well looked after by Hanka and Inez. Don't wait until some disaster prevents your going," he added.

Hilary's view was very much my own. Understandably, I had some concern about leaving Hanka with Hilary. But in spite of my disquiet, I knew that unless I went away, I wouldn't have enough peace of mind to concentrate on learning the new research procedures I had selected.

After I admitted to him my uncertainties about where to go, Hilary suggested, "Attend lectures and work in the laboratories at the Imperial Cancer Research Fund at Lincoln Fields in London. Contact Michael Stoker, director of the Imperial Cancer Research Fund, who's my good friend. He'll accept you as a Visiting Fellow." I followed Hilary's advice and was accepted.

On the day of my departure, Hilary came to see me off at the airport. After we kissed and hugged each other, and just before I went through passport control and security, I looked back. Hilary was standing there without attempting to return to his car. Never before had I seen such an expression of despair as he now had in his eyes. He looked as if his whole world had collapsed because I was leaving him alone. I hadn't realized how he felt about my departure and how much he hated being left alone. I felt intensely happy seeing how much I really meant to him.

During my first few weeks in London I settled down in my apartment, met people at the Lincoln Fields Cancer Research Fund, and began learning organ culture techniques and electron microscopy. I quickly adopted the London lifestyle, going to pubs and theaters.

One day after I had been in Europe for three months, Hilary telephoned to ask me to meet him for a weekend in France and then to accompany him on a trip to Tehran.

I flew from London to Lyon where Hilary had been attending an all day conference on rabies at the Merieux Institute. When I arrived at the Hotel Sofitel where we were going to meet and spend the night, there was a message that Hilary would join me for dinner. An hour later I had on a black silk cocktail dress and we sat at a table by the window looking down at the night lights of the city.

Hilary ordered pâté de foie gras with Pommard 1968 Red Burgundy to whet our appetites before lobster tails and duck, our two main courses. Then he turned his attention to me. "I'm glad that the opening of the cancer research wing is over," he began. "For three days we had people from all over the world coming and going. The event was very successful, but exhausting."

He expected my sympathy. I was dumbfounded. The romantic mood deserted me as I listened to him and I felt as if the world were crumbling around me. "So the new addition to Wistar was a wing for cancer research! I had no idea," I managed to say.

"The National Cancer Institute gave a substantial grant to the Wistar Institute for a new building, Irena," Hilary went on. Hilary must have submitted an application a year or two in advance in order to get this grant. A proposal linking my project with the Wistar Institute's program would have enhanced my chances of getting a grant. He had made such arrangements with other scientists. Did he fear being accused of nepotism if he helped me? Worse, he had kept me ignorant of his plans.

"Why wasn't I invited to the celebrations at the opening of the cancer wing at the Wistar Institute, Hilary?" I demanded in a louder tone of voice.

"Because you were away," he said defensively.

"Didn't you just say that people from all over the world were coming and going for three days? Haven't I been involved long enough in cancer research to be included?" I persevered.

"It was an oversight, Irena," Hilary said in a low and uncertain voice.

His answer sounded lame. Whose oversight had he been referring to, if not his own? I recalled the look of despair on Hilary's face on the day of my departure from the United States. I wondered if he had ceased to think about me altogether when I had been away. Now I felt slighted not only as a cancer researcher, but as a scientist in general.

In spite of my anger and disappointment, I accompanied Hilary to Iran. I had been looking forward to this trip because of my past work in Tehran. I was glad that I had come after I saw the gratifying results of the work I had done at the Tehran Cancer Institute in 1962 on behalf of the World Health Organization. Thirteen years earlier they hadn't even been able to perform routine examinations of Pap smears for cancer cells. Now they had a well-staffed laboratory run by a team of people trained at the Johns Hopkins Department of Cytopathology. Having recently established their own training facilities, the Tehran Cancer Institute had purposely scheduled the official opening of their school of cytotechnology to coincide with my visit. The faculty of the school wanted me to see that my 1962 efforts had been fruitful.

Hilary and I attended joint social functions, shopped, and went sightseeing together, but after we left Iran I returned to London and he to Philadelphia.

Back at Lincoln Fields, I was working on my next proposal for a research grant that would utilize the new techniques I'd learned in London. But my secretary wrote me that Wallace Clark had ordered her to stop working on my application. Nor did he reply to my letters demanding the reason for his action. I was furious and made several person-to-person telephone calls to Philadelphia. After repeated attempts, I finally succeeded in reaching Clark.

"What's going on, Wallace?" I shouted at him. "I'm working hard here to put together a new research proposal, and you stop my secretary from typing it. Why? What's going on?" I was very angry and continued shouting.

"I'm sorry, Irena," he replied in an uncertain voice. "The departmental research committee looked at the draft of your application and didn't think that your proposal was good enough to approve. That's why I had to stop your secretary from typing it. But I can't talk to you now. I have a lecture to give."

So this was it. I was wasting my time during my sabbatical if I wouldn't be able to put to good use what I was learning in London. I was very angry at the Temple departmental research committee. Who were they, anyway? Probably just Wallace Clark and Renato Baserga, who were interested only in their own research. What right did they have to sabotage my efforts to get a grant? Apparently my absence from Philadelphia had given them an opportunity to play games. I felt helpless.

My return home from England began unpleasantly. When my plane landed at Philadelphia airport I looked for Hilary, but he wasn't there. Instead he had sent Christopher to bring me home. "It's good to have you back, Mom," Christopher said, hugging and kissing me. I was very disappointed that Hilary had not met me at the airport. My resentment of his failure to invite me to the Wistar opening returned with full strength.

As we pulled into our driveway, I had the shock of my life. There was Hilary's car pulling out, Hilary at the wheel waving his hand to me in a perfunctory greeting. Sitting next to him with a frightened look on her face was Hanka, who pretended not to see me. My eyes filled with tears. "For heaven's sake, what's going on? What kind of marriage do I have? I've been away for six months and Dad not only fails to welcome me at the airport, but leaves the house with Hanka the very moment that I come home," I cried, deeply traumatized.

Christopher brought my suitcases into the house, and I started unpacking with shaking hands while he sat on a chair watching me silently. When Hilary returned home an hour later, he tried to take me in his arms and kiss me, but I pushed him away. "Why didn't you come to meet me at the airport?" I shouted at him angrily. "Where's Hanka? Where were you taking her the very moment of my return? You owe me some explanation."

"During your absence, Hanka took good care of the house. She also visited Bronislawa frequently. But now that you're back, she wants to free herself from these obligations," he began. "She's enrolled at Temple for the fall semester and found herself an apartment in town. She'll live near Wistar so that I can keep an eye on her and where she'll be able to see the people she knows at the institute." He spoke quietly, ignoring my anger.

Bad news also awaited me at Temple. "Dr. Pen Ming is now using your research laboratory and the rest of your equipment at the medical school, Dr. Koprowska," my secretary informed me. "Dr. Clark brought only your microscope here."

I could hardly believe that anything like this could happen. Three years ago I had established my research laboratory and purchased equipment from my grant money. Now I learned that, during my absence, all this has been taken away from me and made available to Pen Ming, an associate professor of pathology who had no grant of her own, but who instead was working with Renato Baserga under the provision of his grant. I was outraged. I got up, red in the face, excused myself and went to see Wallace Clark in his office.

"Why was my research laboratory with all my expensive equipment taken away from me during my absence, Wally?" I asked angrily.

"Irena, you know the rules. Once you lose your research grant, your laboratory space with all its equipment becomes the property of the department. I was under terrific pressure during your absence," Wally said. But he didn't tell me under whose pressure he had been, and I didn't ask.

Through the opened office door I saw Renato standing in the hall. His head appeared several times at the door, but he didn't enter. Suddenly I realized under whose pressure Wally must have been during my absence. All of a sudden I saw the blocking of my grant application by the departmental research committee in a new light. I strongly suspected it was blocked to make my space and equipment available for someone else.

"Space is at a premium. Your equipment wasn't being used during your absence, but was needed by other people. I couldn't keep it for you, since without your grant you wouldn't be able to use it anyway," Wallace Clark droned on. "Please don't try to enter Dr. Ming's current laboratory. It's off limits for you now, Irena." Then he paused. "I hope that from now on you'll devote your time completely to hospital service, running the Pap smear cytology laboratory and teaching medical students, Irena. This is what the department expects of you." Wallace Clark ended our conversation with this statement.

The next day I went to see the dean. "I'm sorry, Irena, but I must support the decision of the departmental chairman," he said. I became embittered, depressed, and very unhappy as I carried out my institutional obligations. I was uncertain what to do. I thought that this was the end of my career as a scientist.

With no other distressing domestic incidents during the next few weeks, Hilary and I resumed our life together. My anger at Hanka gradually subsided. She began visiting us at home, often on Sundays when Christopher, Bronislawa, and Gene were with us for dinner.

The year following the return from my sabbatical in England was very traumatic. I was so wrapped up in my professional and domestic problems that I never noticed a budding relationship between Christopher and Mary McLaughlin, his classmate at Temple Medical School. Mary was a very bright Philadelphia girl who took out a loan to put herself through medical school. She had an Irish father and a mother of mixed European origin who lived in Holmes, Pennsylvania. Although during his third or fourth year at medical school Chris invited Mary once or twice home for dinner and asked me to accommodate her for the night, he never introduced her as his girlfriend. One day I was looking for Christopher and, in reply to my question where he might be found, another medical student said, "Obviously with Mary." This was my first indication of their interest in each other.

One day Christopher and I were sitting next to each other on the living room sofa. "Mom, I'm very happy at home," he began. "I never want to get married. I'd like to spend the rest of my life with you. Yet I'm thinking of Gene. After Grannie Bronislawa dies, he'll be all alone for the rest of his life. I'm afraid that this will happen to me unless I get married."

He stopped talking for a moment and looked at me, and then asked, "Mom, do you think I should marry Mary?"

I didn't keep him waiting long for my answer: "Chris, if you love her, you should."

Creativity Rechanneled

Christopher and Mary married in 1977, two days after their graduation from medical school. They went to Hawaii for their honeymoon and then proceeded to distribute their possessions between Pittsburgh, where Mary had her internship, and the University of Chicago, where Christopher had his. Their respective internship assignments were made in different locations prior to their decision to get married. They lived separately for the entire first year of their married life, visiting each other every third weekend and accruing incredible telephone bills.

After the excitement of their graduation and wedding subsided, I turned my attention to my own problems. I was very unhappy because I wasn't doing any research and because I had lost all satisfaction from the rest of my work. I still went to work each day and worked efficiently and at the same level of excellence I always had. But my heart was no longer in it. I asked myself why doing research was so important to me. Was it because I believed that I had a chance to free humanity from the scourge of cancer? No, I never had such expectations. I knew enough to realize that there was no such thing as a one-shot cure for cancer, and I wasn't wasting my time looking for it. I knew that this disease develops gradually in a very complex manner, stage by stage. We can't possibly dream of preventing (except in the case of cervical cancer), arresting, or reversing what occurs before any visible tumor appears unless and until we gain more complete knowledge of the mechanism of this development.

I was not enough of a do-gooder to be happy just doing socially useful work. True, I derived satisfaction from it, but not enough to explain the extent of my unhappiness when I couldn't do research any more. I think it was the scientific research process itself that I found most stimulating. But also I was very dedicated to the particular kind of research I had been doing. I thought back over the development of my career. Certainly my engagement in this particular kind of early cancer detection was the direct result of my association with George N. Papanicolaou.

I had then experienced the excitement of participating in his struggle for the recognition of the new method of cancer diagnosis he had created. In my own daily work I acted like a cancer detective hunting for single cells and trying to trace their origin. I was fortunate to have had the opportunity to make contributions to early detection of cancer at various sites of the body by studying single cells in body secretions and by teaching these procedures to students from all over the world. It was very thrilling, and with time led me to even more exciting ventures. Then I began to design and carry out my own experiments in mice, in which I produced cancer of the womb chemically and observed the gradual appearance of increasingly more bizarre abnormal cells in vaginal smears until cancer was well established. It was exciting to be able to initiate the appearance of cancer and watch it grow, because I could control this process by interrupting the use of carcinogens after a certain number of applications. This was experimental cancer research and I loved it.

The extreme satisfaction I derived from these activities must have resulted from some basic need in my nature that I had expressed in a different way earlier in my life. As a small child, I discovered by sheer detective work while listening to Bronislawa's conversation with Grandma Anna that Bronislawa was not my mother and that my mother, Eugenia, had died. As an older child, I would jump out of bed in the middle of the night to write poetry—thus expressing my creativity. Later, making scientific discoveries and thus gaining insight into the mystery of the development of cancer became the main source of satisfaction in my professional life.

After weeks and months of asking myself what exactly made me most unhappy when I had to relinquish my research, I found the answer. I had become deprived of means of expressing my creativity. Perhaps I could satisfy this need in some other way and regain happiness. I had always enjoyed writing, and I wrote easily, although maybe not well. I had had an interesting life. I wondered whether I could improve my command of the English language and my writing skills and one day write my autobiography. I now felt "God's fire" within me. Maybe my life's story contained some messages that would be helpful or interesting to others.

My first move was to take a writing course at night at Lower Merion High School. Then, unexpectedly, a mixture of circumstances conspired to give me my first opportunity to test my writing skills.

One day I experienced a sudden shooting pain down my leg. Hilary had had such a pain in the past because of a slipped disk; now I feared I might also have one. An orthopedic surgeon I consulted sent me to bed for a couple of weeks. While I was flat on my back, I received a telephone call from the Polish-American Medical Association in New York. "Dr. Koprowska, you were named Woman Physician of the Year, and you'll be awarded a gold medal during the annual meeting of our association," the caller announced. "Would you be willing to give a lecture on this occasion at the Polish Institute of Arts and Sciences in New York? We would like you to talk about the history of women in medicine, science, and the arts."

I couldn't believe my ears. This was the first medal I had ever been awarded. I became very excited as I listened. What worried me was the prospect of having to talk about women in medicine. I had never been interested in the history of women in medicine, and I knew nothing about it. But being confined to bed would give me time to learn something about the subject.

"All right, I'll speak about the history of women in medicine," I answered reluctantly after a pause.

Committed to acquainting myself with this topic, I obtained the necessary source material. Lying flat on my back, I had difficulty holding some of the heavy volumes. But in spite of my discomfort, I became fascinated with the topic. In her book, *A History of Women in Medicine from the Earliest Times to the Beginning of the Nineteenth Century*, published in 1938, Dr. Kate Campbell Hurd-Mead traced the role of women as healers all the way back not only to antiquity, but to prehistoric times. Her book became for me the most revealing source of information on this subject.

After several weeks of bed rest, my leg pain stopped bothering me. Soon I was up and around and back to work at Temple. I enjoyed enormously delivering my lecture at the Polish Institute of Arts and Sciences in October of 1977. It was received enthusiastically by the audience, and then published in 1978 in the *Journal of the American Medical Women's Association.*

My next opportunity to write occurred almost simultaneously. The American Society of Cytology in 1977 was preparing the silver anniversary issue of its official journal, *Acta Cytologica,* devoted to the memory of George N. Papanicolaou. I was invited to contribute an article about the personal aspects of working with Dr. Pap because I was one of the very few people who had worked with him long enough to know him as a person. I was delighted by this invitation.

I wrote about Papanicolaou as a creative man, struggling for long-denied recognition of his scientific contributions. But I also wrote how he was afraid that his discoveries might be stolen from him and that the credit for them would be attributed to other scientists. I spoke of his strengths and his weaknesses because I felt it was more important to show him as a man with human weaknesses like the rest of us than to treat him as a monument on a pedestal, which others had done. His biography and several articles that had been published about him were written by people who had known and admired him for his scientific work but may have been unaware of his personal characteristics or didn't want to write about him as a person. I too had great admiration for his work, felt a strong spiritual kinship with his approach to doing science, and loved him as well, but his unpleasant characteristics were undeniable. Anyone who had close professional association with him was aware of them.

I received many requests for reprints of my article about Dr. Papanicolaou, and also of the one I had written about women in medicine. I even began to receive invitations from colleges and universities to give talks on women in medicine. One year I had more invitations to lecture on this topic than to talk on cytology. I enjoyed this new experience and felt I had won a big victory. I pulled myself out of my depression by finding new sources of satisfaction in life. I was very proud of this achievement.

Shortly after the appearance of my article about the role of women in medicine, Lila Wallis, my friend and personal physician, asked me to join the American Medical Women's Association (AMWA). In the past, since I had not felt discriminated against because I was a woman,

I saw no need for a separate organization of female doctors. But my Hahnemann and Temple experiences taught me otherwise. So I joined.

My membership in AMWA involved more than paying dues. Soon after joining this organization, I was appointed chairperson of the Resources Committee of Branch 25, which includes Southeastern Pennsylvania and nearby parts of New Jersey and Delaware. This committee was concerned with the discrimination against women physicians in hospitals, medical schools, and medical societies.

When I became chair of this committee, I focused my attention on female medical students rather than on women physicians because I felt it would be best if they gained insight into the struggles of women physicians early on in their training. I wanted to prepare them to plan their careers and not to be deprived of enjoying a family life if they desired one, since I knew all too well from my own experiences the hardships of women with two careers.

My reputation as a role model for the young women physicians and medical students was already firmly established. I had better communication with them than with women physicians of my own generation because the point of view of these young women corresponded more closely to my own.

I was pleased that my daughter-in-law Liz had a successful dual career as a clinical psychologist and as wife and mother of a beautiful child. Hilary II had inherited his father's big blue eyes with long lashes. He had light blond hair like his mother's Swedish ancestors. Liz and Claude now lived in a lovely house in Rhode Island, and Liz was expecting their second child.

In February 1978, when Hilary II was four years old, Claude called us one day very excited. "We have a daughter!" he exclaimed, announcing the birth of Alexandra. Hilary and I took the first available plane to Rhode Island to see our second grandchild. The birth of our first granddaughter was another of those events that brought us closer together.

After completing his internship, Claude started a residency in orthopedic surgery. When Alexandra was only a year or two old, Liz underwent surgery because of a problem with her knee joint. I took a week off and went to Rhode Island to look after their children and pets. Claude was always a great animal lover and he gave me instructions on how to feed their two dogs, a kitten, and a skunk, which I was told to serve first. Only afterwards were the children to be given their dinner. The first day, I cooked chicken for their daughter Alexandra, but Frosty, their white kitten, managed to eat it as soon as I turned my back. In the meantime Hilary II, who was six years old at the time, made me lift him so that he could reach the top shelf of the refrigerator to help himself to the cocktail olives and onions. I felt guilty, but I played the role of indulgent grandmother and allowed him to do anything he wanted. Spending a full week with my grandchildren was enjoyable in itself, and it provided me with a respite.

In 1978 Fuller, our aged boxer, developed heart trouble. Fearing that we would be left without a dog, Hilary arranged for us to get a French shepherd puppy, whose breed was known by two names: Beauceron and Berger de Beauce. From the moment Porthos arrived, he placed himself at my feet. When Fuller appeared in the driveway and tried to approach me, Porthos started to bark at the big boxer and remained at my feet. Our new dog immediately accepted me as his mistress and began to protect me. He of course didn't scare Fuller, or even make him jealous, and soon the two dogs became great friends and couldn't bear to be apart from each other.

Beth, a student interested in animal technology, lived with us for one year to help us care for the dogs, and she became very helpful to me with other things that needed to be done around the house. Between the help of Beth and our housekeeper Inez, I had the freedom to carry out my professional responsibilities and travel without worrying about the house and the dogs. Once Beth left us, we continued to make similar arrangements with other students or recent college graduates.

In 1980 I discovered that I had a cataract on my left eye, had it removed, and had a new lens implanted.

Every year I was left alone for two or three weeks at a time when Hilary took his annual trip to Rio de Janeiro and Buenos Aires for the Pan American Health Organization. I usually felt lonely the first night after his departure, but then I was pleased to be free of the bulk of my domestic responsibilities in his absence and to have time to write my scientific papers. One year in the early 1980's, I received during his absence a letter from the World Health Organization inviting me to accept a one-month consultantship assignment in India. I showed Hilary this letter as soon as he returned.

"Send them a telegram saying you accept the assignment, and give them the date of your proposed arrival in April," he responded immediately. "Tell them to start processing your documents. An assignment to India sounds to me like an interesting proposal. I wouldn't miss it."

I know I was lucky to have a husband who was supportive of my career, but I awaited signs that he would mind the prospect of our pending separation. He showed none. However, I felt that he had given me good advice, and I started making preparations for my trip. After the recent lens implantation, I wasn't back at the microscope yet. I thus felt free to make plans to stop in Munich on my way back to attend an International Cytology Congress and to give my eyes a longer period of rest.

"After Munich, I'd like to go to Paris and visit my cousin Irene Binois," I told Hilary. "Can you join me there?"

"I'll be with Carlo Croce attending meetings in Israel and in Italy when you'll be in India and Munich," he suddenly announced. I hadn't known of these plans. "But I can meet you in Paris in May." The idea of meeting Hilary in Paris was appealing.

On the day of my flight to New Delhi, I was still packing when Hilary left for Wistar in the morning. "I'll come back home to accompany you to the airport," he said.

When he returned home that afternoon, he handed me a small square box. I opened it and found a twisted gold wire pin of an intricate design with a large cluster of sapphires in the center. "Wear it on your trip to remember me," he said.

I was thrilled with his gift, and I put it on immediately. It made me feel good, not just because it was lovely and valuable, but because of Hilary's thoughtfulness.

Lung cancer had increased in northern India because of the growth of industry and the resultant pollutants. This worrisome cancer rate was why, in addition to being invited as a consultant, I also was asked to give a course on the early diagnosis of lung cancer. I was proud of this assignment, and my course in New Delhi was well attended. One of the participants, a woman pathologist, invited me to visit her in her native Kashmir, where I went sightseeing for a long weekend. I enjoyed living on a houseboat and felt a malicious satisfaction that my experience in India was more exciting than Hilary and Carlo's trip to Israel.

After completing a month in India, I went to Munich, as planned, to attend the International Cytology Congress. Many of my colleagues were envious of my W.H.O. consultantship, and that made me feel good. For among them were some who had kept me from holding prestigious offices and receiving honors at national and international meetings. Sometimes I wondered why, and once I discussed this situation with my highly devoted cytotechnologist, E. Lou Bridges. When I asked her why it was so, her answer was, "There are only so many places at the top." This is true, but I think there may have also been other reasons. I was still Papanicolaou's research fellow when some of the cytopathologists that I taught cytology courses to at Cornell had been heads of academic departments, and they therefore were more likely to be selected to prestigious positions. Fortunately, I had friends at the World Health Organization, and thanks to them I had been chosen for this important assignment.

On my flight from Munich to Paris, I began to long to see Hilary. But there was no message from him in Paris at my cousin's apartment. I was disappointed and began to worry. Then the telephone rang. "It's for you," my cousin said as she passed the receiver to me.

"Everything is all right, Mom. Don't get scared, but Dad is in the hospital." I heard Christopher's voice, and I felt the blood rushing through my neck arteries.

And so I learned that Hilary had gone to an important meeting in Washington straight from Italy, before he returned home. On his way back to Philadelphia he felt very weak. He called Mary, who arranged for him to be rushed to the hospital where they diagnosed a stomach hemorrhage.

Immediately I called the airlines to get a reservation on the first available flight back home. Twelve hours later I ran upstairs to our bedroom. Hilary was in bed, looking pale, somnolent, and unusually quiet. But as soon as he became aware of my presence, a smile appeared on his face. He was obviously relieved to see me. An hour later, when he started complaining about being uncomfortable, asking to have his pillows rearranged and making other demands, I realized that he must be getting better.

Several years earlier Hilary had bought a boat with an understanding that Claude and Liz would use it and take good care of it. Since then we spent some vacations on the boat with Claude and his family. Until 1977 Hilary and I had only summer vacations, but we had a Caribbean vacation with Claude and Liz almost every winter between 1977 and 1987. Our marriage had entered a phase of new happiness. We became more tolerant of each other, and the scare of Hilary's gastric hemorrhage had made it clear how much we meant to each other.

I loved the magnificent sunsets on the Caribbean waters, which all of us watched together, adults sipping rum punches and the children having soft drinks. "Peli, Peli, Peli!" little Hilary and Alexandra shouted to the pelicans, as these birds in search of fish suddenly dropped from the sky in a straight line to the surface of the water.

Most of the time our entire family was happy being together on the boat in Caribbean waters. We would stretch our evenings so that they lasted a long time. Steaks were broiled on the boat's barbecue. Then we would sit drinking more rum punches in the gathering darkness, talking about the past, and making plans for next year's vacation. A conflict of commitments usually prevented Christopher and Mary from sharing these boat vacations with us and neither Bronislawa nor Gene would join us.

Bronislawa was now eighty-eight. I found for her and her health aide, whom she now needed, an apartment large enough to also accomodate Gene whenever he was able to come and stay there during weekends. Gene showed unending patience with her and continued being an affectionate son. Once I dropped in when Bronislawa was lying down on the sofa and Gene sat on a chair next to her holding her feet in his hands and caressing them lovingly. At such moments their strong bonds and mutual attachment were apparent.

Decade of Insights

Following the upheavals of the 1970's, I gained the peace of mind that allowed me to better understand myself and find alternate sources of satisfaction in life.

Amanda, a redheaded girl, Christopher's first child, was born in 1980. She was a healthy and beautiful baby except for a vascular birthmark close to her right eye. This became a source of much anxiety to all of us for several months, although it did not endanger the vision and, as predicted by the pediatrician, eventually disappeared. Chris and Mary became devoted and happy parents. Mary returned to work soon after a brief maternity leave and hired a reliable middle-aged babysitter to take care of Amanda. Christopher surprised me by his loving participation in bathing, feeding, and changing diapers. They lived now in their own house in Havertown, ten minutes by car from us, and we usually saw them during weekends.

By then, Hilary had achieved many of his scientific goals. Since he had become its director in 1957, the Wistar Institute was recognized as one of the leading medical research institutes of the world. Hilary's energies never were exclusively focused on scientific goals and career achievements. Besides his interest in music, art, and history, he was very interested in people. He acted as a father confessor to numerous friends, colleagues, associates, graduate students, technicians, and secretaries.

One summer evening in 1981, I returned home late from Temple in a torrential rain storm to find Fuller dead on the floor of our living room. The poor animal was always afraid of thunder and must have died of a heart attack. Porthos was running around the corpse, upset that he couldn't get Fuller to play with him. It was a heartbreaking sight.

After refusing to eat and mourning his playmate for two weeks, Porthos redirected all of his affection towards us. He followed Hilary and me wherever we went. He had dinner with us in the dining room, and he slept in our bedroom. Hilary's father's sofa, which we brought home from Manchester, became his bed.

By now I'd become less jealous of Hilary's attention to other women. My marriage had not only survived, but was happier than ever.

In Boston in 1982, Hanka married Mark Weiner, then a graduate student at the University of Pennsylvania. Because her parents were in Poland, almost all of our family attended the wedding. After the wedding, the young couple returned to live near us on the Main Line in Rosemont. Hanka took a job as a nurse's aide.

During the seven years I was without a grant from the National Cancer Institute, I ceased to be involved in cancer research and was bored by my routine work at Temple. Then in 1982, the Bender Pharmaceutical Company in Austria, which had a research division interested in diagnostic tests, unexpectedly offered me their support to develop an immunologic test for early detection of cancer of the womb based on the use of monoclonal antibodies. Monoclonal antibodies are proteins produced in the laboratory which, in contrast to naturally occurring (polyclonal) antibodies, are derived from a single clone of cells. They bind single specific (tumor) antigens.

I owed my initial contact with Bender Company to Hilary, who had been working for years at Wistar with the monoclonal antibodies in an attempt to develop immunotherapy of cancer. His present attitude toward me as a scientist was in marked contrast to the past, as when he ignored my existence and status at the time of the opening of the cancer research wing at the Wistar Institute. I felt that his respect for my work had increased as our emotional ties became stronger. My situation at Temple improved at the same time because, as soon as I received the research grant and became involved in experimental work, they had to provide me with additional laboratory facilities.

I hired a young man to become my research technician and sent him to Wistar Institute to learn how to develop monoclonal antibodies (MAB's). Within the next couple of years he succeeded in producing several MAB's, which I needed to test to see if they would bind to tumor antigen of cancer of the womb. But I ran into the unexpected problem of where to find the tumors to test them against. In the United States, thanks to Pap smears, these cancers are being picked up early and treated before they progress to sizable tumor masses of the sort I needed for testing. I ended up going to Poland where early detection of cancer of the womb by Pap smears had become so neglected that many large untreated tumors were commonly seen in some gynecological clinics. Through cooperation with Polish gynecologists in Silesia, I obtained and brought with me imprints of such tumors removed in the operating room. After testing our monoclonal antibodies, I found out that they did indeed react with cervical cancer.

But all this was still preliminary work. Now we had to find out if any of these new monoclonal antibodies could be used to detect early cervical cancer in vaginal smears using immunoperoxidase stain reaction. One of our monoclonal antibodies appeared to give a positive reaction in vaginal smears of women whose smears had been suggestive of a carcinoma in situ by a concurrently used Pap smear. This was very exciting, and I became enthusiastic because now further study of this MAB became warranted.

In the meantime Wallace Clark resigned from the departmental chairmanship to accept a position at the University of Pennsylvania. Then, in 1982, Renato Baserga once more became chairman of Temple's Department of Pathology. Several months later, sitting in my office and feeling full of energy at sixty-six, I received a letter from him advising me that the following year I would reach Temple's retirement age. But because of my "great value to the department," Baserga invited me to continue directing the Temple University Cytology Laboratory for another three years which, according to him, was as long as he would be able to postpone my retirement. Of course, I would be free to continue doing research beyond that time as long as I had an outside source of support, but according to institutional rules I would have to step down from the administrative responsibilities of directing a diagnostic laboratory at the age of seventy.

Neither I nor Hilary had any intention of retiring as yet. We both felt full of vitality and thought that we still had much to contribute. While we had to face the problem of my not-too-distant retirement, we had happy personal events. It was a decade of growth for Christopher's family. His second daughter Agatha, a blue-eyed little devil, was born in 1983. His long-awaited first son, Paul, was born a year later.

During the next two years I was busy working hard on my research project, trying to determine if a MAB test for early cervical cancer would be of value. Most cases of CIS detected by Pap smear precede the appearance of cancer, although it is not possible to predict which individual CIS will progress to cancer. But it is conceivable that a positive MAB test could be a more specific predictor of such progress to cancer. In such a case it would serve not only for the detection of CIS, but also as a useful basis for the selection of an appropriate treatment. The answer to this question could be provided by a large clinical trial with a long follow-up in which the ultimate outcome of CIS detected by MAB would be established.

Bender Company became interested in such a trial, but they did not have as much experience as Organon, a much larger Dutch pharmaceutical company with whom Bender had an established connection. Therefore, I was invited to Holland to plan a clinical trial in conjunction with a large-scale cancer detection program involving twenty thousand women in Austria. After this meeting I went to Amsterdam to join Hilary, who was there attending another conference.

Hilary had taken a suite in an elegant hotel and had bought us tickets for an evening concert. We had plenty of time, and were happy to be together and to chat while enjoying the remarkable view of a canal from our window. We had drinks, and Hilary suggested an afternoon nap. I woke up before Hilary did and reflected how much both of us had changed. In the past, Hilary's secretive nature, his hiding the truth for the sake of avoiding scenes and confrontations, puzzled and annoyed me. But he seemed to now be more straightforward with me.

I wondered how I had changed. I had been spoiled as a young girl because my father and Bronislawa always tried to satisfy all my wishes without expecting anything from me in return. When my half-brothers were born, I felt lonely, no longer being the center of parental affection. I also considered myself a very special girl.

During the war I became both inventive and aggressive, but my aggressiveness was much more apparent in life-threatening situations than in my attempts to climb the academic ladder. In dealing with my career, I saved my energies and action for my research. If I had been more assertive at work, I probably would have gotten further ahead in this world and received more rewards, as more ambitious people do. But that simply wasn't my style. I never asked for a raise or sought membership in any medical school, hospital, or professional society's committee. I never solicited invitations to be a speaker or to play a prominent role at a scientific meeting. I never asked to be invited to any social occasion. The few honors I received came to me without any solicitation, and they came as a surprise. The only exception I can recall is asking for my promotion to full professorship, and even this I did at Hilary's suggestion. I hadn't aspired to a departmental chairmanship, although I had two opportunities to achieve it. But then it is possible that it wasn't as much my passivity as my lack of interest in executive-type administrative positions and a dislike of the dog-eat-dog politics of academic medicine. I felt that, although not exactly passive, I exhibited a tendency toward emotional dependence upon important people in my life, such as Hilary and Dr. Papanicolaou.

In retrospect, I consider that the extraordinary endurance, courage, and resourcefulness that I demonstrated at critical moments in my life, especially during the war in Poland and then in France and in Brazil, stemmed from my relentless efforts to be with Hilary at all cost. It was that very love for Hilary and the desire for his love that made his flirtations with other women so hard on me, yet had me remain with him despite the humiliation.

It really wasn't until well into the sixth decade of our lives that we established our relationship on the basis of genuine love and mutual trust.

In the past, I tried to explain Hilary's ambiguous pattern of behavior towards me on the basis of his chameleon-like personality. But now, as I thought about our relationship, I started considering changes in my perception of Hilary's behavior and attitude towards me. Marcel Proust imagines personalities as impenetrable shadows in *Remembrance of Things Past*. He describes how he realized no person is constantly endowed with good or bad qualities. We perceive their multiple images on the basis of incomplete reflections, such as what they say and do. Thus, at times they may express with equal probability sparks of their love for us, at other times hatred or indifference.

Proust's descriptions express well my experience with Hilary. My perception of Hilary's personality changed as I have changed.

I never succeeded in freeing myself from my tendency to day-dream, which I did sometimes when I was alone and sometimes when with other people. My family was well aware of this and made fun of me because of my frequent unawareness of what they were talking about. Often I would not pay attention to what they were saying, which sometimes was irritating to Hilary, Claude, and Christopher. It bothered Christopher from the day I insisted on speaking French to an American man in Agay, France, during our vacation in 1957.

"Mom, you don't listen to me," he would say. And he was right. "I knew when I was six years old that you were 'out to lunch'—ever since that summer in Agay," he added.

When Hilary woke up, I shared some of my reflections with him and said that I was much happier with him now after forty-eight years of marriage than ever before, and that I felt that both of us had changed. "Yes," he said. "We became more tolerant of each other," and he gave me a big hug.

In 1986 I received a second letter from Renato—a follow-up to the one he sent me two years before. He advised me that I would be seventy years old in 1987 and would have to retire. Although I might have expected such a letter, its arrival came to me as a painful shock. I showed Baserga's letter to Hilary as soon as he came home for dinner.

"You can fight Temple and win, Irena, if you want to. It's illegal to discriminate against age in the city of Philadelphia," he said rightly or wrongly. Whenever I had problems, I always discussed them with Hilary, who would stand by me and usually encourage an energetic response. Hilary always favored positive action. Only six months older than I, Hilary didn't want to think about his own retirement. As the director of an independent scientific institute, he was not subject to the University of Pennsylvania's retirement rules.

"I'm not sure it's worth fighting. Suing a university is an expensive, long, and involved process with an uncertain outcome," I told him. "I'd make enemies and suffer aggravation, Hilary. I have to retire at some point, and if they no longer want me at Temple, I'm not sure that I want to remain there."

I assessed my situation realistically in refusing to fight. I did not have enough support to conduct research at Temple, where I was bored by my routine hospital activities and disliked the negligible role of cytology in the department's teaching program. It wasn't worthwhile fighting to continue a job I didn't need, at which I was no longer wanted. I was ready now for a different kind of activity, and I returned to an idea conceived ten years before. I began writing my wartime memoirs.

Bronislawa, at ninety-five years of age, stopped recognizing her great-grandchildren and then her grandsons. In early March of 1987, when she was ninety-seven years old, she suffered several minor strokes. Sometimes she didn't know even Gene or me. After a major stroke, however, I had her transported by ambulance to the hospital, where she remained without regaining consciousness. Gene arrived from Washington, and he and I visited her daily. Gabriel joined us after it became apparent that she was dying.

On March 29, 1987, we were all sitting at the dinner table when the telephone rang. "I'm sorry to tell you that your mother just passed away," Bronislawa's doctor told me. "She died peacefully without suffering."

Half an hour later, all of us stood by her bed watching her motionless body and her sad face, immobilized by death. We were all silent. There were no tears or sobbing at her deathbed.

Bronislawa's death brought more relief than sorrow even to Gene. Gene was the most sacrificing son I ever knew. He had never married and he lived in very modest financial circumstances. In spite of this, he managed to provide a comfortable life and tender care for Bronislawa. His relationship with her was very different from Gabriel's and my own. We were married and had other ties and obligations towards our families. Three weeks later when I returned with Gene to the cemetery, the orchids were just as fresh as on the day I brought them.

When I think about Bronislawa and the long-dead Sofia Semeonovna, two such important personalities in my life, as different as these two women had been, they had an important characteristic in common: extreme possessiveness towards their sons.

In July 1987, at the age of seventy, I reached Temple University's mandatory retirement age and had to step down from my directorship of the Cytology Laboratory, which I had assumed in 1970. I now became professor emerita. I still had modest outside support to retain a tiny office and a well-equipped research laboratory on the campus for several more years.

Prior to the end of the clinical trial of my monoclonal antibody, I went to Vienna in August of 1987. On the eve of the day of the meeting of the advisory committee, I had a few hours of leisure. A short walk from my hotel took me to a nearby park, where I sat in an outdoor café facing a stand for the orchestra. Viennese waltzes filled the air. I treated myself to a cup of coffee with whipped cream and to a slice of Sacher torte, and I enjoyed the old-fashioned European atmosphere. The waltzes were followed by a popular potpourri with a predominance of schmaltzy Hungarian dances.

Suddenly, two old women got up and began to dance. One wore an old-fashioned two-piece beige suit, the other a red dress that had seen better days and a straw hat. Neither of them had the posture or grace of dancers, but both moved their legs skillfully high in the air, as if they were dancing the cancan in a cabaret performance. The sight of these dancing women reminded me of how much more life there was to live and enjoy.

The waiter came to wipe my table. I got up and returned to my hotel. I prepared my talk and selected a new sheer navy wool suit with a double-string pearl necklace and navy shoes to wear to the meeting. I always thought that a woman scientist should never forget her appearance. The clinical trial had been approved for a period of two years, during which the progress of testing the value of my monoclonal antibody had to be evaluated. The first preliminary results had been discussed during the second day of our meeting, but it was too early to draw any definite conclusions. It was apparent that Bender Company was reluctant to make a long-term commitment, which I knew would be necessary to establish the diagnostic value of this antibody. The following day I left Vienna and flew to Paris to visit Irene Binois. I returned to Philadelphia two days later.

In November of that same year, 1987, at the annual meeting of the American Society of Cytology, I was honored with the Papanicolaou Award, the highest award of the society, for my contributions to cytology. There was a standing ovation as I walked to the podium to receive it.

"You should have received it years ago," Leo Koss told me. He was right, but why hadn't he or other prominent members of the American Society of Cytology seen to it that I was so honored?

Fiftieth anniversary of the completion of the last pre-war class at Warsaw University School of Medicine. Hilary and Irena sitting in first row, far right.

Unfortunately, the decision of the Bender and Organon Companies to discontinue their support in 1989, after two years of clinical trials, precluded any valid conclusions from my research with monoclonal antibodies. Without at least three more years of funding, it was impossible to determine whether our monoclonal antibody was a reliable predictor of cancer. I was disappointed that the potential diagnostic value of a promising monoclonal antibody—the result of my arduous research—wasn't conclusively established.

However, once Bender terminated their support of the clinical trials, my further involvement in the project ended. I then left Temple and began to write my autobiography in earnest.

One Saturday, Hilary, Porthos, and I are on the way to our mountain retreat on Timber Trails Lake in the Poconos. We're looking forward to a relaxing weekend.

We arrive in time for lunch. I open our coolers and set the table with bread, butter, Nova Scotia salmon, cold meats, cheeses, fruit, and a cinnamon ring. Hilary fixes us Bloody Marys, and I brew coffee. We eat and drink, and then go for a long walk on the beach. The sun is out, and the ice is melting on the lake. We breathe the fresh cold air with delight, and Porthos is ecstatic, gamboling without restraint. There's not a soul in sight.

"What's the current status of your wildlife rabies vaccine, Hilary?" I ask, well aware that the lack of recognition of his discovery of the live polio vaccine didn't discourage him from developing other vaccines.

"Well, we've finally prepared an oral vaccine for raccoons who transmit rabies. They like the taste of the vaccine, but other animals don't, so it won't be wasted on those who don't transfer the disease. We call this vaccine 'rac-snacks.'"

We begin watching the ducks on the lake. Hilary is all bundled up in wool, and I can only see his blue eyes and pink cheeks. He tells me about the review of an autobiography he has just read. "An autobiography is an unfaithful representation of character, the reviewer asserts. A biography written by someone else is more objective and can tell you more about a person. Isn't this true, Irena?"

Hilary is obviously anxious to talk about the autobiography I've been writing for over two years, of which I thus far haven't allowed him even a glimpse. "You're absolutely right,

Hilary. I agree. In writing my autobiography I sometimes discover that I can't remember what I felt at the time of an important event. But since it's creative writing, I'm free to be inventive, fill in the gaps in my memory and create images of myself and of other people. No doubt it's different from the way someone else might see me," I reply.

Hilary doesn't say anything.

"Remember Rashomon?" I ask. "Each participant in the event portrays himself as the murderer."

Hilary still doesn't reply. I recall the mistake I made in showing Claude some of what I had written. "I never knew you to be such a liar, Mother. What you say about my reasons for dropping out of Princeton are not true. Something completely different happened," Claude had told me, upset by my description of these circumstances.

I want this conversation to continue. It provides me with an opportunity to ask Hilary questions that have puzzled me ever since I met him and to which he has never given me satisfactory answers. In our mountain retreat suddenly he has become my captive audience. "I find it difficult to write about myself," I confess. "The process of writing requires better insight into my own feelings than I've ever had. I'm struggling now to understand myself at last. But you're the most important person in my life and my biggest difficulty is understanding some of *your* behavior. I still don't know you very well," I tell him. "Perhaps you'll help me understand you better."

"I'll do it over a martini, which I'm about to fix for us. What about you making some snacks?" Hilary at last responds.

"I'm ahead of you this time, Hilary. They're ready."

A few minutes later we're sitting next to each other on the sofa in front of the fireplace with Porthos at our feet. As we raise our cocktail glasses, we stare at the lake from our living room windows.

"Why did you leave me alone only weeks after our secret wedding and go to Manchester?" I blurt out.

"I would really have to think about it. It was so long ago, I don't remember," Hilary predictably evades me. At least he doesn't repeat the unconvincing story he told me fifty years ago. Then he said that he was angry because I changed my maiden name to my married name at the medical school without his permission. I find it amazing that even now he doesn't want to tell me the truth. I don't want to make a scene and spoil our evening, so I change the subject.

"All right, Hilary, take your time to decide what you'll tell me about your Manchester escapade. But perhaps you can answer a different question. I've always wondered at what point you finally realized that your mother was doing everything she could to destroy our marriage, and why you let her make me suffer as much as you did?"

"Don't exaggerate your suffering, Irena," he says. "In spite of her behavior, we had our good times when we were young." He pauses for an instant.

"I know that my mother didn't behave properly toward you," he goes on. "But you must understand that you were a threat to her. She suffered from illnesses and had an unhappy marriage. I was her only child. I meant everything to her and, until you entered the family, she had me under her total control. You made her unhappy, just as she made you suffer."

I don't interrupt him. And in part I agree with him. You can't blame a man for trying to justify his mother's behavior. Hilary's position in our triangle wasn't enviable either. He catered to his mother's wishes and for a long time behaved like an immature and unfeeling young man towards me just because he didn't want to hurt the feelings of his possessive mother. Only in Brazil did it become apparent to me that Hilary realized how destructive to our marriage his mother had been. But even then he never told me that our marriage was really important to him.

We sit quietly while I organize my thoughts. "What kind of wife have I been to you, Hilary?" I suddenly confront him.

"You've been a monster!" He smiles when he says that, but I know that it isn't a total joke.

"But haven't I changed at all since you married me?" I hope that he will sweeten his bitter remark.

"As a matter of fact you have, Irena. When I married you, you were a very spoiled and impatient girl with outbursts of temper. Now you're a most loving wife which, in the early days of our marriage, I never believed that you could become. And I'm the most important person to you," Hilary said, looking at me tenderly.

"You're only repeating what I said about you being the most important person in my life," I reply, disappointed. "It's true, but when you say it that way it sounds as if you take me for granted. In fact, I don't believe that you feel I'm the most important person in your life, Hilary." I can't help but express some of my old bitterness.

Suddenly I see us at nineteen wandering through the snow-covered hills in Bukowina with our arms around each other. We enter an inn where Hilary immediately notices a piano. Leaving me behind, he walks to the piano, sits down on the stool, and begins to play. In no time at all a small group of music lovers among the inn's guests assembles around him. I move to the side, feeling that I don't exist for him at all. From that moment I knew that he would never belong to me totally.

"But you *are* the most important person in my life, Irena," Hilary replies immediately.

Yet I know that as important as I may have become to him by now, there will always be aspects of his life that I'll never share.

Unexpectedly, a few weeks later, I did get an answer to one of the most perplexing puzzles of my life. It was during a quiet weekend when we had no guests or outside commitments. On Friday evening Hilary returned home holding several stapled, typed sheets of paper in his hand. He had mentioned the night before that he had to write an introduction to the book written by the recipients of the Paul Koprowski Memorial Fellowship at the University of Manchester, which he had established for deserving students. He asked for my help.

"Promise me you'll edit these pages during the weekend, Irena," Hilary asked, obviously anxious to have me drop everything to edit his manuscript.

"I'm not much of an editor," I remarked mildly. "But I'll do what I can." I thought to myself that this task would leave me no time for working on my autobiography, and I resented it. The very mention of Manchester was upsetting to me even after more than fifty years. Still, I couldn't refuse to edit these pages without hurting his feelings, which I didn't want to do, his past behavior notwithstanding.

We installed ourselves in our familiar recliners in the den, and while Hilary read a book, I worked on his draft. Suddenly I found myself reading about Hilary's long-established ties with the University of Manchester. In his essay he remarks that at one time he thought of transferring from a Polish medical school to the University of Manchester.

"I never knew that you planned to transfer to a foreign medical school, Hilary," I remarked. "Was this why you went to Manchester and left me alone? Were you planning to leave me and get out of our marriage?" I asked. My heart was racing.

Irena on a family vacation (Galapagos Islands, 1993). Front row l to r: Paul, Amanda, Hilary II, and Agatha. Back row l to r: Claude, Christopher, Hilary, Alexandra, Irena, Liz and Mary.

"Yes," he replied in a firm tone of voice. He considered ending our marriage, but didn't.

"Was it because you married me believing that I was pregnant, and I told you during our wedding night that I wasn't?" I persisted.

"Yes," Hilary repeated this one word again. It sufficed.

Suddenly the mystery was solved. I started menstruating on the morning of our wedding, but concealed this from Hilary so that we would go through with the wedding. I cheated him, and he wasn't going to forgive my cheating. He married me only because he believed that I was pregnant. Once he discovered I had lied to him, he almost abandoned me for good. Then he changed his mind. He returned to me lovingly, and never left me again.

I wasn't sure whether Hilary realized how much this truth was painful to me, even after so many years. But finding a truthful answer to a great puzzle for me was worth this pain. Maybe many happy marriages depend on less than complete openness. We lived nearly all our lives with this secret, yet I believe that we're as happy as a couple can be.

Appendix

A condensed version of an unpublished lecture, "Frontiers of Virology: Development of Vaccines Against Polio Virus," by Hilary Koprowski at the Medical School of the Hershey Medical Center, June 18, 1980.

I took a lesson from the development of the yellow fever vaccine from the late Max Theiler, Nobel Prize winner and developer of an attenuated live virus vaccine against yellow fever, with whom I had numerous discussions in New York at the Rockefeller Foundation laboratories. I decided to first attenuate poliomyelitis virus, then to find out whether it was possible to develop a vaccine that would replicate in human gut without causing signs of disease, and then to immunize people by feeding them this vaccine. This would be the first oral viral vaccine.

We obtained a strain of virus from the late Dr. Kessel in California. We passaged this virus once in monkeys, the animal of choice, and then obtained monkey cord and injected it into mice, which then showed signs of paralysis. After several passages, we isolated a strain of poliomyelitis virus that we called the TN strain because the man who assisted me in this work was T. Thomas W. Norton. After several passages in mice, we decided to adapt this strain to cotton rats. Cotton rats were, at that time, a relatively common laboratory animal. The virus was injected intracerebrally, and after 3, 10, 15, and 20 passages we started to check for attenuation. How was polio virus checked for attenuation? There was only one way to check it, and that was to inject it into a susceptible primate host, i.e., the rhesus monkey. We made an emulsion of the rat brain, injected it at different passage levels into monkeys, and found that at level 1 to 5 or 5 to 10, not a single monkey became paralyzed. They instead developed antibodies and were resistant to challenge with a virulent strain of the virus.

We started this work in 1946, and it took four more years before we dared administer it to human beings. Prior to administration to human subjects, we tested the animal closest to man by feeding virus to a number of chimpanzees. We observed them very closely and found that the attenuated virus was excreted in feces and that all the chimpanzees fed developed antibodies to this strain.

We next faced the problem of whom we would vaccinate. Near Pearl River, New York, there was a state institution for abnormal children called Letchworth Village. The chief pathologist of Letchworth Village was Dr. Jervis, who was a close friend of ours. Dr. Jervis first asked us to determine whether children in the wards at Letchworth Village had antibodies against polio virus. Because of the frequent intercontamination of the children with fecal material, he feared a pretty bad polio epidemic if no antibodies were present. Sure enough, in our original test approximately 60 percent of these children had no antibodies to the type of polio virus that we had used. Once we informed Dr. Jervis about the possibility that the children would be exposed to and contract poliomyelitis, he requested us to administer the attenuated polio virus to this group of children.

I realized then that I would never get official permission from the State of New York. Therefore, we asked permission from the parents of these children. The parents gave us permission to feed vaccine to their children. On February 27, 1950, the first human subject was immunized with poliomyelitis virus by drinking an emulsion of cotton rat brain and cord which, when I took it, tasted somewhat like cod liver oil. Thus, cod liver oil provokes the first memory of this vaccine. The fact that we drank the vaccine was absolutely immaterial because we all had antibodies against polio; however, the boy had no antibodies, and we isolated the virus from his stools during the first 10 or 12 days after feeding. This boy developed high titer neutralizing antibodies after a few weeks. Then we increased the number of children to 5, to 10, and ultimately ended with 20 children, 12 of whom had no antibodies to poliomyelitis. All of them developed such antibodies. All of them, except one, excreted the virus in stools and were immune to the virus.

We debated a long time and decided to take advantage of a conference called by the National Foundation for Infantile Paralysis in Hershey, Pennsylvania, at the Hotel Hershey on March 15, 16, and 17, 1951. That is why I told you the second smell is that of chocolate. I do not know if Hotel Hershey still exists, but whenever we walked out to the hotel, the smell of chocolate accompanied us. It had to be done by subterfuge because I was invited to talk in general about attenuation of viruses, e.g., attenuation of rabies virus, but I wanted to talk about our trials at the same time. Therefore, I asked Dr. John Paul, chairman of Epidemiology at Yale University, if I could comment on the results I had obtained. "Well," he said, "I will ask you to give your comments after Salk's paper."

Finally, I was called to give a talk. I had given my discussion on attenuated viruses the day before, and if I remember correctly, on March 16, 1951, the chairman Dr. Paul said, "Well, do you have any comments to make?"

Sabin was quite vociferous at the meeting. Now Sabin questioned my daring. How did I dare to feed children live polio virus? I replied that somebody had to take this step. Well, he turned round and round saying, "How do you dare to use live virus on children? You are not sure about this, you are not sure about that, you may have caused an epidemic." Even kind Dr. Stokes, with whom we later collaborated, asked whether I had checked the possibility that the Society for Prevention of Cruelty to Children would sue me for what I had done.

Only one person out of the whole group of 30 called and gave me strong encouragement, and he was probably the most eminent scientist of all, Jules Freund. He approached me and said, "Hilary, this is the way to approach immunization against poliomyelitis. You have the right way and they have the wrong way." In 1952 the paper was published, and was again followed by stony silence.

In the meantime, however, we became interested in doing more work and wanted to enlarge our group. Dr. Karl Friedrich Meyer was probably the most eminent microbiologist in the United States at that time and was director of the George Williams Hooper Foundation at the University of California.

Dr. Meyer met me at the Barbizon Plaza during a meeting of the New York Academy of Sciences, and was very interested in collaboration. In typical Karl F. Meyer fashion, in California he did it big.

He obtained the help of Mr. Coblentz, who was a very powerful man in California. He enlisted the help of Paul DeKruif, a friend, a very good public relations man for microbiology, and author of *Microbe Hunters*. We then went to the California State Department of Health and discussed whether it would be possible to undertake work at the Sonoma State Home. It was a much larger home than Letchworth Village and during the survey, we again found a large number of children who had no antibodies. Since there was again an enormous exchange (if I may use this term) of fecal material, the possibility existed that if one got sick, there would be an immediate epidemic of poliomyelitis. The authorities wanted to avoid exposing these children, who had abnormalities of the central nervous system, to poliomyelitis, and we received official permission from the state, thanks to Meyer, Coblentz and DeKruif, as well as permission from the parents. Thus, this was the second group of children to be vaccinated against poliomyelitis. This trial took place in California in the beautiful Valley of the Moon (which Jack London described) in Sonoma in 1952.

At the time of our trial in Sonoma State Home, the first Salk vaccine (after conferences) was injected into human beings, starting what was called the "Carter Episode." It was found that the virus used by Salk was not sufficiently killed and that it caused a number of inoculated children to develop poliomyelitis from live virus present in the vaccine. The National Foundation supporting Salk was taken aback and did not know what to do next. At the same time, we were working with live virus vaccine, but still were not supported by any grants from the National Foundation. Again the second trial was published, if I remember correctly, in the *Journal of the American Medical Association*. Then there were similar trials. One of the most interesting was in a home similar to the Sonoma State Home. We immunized normal children in the New Jersey State Prison for Women, which was not far from Flemington on Route 22.

At the same time we were doing these trials, we got publicity in the New York newspapers. There was a federation meeting in New York City in April 1954, where a journalist asked Bodian about the polio vaccine. "The Foundation has been collecting all the dimes from the population for ten years. Where is the vaccine?" He said, "Well there already is a vaccine. There is a paper that was published in January 1952 by Koprowski and his associates describing a successful immunization of children." Suddenly, not knowing anything about it because he never told us, we opened the now defunct *New York Herald Tribune* and there, on the first page in an April issue, was printed "Poliomyelitis vaccine fed to children: all found immune," written by Earl Ubell, who was quite a good science reporter. Then, of course, the foundation had to do something, and what they were doing was perfecting the Salk vaccine. The Salk vaccine reappeared between 1954 and 1955, and a large number of children here, in Europe, and in Sweden, where it is still used today, received the inactivated vaccine. Children in England were vaccinated with a killed virus vaccine. Again, our work was sort of pushed aside, but not by silence. It would not be silenced because we had been invited to conferences at the National Foundation. However, publicity was always pushed on Salk.

In the meantime, Albert Sabin, who criticized me for using live polio vaccine in children, started working himself on a live polio vaccine. He obtained three other virus strains from other scientists and did what we had done; he passed virus in monkey kidneys and tissue culture and, after several passages found that it lost its virulence when injected intracerebrally into Rhesus monkeys. Then, of course, he started to push the vaccine, against the wishes of the National Foundation. Essentially there were two competitors in the live virus vaccine area. Sabin's first paper appeared in 1956; this is the only paper where he graciously quoted my work. From then on, he quotes only his 1956 paper, but he had to have a precedent, so he quoted my paper from 1952. The Salk vaccine was pushed by the National Foundation.

There were two things that we were looking for: an epidemic of polio, so that we could actually intervene with the live virus vaccine and stop the epidemic; and the opportunity to apply mass polio virus vaccination on a large scale.

We found such an epidemic in the Belgian Congo. The Belgian Congo presented classical, typical infantile paralysis. The paralytic cases were limited to children less than one year old. By the age of three, every single child in the Congo we investigated had antibodies to all three strains of polio. One such epidemic developed in the Ruzizi Valley. Dr. Flack from the Clinton Farms and Dr. Jervis went there to vaccinate 250,000 people who stood in line to get this vaccine for their children. They squirted a 1-cc suspension of live polio virus in slightly salty water by automatic syringe; apparently, the people like salty water, and the children were very happy to swallow salty water. I have pictures showing the procedure, and in six weeks 250,000 children were vaccinated. This was the first mass trial against polio. To tell you that it stopped an epidemic would be very difficult because trial conditions allowed cases to escape. But at least the Belgian authorities claimed that there were definitely fewer cases after the vaccination and they couldn't report any cases in the Ruzizi Valley.

Sabin did not sleep. He also was looking for an epidemic and for a mass population. He then did a very smart thing. He went to the Soviet Union. Even though Stalin was still alive, there was much closer collaboration between Soviet and American scientists than today because the gates had been opened after the war and Soviet scientists were avid for collaboration. Two men, Smorodinsev and Chumakov, decided that they would take up Sabin on his offer to vaccinate their population. Whatever the Russians do, it is done in a big way. Not always in a safe way, but in a big way. They never would start a vaccination program in the Russian republic, so when Sabin sent them his three attenuated strains (about 1957) they decided to vaccinate people in the Lithuanian and Moldavian republics. If those children survived, then they would move slowly and finally end in the Russian republic.

They immediately fed the virus to a thousand children and increased the number in such a rapid way that, by the time a conference on poliomyelitis was held in Washington in 1959, they had probably vaccinated two million people. I will never forget a report by Chumakov, who said that there was not a single case of complication. When one American scientist asked whether there was not a headache in one of two million, whether nobody vomited, he said, "Nobody." This gives you an example of how they did their work and how they still do their work today.

Finally, by 1961, the pressure of Sabin on the United States government was so great that they had to license a live polio virus for immunization in the United States. The committee consisted of Bodian, Smadel, and other people—but not us, of course—who had worked on live virus vaccines. The committee announced that they would license only the Sabin polio virus strain, although they recognized and announced that the other attenuated strains were probably similar.

When I want to make a joke and to discuss the old times, I introduce myself as the developer of the Sabin poliomyelitis vaccine. However, I do not consider it wasted time—for one reason. When I look at my colleagues, with all respect, Sabin and Salk became public figures after all these events. They were moved from the realm of science to the realm of public relations, receiving medals and decorations, being seen by presidents and prime ministers, and having to live up to it. Sabin, in addition, insisted that any vaccine manufactured from his polio virus strains had to be personally inspected by him. So while they were doing those things, during the past two, now almost three decades, I have been enjoying my scientific work. From that point of view, I don't think there was any waste of time, in spite of being disappointed in a tragic way that my vaccine was not licensed. However, it was used in two countries, but this was disregarded. Nine million children in Poland were fed my virus, and the number of paralytic cases dropped from 569 to 3.

A Selected Bibliography

Bogacz, J. and Koprowska, I. (1961). A cyto-pathologic study of potentially carcinogenic properties of air pollutants. *Acta Cytologica 5(5)*, 311–319.

Chaudhuri, S., Koprowska, I. and Rowinski, J. (1975). Different agglutinability of fibroblasts underlying various precursor lesions of human uterine cervical carcinoma. *Cancer Research 35*, 2350–2354.

Hurd-Mead, Kate Campbell. (1938). *A History of Women in Medicine From the Earliest Times to the Beginning of the Nineteenth Century* Haddam, CT:The Haddam Press.

Koprowska, I. (1953). Principles and present day applications of exfoliative cytology for the detection of malignant neoplasms of various organs. *The Indian Journal of Medical Sciences 7(6)*, 267–277.

Koprowska, I., and Koprowski, H. (1953). Morphologic and biologic changes in a mouse ascites tumor following induced infection with certain viruses. *Cancer Research 13(9)*, 651–660.

Koprowska, I., and Koprowski, H. (1956). Susceptibility of induced cervical carcinoma of mice to viral infection. *Proceedings of the American Association for Cancer Research 2(2)*.

Koprowska, I., and Koprowski, H. (1957). Enhancement of susceptibility to virus infection in the course of a neoplastic process. *Annals of the New York Academy of Sciences 68(2)*, 404–418.

Koprowska, I., and Bogacz, J. (1959). A cytopathologic study of tobacco tar-induced lesions of uterine cervix of mouse. *Journal of the National Cancer Institute 23(1)*, 1–19.

Koprowska, Irena, M.D. (1977). "George N. Papanicolaou — As We Knew Him", *Acta Cytologica 21(5)*, 630–638.

Koprowska, Irena, M.D. (1978). "The Role of Women in Medicine, Science, and Arts" *Journal of the American Medical Women's Association 33(1)*, 453–458.

Koprowska, I., Zipfel, S., Ross, A.H., and Herlyn, M. (1986). Development of monoclonal antibodies that recognize antigens associated with human cervical carcinoma. *Acta Cytologica 30(3)*, 207–213.

Koprowska, I., and Wheeler, J. (1986). Preceptorships for premedical students with women physicians. *Journal of the American Medical Women's Association 41(5)*, 160–161.

Koprowska, I., and Zipfel, S.A. (1988). A monoclonal antibody that binds to tumor-associated antigens of exfoliated cells in the smears of patients with cervical intraepithelial neoplasia. *Acta Cytologica 32(3)*, 293–297.

Lillenfeld A., Archer, P.G., Burnett, C.H., Chamberlain, E.W., Chazin, B.J., Davies, D., Davis, R.L., Haber, P.A., Hodges, F.J., Koprowska, I., Kordan, B., Lane, J.T., Lawton, A.H., Lee, L., Jr., MacCallum, D.B., McDonald, J.R., Milder, J.W., Naylor, B., Papanicolaou, G.N., Stutzker, B., Smith, R.T., Swapston, E.R. and Umiker, W.O. (1966). An evaluation of radiologic and cytologic screening for the early detection of lung cancer: A cooperative pilot study of the American Cancer Society and the Veterans Administration. *Cancer Research 26*, 2083–2121.

Papanicolaou, G.N., and Koprowska, I. (1951). Carcinoma in situ of the right lower bronchus. A case report. *Cancer 4(1)*, 141–146.

Proust, Marcel. *À la recherche du temps perdu*, 1919–54 Gallimard Éditions. [Original translation entitled *Remembrance of Things Past* by C.K. Scott Montcriel was followed by his joint translation with Terrence Kilmartin, published by Random House, New York, in 1981.]

Travell, J., Koprowska, I., Hirsch, B.B., and Rinzler, S.H. (1951). Effect of ethyl chloride spray on thermal burns. *The Journal of Pharmacology and Experimental Therapeutics 101(1)*, 36.

Ultmann, J.E., Koprowska, I., and Engle, R.L., Jr. (1958). A cytological study of lymph node imprints. *Cancer 11(3)*, 507–524.